the *Father* is not the *Son*

Godhead or Trinity?

Ramon D. Smullin

CAMDEN COURT PUBLISHERS, INC.
PO Box 901875
Sandy, UT 84090

The Father Is Not The Son: Godhead or Trinity?
Copyright © 1998 Ramon D. Smullin. All rights reserved.

All rights reserved under International and Pan-American Copyright Conventions. This includes the right to reproduce this book or portions thereof in any form whatsoever except as provided by the U.S. Copyright Law.

This work is not officially endorsed or supported by The Church of Jesus Christ of Latter-day Saints nor is meant to add to or detract from official policy. The author takes full and complete responsibility for the statements within.

ISBN: 1-890828-07-6

1st Edition: Spring 1998
2nd Edition: Fall 1998

PRINTED IN THE UNITED STATES OF AMERICA.
10 9 8 7 6 5 4 3 2

To my wonderful wife Louise
and my children Brian, LeAnn, and Kevin.

Contents

Preface	*vii*
1. Revelation versus Tradition	*1*
2. Are They The Same Being?	*15*
3. The Unity of God	*33*
4. Does God Have A Body?	*51*
5. The Generic God	*75*
6. Who Is Christ?	*85*
7. The Offspring of God	*107*
8. Their Hearts Are Far From Me	*123*
9. The Nicene Council	*141*
10. Defining *Homoousios*	*155*
11. The Athanasian Creed Develops	*179*
12. Aquinas and Luther	*199*
13. They Are Real Beings	*213*
Bibliography	*229*
Index	*237*

Preface

Members of the Church of Jesus Christ of Latter-Day Saints (LDS Church) have often been accused of worshipping the wrong god because they reject the traditional definition of the Trinity as contained within the Nicene and Athanasian Creeds.

But there is another doctrine which precedes the Nicene Creed. This doctrine runs contrary to Trinitarian doctrines but has been accepted by every Christian council which has ever been convened.

Novatian wrote that "the distinction however remaining, that *he is not the Father who is the Son, because he is not the Son who is the Father*."[1]

Later, Fathers like Augustine and Thomas Aquinas made the Father, Son, and Holy Ghost into part of the same substance. A review of the writings of these men reveals that they made these changes because *they thought there were errors in existing Christian doctrine*. Terrible things happen when one changes the teachings of

Jesus Christ because one thinks one knows better.

Here are some of the historical developments which resulted because of this change:
1. Thomas Aquinas and other church leaders began writing huge works seeking to prove that God does exist.
2. Armed with the premises of the Trinity, critics of the Christian church began to argue that God is dead.
3. Martin Luther argued that one could call the Trinity by the name of any of the three Persons. He chose the name of Jesus Christ.
4. Jesus intercedes with the Father in our behalf. When the people heard all three Persons were in the same substance, they searched for another intercessor. This is when people began to pray to saints and to rely upon the works of these dead people (in the mass and in indulgences) to cleanse them from their sins, instead of Jesus Christ.
5. Huge numbers of heresies arose. These happened because everyone was trying to understand what the difference between the three Persons was if God was one substance;
6. Rivers of blood were shed by Christian churches trying to enforce their own version of these creeds.
7. The message of the Bible was declared to be anthropomorphic in order to protect the Trinity.

These developments happened because the doctrines of the Trinity were incorporated into Christian doctrine. Jesus said:

> Ye shall know them by their fruits. Do men gather grapes of thorns, or figs of thistles? Even so every good tree bringeth forth good fruit; but a corrupt tree bringeth forth evil fruit. **A good tree cannot bring forth evil fruit, neither can a corrupt tree bring forth good fruit.** Every tree that bringeth forth not good fruit is hewn down, and cast into the fire. **Wherefore, by their fruits ye shall know them.**[2]

I invite the reader to examine with me the fruits of the Trinitarian doctrines. Although I have attempted to encapsulate the beliefs of the Church of Jesus Christ as well as the message of the scriptures and the evidence of historical records, I alone am responsible for the contents of this book.

Preface — ix

I wish to thank my wife Louise and my three children—Brian, LeAnn, and Kevin—for their support and love.

Those who gave me valuable suggestions and provided words of encouragement after reading the manuscript include Mike Olsem, Bob Durocher, Daniel Peterson, Ila Muhlestein, Jeff Collett, and Kent Buckner. I am also indebted to the Salt Lake County Inter-Library Loan Department for locating many old and out-of-print manuscripts for me. Without their assistance, this book would not have been possible.

I thank Brother and Sister Glenn Taylor, the stake missionaries who brought the gospel to our home. I thank the late James L. Barker, who wrote *Apostasy From the Divine Church*, a book which I recommend to the reader without reservation.

Lastly, I thank a loving Heavenly Father who cared so deeply for me (and all of mankind) that he sent his son, Jesus Christ, to the earth. I owe a deep debt which I can never repay to Jesus Christ for paying the debt for my sins, for dying upon the cross, and for being resurrected so that all men can have the opportunity to return to the presence of God the Father. I thank the Holy Ghost for bearing witness of the Son. In short, I echo the words of Joseph Smith:

> And now, after the many testimonies which have been given of him [Christ], this is the testimony, last of all, which we give of him: that he lives!
> For we saw him, even on the right hand of God, and we heard the voice bearing record that he is the Only Begotten of the Father—
> That by him, and through him, and of him, the worlds are and were created, and the inhabitants thereof are begotten sons and daughters of God.[3]

And though I saw neither the Father nor the Son, the Holy Ghost has borne witness to me that they do live. I testify of this in the name of Jesus Christ, Amen.

PREFACE REFERENCES

1. Novatian, *Concerning the Trinity*, XXVII
2. Matthew 17:16–20
3. D&C 76:22–24

1
Revelation vs. Tradition

During the 1980s a group of Evangelicals left a book on my doorstep which accused me and all other members of my faith—The Church of Jesus Christ of Latter-day Saints (LDS Church)—of not being Christians. We are not alone. Any Christian faith which refuses to accept Trinitarian doctrines has been so targeted. One of the foremost authors of this attack was the late Dr. Walter Martin, the "Bible Answer Man" who is quoted as saying:

> ...the tie that binds this diverse group together, despite their many differences, is the acceptance of two fundamental doctrines they regard as being central to historic Christianity.
> Any group which does not accept these tenets but claims to be Christian is, by Dr. Martin's definition, a **cult** of Christianity—an apostate offshoot, disassociated from the true body of Jesus Christ. The two dogmas which that have become the hallmark of this ecumenical movement are (1) the Trinity and (2) the doctrine of salvation by grace without works.[1]

These evangelicals clearly believe in the doctrinal efficacy of the Nicene Creed, which was codified in 325 A.D. and the Athanasian Creed, which was codified thereafter. Both of these documents defined what the Trinity was. The Athanasian Creed specifies that "He therefore that will be saved must think of the Trinity."[2]

For almost two thousand years any Christian who dared to question the doctrine of the Trinity has been persecuted. J. M. Carroll, in a pamphlet entitled "The Trail of Blood" (published by the Ashland Avenue Baptist Church), points out that "rivers of blood" have been shed over this doctrine. *But neither force nor ridicule can establish the validity of an idea.* The Trinitarian doctrines are false and all the persecution in the world cannot change the facts.

Members of the LDS Church disavow the doctrines of the Trinity, claiming that *Jesus Christ appeared to Joseph Smith in 1820 and denounced Trinitarian ideas*:

> I was answered that I must join none of them, for they were all wrong; and the Personage who addressed me said that all their creeds were an abomination in his sight, that those professors were all corrupt; that: "they draw near me with their lips, but their hearts are far from me, they teach for doctrines the commandments of men, having a form of godliness, but they deny the power thereof."[3]

Later, the Savior gave a direct revelation in which he expressed exactly what the natures of the members of the Godhead are. He said that "The Father has a body of flesh and bones as tangible as man's; the Son also; but the Holy Ghost has not a body of flesh and bones, but is a personage of spirit. Were it not so, the Holy Ghost could not dwell in us."[4]

What is so offensive about the doctrine of the Trinity? John O'Brien summarizes the Roman Catholic version of the Trinitarian doctrine. Note that *he identifies the true view of deity as "one god in three personages" and alludes to "a substance."*

> The Christian religion teaches that there is one God in three divine Persons, equal and distinct, the Father, the Son, and the Holy Spirit. This is called the mystery of the blessed Trinity, a truth not against our reason but above it. We believe it because it has been divinely revealed to us in Holy Scripture. God the Father is the Creator of the world, God the Son is the Redeemer of mankind, and God the Holy Spirit is the Sanctifier.
>
> Our Christian faith teaches us that Jesus Christ is divine in His personality and possesses two distinct natures, human and divine. "**He is God of the substance of the Father**, begotten before time," says the Athanasian Creed, formulated in the fourth century, "He is Man of the substance of His mother, born in time."[5]

The insertion of the idea of a divine substance has been the cause of innumerable difficulties in Christian theology. It was the insertion of this essential premise of Pantheism (the doctrine that all nature of the universe is God) which caused the bloodshed already mentioned.

It will be observed that in order for any belief to be mandatory for our faith, it would have to be clearly defined in the Scriptures. The Trinity, as defined in the aforementioned creeds, does not appear in the Bible.

Religious scholars have sought to give validity to the Trinitarian doctrines by searching the Scriptures. It shall be demonstrated that the Bible does not contain the premise that there is a substance which fills the universe and which contains the Father, Son, and Holy Ghost. C. Draina noted that "the mystery of the Holy Trinity was not revealed to the Chosen People of the OT [Old Testament]."[6]

But Draina is not alone in these conclusions. William Fulton states that a representation of the Trinity cannot be found in the Old Testament, saying that "The Old Testament could hardly be expected to furnish the doctrine of the Trinity, if belief in the Trinity is grounded upon belief in the incarnation of God in Christ and upon the experience of spiritual redemption and renewal through Christ."[7]

Furthermore, Trinitarian doctrines cannot be found in the New Testament. Of course, the Father, Son, and Holy Ghost are mentioned, but this is a representation of the Godhead. In the godhead preached by the LDS Church and the Bible, each of the three maintains his own individuality and is a real being. Fulton further explains that the New Testament does not contain the complicated formulas of the Trinity which describe them as being three in one, noting that "In the New Testament we do not find the doctrine of the Trinity in anything like its developed form, not even in the Pauline and Johannine theology, although ample witness is borne to the religious experience from which the doctrine springs."[8]

Other Trinitarian experts have given up any hope of finding a formal declaration of the present creeds in the Bible. Instead, they now try to prove that the ideas which are contained within the creeds are implied in the New Testament.

> We do not intend to seek in the Old Testament and in the New Testament what is not there, a formal statement of trinitarian doctrine. Our aim is to gather together the Biblical concepts that lie behind the doctrine of the Trinity and to find what the sacred writers say and imply about God that could lay the foundations for a later formulation of the doctrine of the Triune God.[9]

Let us be clear about the implications of this discovery. *If the Trinitarian doctrines cannot be found in the Bible, then Jesus Christ and his apostles did not teach those doctrines.* If Jesus Christ and his apostles did not teach them, then belief in such doctrines is not mandatory for salvation. If Trinitarian doctrines are not mandatory for salvation, they cannot be used as a litmus test for membership in the Christian community.

The question is not whether the teachings of Jesus and the apostles can be understood in a Trinitarian way but whether Jesus and the apostles understood them to have that meaning. If they did not, then mankind is guilty of changing the doctrines of Christ to justify its own private theories. Cardinal R. L. Richards admits that the writers of the Bible do not appear to have even conceived of God in a way which would be harmonious with the idea expressed in modern Trinitarian doctrines.

> ...the formula itself does not reflect the immediate consciousness of the period of origins; it was the product of 3 centuries of doctrinal development. But current preoccupation and current emphasis is far less with the subsequent articulations of Christian dogma than with the primitive sources, chiefly the Biblical. It is this contemporary return to the sources that is ultimately responsible for the unsteady silhouettes.[10]

In fact, the word "trinity" does not appear in the Bible. It was not used by any Christian writer before the third century. Why should we accept a word which cannot be found in the Scriptures? Kung notes that "The Greek word trias was first used by the apologist Theophilus of Antioch in the second century, the Latin trinitas in the third."[11]

Since the current Trinitarian creeds did not come from the Bible, they must have come from some other source. Who formulated them? They are developed in the writings of Tertullian, Origen, Athanasius, Augustine, Anselm, Basil, Gregory of Nazianzus, Thomas Aquinas, and many others. These men lived hundreds of years after the Bible was written. They never claimed to have received a revelation from God. However, it was these men who codified the doctrines of the Trinity. In fact, they defined all of the doctrines of the Catholic Church.

The authors whom I have cited are often referred to as the Fathers of the church. They attempted to explain to a pagan world what the Scriptures mean. However, the Fathers went beyond mere interpretation and began to add doctrines of their own to the sacred messages. Pelikan explains that "What [the apostles] spoke in brief form, that [the orthodox theologians of the church] expanded to greater length...by gathering together the statement of many who had gone before and expanding these more profoundly in what they added to them."[12]

These personal ideas became so deeply entrenched in Christianity that they became regarded as sacred concepts. When a scripture conflicted with such a tradition, the Catholic Church assumed that the scripture was being interpreted incorrectly. Thus, those who disagreed with the ancient Fathers were accused of being heretics. Pelikan further says that "One could define a heretic as someone who by his own wicked ideas sought to destroy the teachings of the fathers...more precisely, *scripture was properly interpreted only when it was seen as standing in agreement with tradition.*"[13]

It will be observed that the Protestant churches do not venerate the teachings of the Fathers. However, they do accept the definitions of the Trinity which were formulated by the Fathers. Therefore, in order to prove the antiquity of their own doctrines, the Protestants must refer to the writings of the Fathers. Otto Bardenhewer explains that:

> The Fathers of the first centuries are and remain in a special way the authentic interpreters of the thoughts and sentiments of the primitive Christians. In their writings were set down for all time documentary testimonies to the primitive conception of the faith. Though modern Christian sects have always denounced the Catholic principle of tradition, they have been compelled by the logic of things, to seek in ecclesiastical antiquity for some basis or countenance of their own mutually antagonistic views.[14]

The teachings of the Fathers are really a two-edged sword. Although they do establish that the teachings of the Catholic Church are very old, they also establish that such doctrines have been changed many times since the time of the Savior. Joseph Martos, a Roman Catholic scholar, explains that this has ocurred in the Catholic idea of the seven sacraments. But if this could happen in the case of the sacraments, did it not also happen in the doctrines of the Trinity? We affirm that it did. And just as the many historical records show that the sacraments have changed, they show that ideas about the nature of God have also been changed.

> ...the sacramental rituals themselves were assumed to have remained substantially unchanged for nineteen hundred years, even though there was no direct evidence that this was actually so. Yet it is not as though Catholic theologians intentionally decided to ignore historical facts in developing their explanations of the sacraments. **Many of the facts were simply unknown, buried in the archives of the Vatican and other old libraries.** More importantly, though, the reason why they did not bother to dig through these documents was because they believed that the truths of faith were changeless and unaffected by history.
>
> But historical research in the nineteenth century made Catholics begin to reevaluate this position, and by the twentieth century

it was generally accepted that many of the Roman church's beliefs had indeed changed through the years.[15]

Doctrinal changes can be traced through historical evidence. Therefore, we propose to trace the development of the doctrine of the Trinity. This will enable us to demonstrate that such ideas were not instituted by the Savior.

> Shall we not do well to ask: What was the first germ of evil which found an entry into the minds of the faithful and well-meaning men? Can we trace its introduction, or at least detect its early presence?[16]

A search for a historical justification of Trinitarian doctrines must begin with the first Fathers. These include such individuals as Polycarp, Papias, Irenaeus, Clement of Rome, Ignatius, and books such as the Shepherd of Hermas, the Didache, and the Epistle of Baranabas. These are the earliest Christian sources besides the Bible. A review of these sources shows that they do not contain the modern Trinitarian doctrines. They did, of course, teach that God the Father, Jesus, and the Holy Ghost are divine. However, these early writers did not have a complete Trinitarian theory which is similar to the one which most Christian churches teach today.

Keller writes that "If one claims that Mormons are not Christian, because they do not hold the same view of the Trinity that persons of the Catholic or Reformed traditions do, does that also mean that the early believers of the first two or three centuries were not Christian, since the full trinitarian doctrine did not originate for several hundred years?"[17]

Edward Fortman, a Roman Catholic scholar, explains that:

> In the...Apostolic Fathers there is solid evidence of a belief in three pre-existent beings, both from their actual words and more especially from the fact that they ascribed strict divinity to the Father, Christ and the Holy Spirit. There is in them, of course, no trinitarian doctrine and no awareness of a trinitarian problem.[18]

These Christian sources spanned the first two hundred years of the history of the Christian Church. If the doctrines of the Trinity do not appear within this period, they cannot be said to have always been taught by the Christian Church. Cardinal John Henry Newman, one of the foremost Roman Catholic authorities upon this subject, writes:

> First, the Creeds of that early day make no mention in their letter of the Catholic doctrine at all. They make mention indeed of a

Revelation vs. Tradition

Three; but that there is any mystery in the doctrine, that the Three are One, that They are coequal, coeternal, all increate, all omnipotent, all incomprehensible, is not stated, and never could be gathered from them. Of course we believe that they imply it, or rather intend it. God forbid we should do otherwise! But nothing in the mere letter *of* those documents leads to that belief. To give a deeper meaning to their letter, we must interpret them by the times which came after.[19]

Why did they need to interpret the nature of God by "the times which came after"?

The only reason why such a condition would exist is if a new doctrine had been installed into Christianity which had not been there before. This new doctrine (the Nicene Creed) was one of many which were codified during the period of 300–350 A.D. Others were invented during the same period were a new organization for the "Catholic" Church, the format of the worship service, the doctrine concerning the meaning of the sacrament meal, faith, repentance, baptism, confirmation, and so forth. In other words, every doctrine was set in place which was necessary for the establishment of a new religion.

A review of the councils which accepted these ideas reveals that they were merely bowing to the wishes of the Roman government. The bishops present rejected the idea of constructing a creed which was based upon the Scriptures, choosing instead to incorporate the insertion of Constantine that the substance of God was *homoousios* and could not be divided. This premise was Greek in origin and had already been rejected as a heresy by two councils.

History reveals that 316 out of the 318 bishop present chose to sign rather than suffer exile. Later, over 1800 bishops signed documents repudiating the premises used in the Nicene Creed. Duchesne said, "Neither in the West nor in the East was there a single bishop in office who had not declared himself against Athanasius and the Nicene Creed."[20]

Why did these bishops rebel against the Nicene Creed? A review of the Nicene Proceedings reveals that the bishops present complained that the language was neither scriptural nor accepted doctrine.

The Nicene Creed was ratified in 325 A.D. Let us do some rapid math. Jesus was crucified in approximately 33 A.D. If we accept the premesis that twenty-five years equals a generation, then twelve generations had passed away before this council. Reason tells us that the people must have believed *something*. What was it? They taught that "the Father is not the Son and the Son is not the Father."

Constantine and the Roman emperors burned the writings of those who disagreed with them and employed men (bishops were on the empire payroll) to compose theology to explain what the new doctrines were and to compose a history which would harmonize the innovations with what had happened before. Some of these individuals were Ambrose, Augustine, Gregory the Great, Gregory of Nazianzus, Hilary of Poiters, and others. They were men who were trained in Greek theology and reason and are known as the Fathers.

Since the Catholic and Protestant churches teach that no public revelations were received after the Biblical era, the Trinitarian ideas which developed later have to have been taken from some other source. But what other source had a correct idea of the Father, the Son, and the Holy Ghost? The Fathers decided to borrow from the theories of the Greek (pagan) philosophers.

Jean Danielou quotes Clement of Alexandria: "The revelation of Christ takes the forms appropriate to the various cultures. If Christianity spreads in the Greek world, it must doff its Semitic form and put on a Hellenist form, it must speak the language of Plato and Homer and take the attitudes of Hermes and Ulysses."[21]

The annals of history bear witness to the fact that Christians plagiarized the doctrines of the pagans. Some of the Fathers were so brazen that they bragged about what they were doing. Augustine, for example, wrote to encourage his contemporaries in this activity. He used a strategy which he called "spoiling the Egyptians". This meant that he would steal the most popular ideas from Platonism. He justifies his actions by pointing out that Christianity had used this practice many times and even names some of the practitioners. Each and every one of them had introduced pagan ideas into Christianity—and Augustine was proud of it!

> Now these are, so to speak, their gold and silver, which they did not create themselves, but dug out of the mines of God's providence which are everywhere scattered abroad, and are perversely and unlawfully prostituting to the worship of devils. These, therefore, the Christian, when he separates himself in spirit from the miserable fellowship of these men, ought to take away from them, and to devote to their proper use in preaching the gospel. Their garments, also—that is, **human institutions** such as are adapted to that intercourse with men which is indispensable in this life—**we must take and turn to a Christian use.**
>
> **And what else have many good and faithful men among our brethren done?** Do we not see with what a quantity of gold and

silver and garments Cyprian, that most persuasive teacher and most blessed martyr, was loaded when he came out of Egypt? How much Lactanius brought with him? And Victorinus, and Opatus, and Hilary, not! to speak of living men! How much Greeks out of number have borrowed!"[22]

But the pagan doctrines did not agree with the Bible. It was necessary to argue that certain Bible passages did not mean what they said. The accounts of God's appearance to prophets were, for example, discounted as being anthropomorphic because the Greek element would not agree that God does have a body.

> In the earliest parts of the Bible there are many passages which speak of God in a way which seems to us anthropomorphic, i.e., feelings and thoughts and acts are attributed to Him which belong to man and not to God; e.g., God is said to walk in the Garden of Eden in the coal of the day, Gen. 3:8; He is said to have repented that He had made man on the earth, and to have been grieved at the heart; Gen. 6:6, see also Gen. 11:5–7; 38:32; 32:24–32. As time went on men perceived that such language was metaphorical; but during the childhood of the race it was the most natural way in which to express man's beliefs about the ways and thoughts of God.[23]

What are the Syndics of Cambridge really saying? They are saying that the prophets of the Old Testament did not really understand what God is really like. Clement of Alexandria gives voice to the theory of anthropomorphism by explaining that "We must not even think of the Father of all as having a shape, or as moving, or as standing or sitting, or as being in some place, or as having a left and a right hand, **even though the scriptures say these things about him.**"[24]

As this process continued, a new vocabulary became popular in Christian theological discussions. It was made of words and concepts which had been previously used only by the pagan philosophers and religions.

> Instead of resting on historical facts, it now built itself on certain speculative assumptions. This is the secret of the remarkable change from the confessional character of the Apostle's creed to the transcendental metaphysics of Nice and Chalcedon. It is a fact which theologians have been slow to learn, that the metaphysical words so freely used by the Greek Fathers in theological controversy were all borrowed from the philosophical nomenclature of Plato and Aristotle. This becomes especially apparent in what may be called the scholastic period of Greek theology, and is well illustrated by John of Damascus, who prefaces his great work,

"On the Orthodox Faith," with an explanatory dictionary of Aristotelean terms.[25]

But can we discover the nature of God by studying the writings of the philosophers? Paul did not think so. We must remember that he was a very well-educated man who had already studied the writings of the philosophers. And he did not approve of their teachings. In fact, he found them to be opposed to the teachings of Christ.

> As ye have therefore received Christ Jesus the Lord, so walk ye in him:
> Rooted and built up in him, and established in the faith, as ye have been taught, abounding therein with thanksgiving.
> Beware lest any man spoil you through philosophy and vain deceit, after the tradition of men, after the rudiments of the world, and not after Christ.[26]

This was not the only time when Paul commented upon the dangers of philosophy. He also wrote to the Corinthians about this same subject.

> Where is the wise? where is the scribe? where is the disputer of this world? hath not God made foolish the wisdom of this world?
> For after that in the wisdom of God the world by wisdom knew not God, it pleased God by the foolishness of preaching to save them that believe.
> For the Jews require a sign, **and the Greeks seek after wisdom**:
> But we preach Christ crucified, unto the Jews a stumblingblock, and **unto the Greeks foolishness**;
> But unto them which are called, both Jews and Greeks, Christ the power of God, and the wisdom of God.[27]

Paul declared that the truths of God cannot be discovered by studying the writings of the philosophers. Instead, they were given to mankind by revelation. The Viscount Rene DeChateaubriand agrees with this view. He feels that Christianity is, and must always be, a revealed religion.

> Christianity, therefore, is not the work of men. If Christianity is not the work of men, it can have come from none, but God. If it came from God, men cannot have acquired a knowledge of it but by revelation. Therefore, Christianity is a revealed religion.[28]

We agree with DeChateaubriand that the true Christian doctrines were revealed from heaven. However, mankind has placed other doctrines in the church. The Savior has declared that such interpolations are not to be accepted. He declared, "But in vain do they worship me, teaching for doctrines the commandments of men."[29]

The doctrines of the Trinity have been examined and found to be the ideas of men. Dr. Harry Emerson Fosdick gives the verdict:

> A religious reformation is afoot, and at heart it is the endeavor to recover for our modern life the religion of Jesus as against the vast, intricate, largely inadequate and often positively false religion about Jesus. Christianity today has largely left the religion which he preached, taught and lived, and has substituted another kind of religion altogether.
>
> If Jesus should come back to earth now, hear the mythologies built up around him, see the creedalism, denominationalism, sacramentalism, carried on in his name, he would certainly say, If this is Christianity, I am not a Christian.[30]

Dr. Fosdick theorized that if Jesus appeared he would disavow the existing theories about him. Indeed, many sincere people have been expecting him to do precisely that. James Mosheim wrote:

> Some of this class of people, perceiving that such a church as they had formed an idea of would never be established by human means, indulged the hope that God himself would in his own time erect for himself a new church, free from every blemish and impurity; and that he would raise up certain persons, and fill them with heavenly light for the accomplishment of this great object.[31]

In 1534 Rothman declared:

> The world has fallen from the truth, in that it has been misled by the papacy and by the so-called Evangelical teachers, but the time is at hand when Christ shall restore the world lost in sin, and this restitution or restoration of the world shall take place by means of the lowly and unlearned.[32]

In 1713 Peter Poiret wrote:

> Christianity, having degenerated into a beast and Harlot, receives sentence of condemnation, which God is pleased not to execute without calling men to repentance by one more, and that the last dispensation of his Grace...
>
> In the world's sixty, which is its old age, it shall by the favor of Jesus Christ receive one more Dispensation of his Grace, which will be the last the wicked world is ever to expect. It will consist, as the former did, in appearing, revelation and reestablishment of some ordinances.[33]

All of these people recognized that the teachings of the churches of their day had not been established by Jesus, They knew, however, that these new revelations would be in full harmony with the teachings of the Bible.

> It will be a newer theology than anything else we have had, and yet it will be recognized as the old. The hearts of men will leap in response to it, and will say, "This is true. This is what we have been waiting for." And we shall preach it with a consciousness that we are in line with all the faithful preachers of the past, and yet that we preach in a language that is understood by the present generation.[34]

All of these people acknowledged that a restoration of the gospel of Jesus Christ was needed. Indeed, many of these cited experts fully expected that such a restoration would take place. Why did they believe this? Because they believed that God actually lived and could answer their prayers. They lived for such an occurrence and prayed for it. And, in 1820, God the Father and his son Jesus Christ appeared to the prophet Joseph Smith. The faith, prayers, and longing of these righteous people had been rewarded.

John had seen this day (in vision) and had written:

> And I saw another angel fly in the midst of heaven having the everlasting gospel to preach unto them that dwell on the earth, and to every nation, and kindred, and tongue, and people.
> Saying with a loud voice, Fear God, and give glory to him; for the hour of his judgement is come: and worship him that made heaven and earth, and the sea, and the fountain of waters.[35]

I bear my testimony that heavenly messengers have come to the earth once again. They have restored a true knowlege of the nature of the Father, Son, and the Holy Ghost. The following chapters will contrast this true knowledge with the theories of the Fathers.

CHAPTER 1 REFERENCES

1. Hopkins, *Biblical Mormonism*, 11
2. Brantl, *Catholicism*, 71
3. Joseph Smith History 1:19
4. Doctrine & Covenants 130:22
5. O'Brien, *The Faith of Millions*, 17
6. *New Catholic Encyclopedia*, 14:306, Article "Holy Trinity"
7. *Hastings Relig. Encyclopedia*, 12:458, Article "Trinity"
8. Ibid., 458
9. Fortman, *The Triune God*, xxvii
10. *New Catholic Encyclopedia*, 14:295, Article "Holy Trinity"
11. Kung, *On Being A Christian*, 472
12. Pelikan, *The Christian Tradition*, 1:337
13. Ibid., pp. 336–337
14. Bardenhewer, *Patrology*, 4
15. Martos, *Doors to the Sacred*, 3–4
16. Tymms, *The Evolution of Infant Baptism*, 17
17. Keller, *Reformed Christians and Mormon Christians: Let's Talk*, 143
18. Fortman, *The Triune God*, 44
19. Newman, *An Essay on the Development of Christian Doctrine*, 15–16
20. Duchesne, *Histoire Ancienne de l'Eglise*, 2:269 as cited by Barker, *Apostasy From The Divine Church*, 306
21. Danielou and Marrou, *The Christian Centuries*, 1:42
22. Augustine, *On Christian Doctrine*
23. The Syndics of the Cambridge University Press, *A Concise Bible Dictionary*, 65
24. Stromata V, 4 as cited in Lonergan, *The Way to Nicea*, 116
25. Paine, *A Critical History of the Evolution of Trinitarianism*, 32
26. Colossians 2:6–8
27. 1 Corinthians 1:20–24
28. DeChateaubriand, *The Genius of Christianity*, 1:685
29. Matthew 15:9
30. *Liahona*, Vol. 23, No. 22, p. 424 as cited in Richards, *A Marvelous Work and a Wonder*, 29
31. Mosheim, *Institutes of Ecclesiastical History*, Book IV
32. E.B. Box, *Rise and Fall of the Anabaptists*, 63 as cited in McGavin, *Cumorah's Gold Bible*, 14

33. *Economy of the Restoration of Man*, IV:205 as cited in Ibid., 13
34. Walters, *The Deseret News*, Aug. 4, 1934, as cited in Ibid., 31
35. Revelations 14:6–7

2
Are They The Same Being?

Many centuries ago, in the land of Palestine, Jesus asked his apostles an incredibly important question.

> And when Jesus came into the coasts of Caesarea Phillipi, he asked his disciples, saying, Whom do man say that I the son of man am?
> And they said, Some say that thou art John the Baptist; some, Elias; and others, Jeremias, or one of the prophets.
> He saith unto them, But whom say ye that I am?[1]

Many years have passed since that moment, but man is still asking that same question. And many answers have been formulated. Some say that Jesus was a scoundrel, while others acknowledge that he was a great teacher. Still others have decided that Jesus is God the Father. None of these answers are right, for Peter gave the right answer.

> And Simon Peter answered and said, Thou art the Christ, the Son of the living God.
> And Jesus answered and said unto him, Blessed art thou, Simon Bar-Jona: for flesh and blood hath not revealed it unto thee, but my Father which is in heaven.[2]

What is the meaning of this passage? It is that Jesus is the Son of God the Father. Jesus praised Peter for giving this answer and said that the apostle had been given the answer as a revelation. Therefore, we accept Peter's declaration as an eternal truth—that Jesus is the Son of God.

But many Christians do not share this conviction. In their minds, Jesus is God the Father. The reason for this error is not difficult to understand. They have been taught to believe in the Trinity. The Trinitarian Creeds state that the three persons—Father, Son, and Holy Ghost—are really one god. As a result, they choose to designate Jesus as the one God. A. C. McGiffert states that "...the distinction of the Son from the Father is a philosophical element, 'the product of metaphysics' without which the religious element in Christian faith can maintain itself very well."[3]

Richard Niebuhr noted this trend with alarm. He saw some very real problems in this type of theology and tried to warn other clerics that they were, in actuality, denying the reality of God the Father.

> Yet as in the case of Biblicism it is hardly necessary to await the outcome of many inquiries before concluding that substantial error involving many further confusions is present when the proposition that Jesus Christ is God is converted into the proposition that God is Jesus Christ...however the doctrine of the Personae is stated it must still be affirmed that **the father is not the son and the son is not the father and the spirit cannot be equated with either.** Yet in many churchly pronouncements the faith of Christians is stated as if their one God were Jesus Christ; as if Christ's ministry of reconciliation to the Creator were of no importance; as if the Spirit proceeded only from the Son; as if the Christian Scriptures contained only the New Testament; as if the Old Testament were relevant only insofar as it contained prophecies pointing to Jesus Christ; as if Jesus Christ were man's only hope. **When this is done the faith of Christians is converted into a Christian religion for which Jesus Christ in isolation is the one object of devotion and in which his own testimony, his very character, his sonship, his relation to the one with whom he is united, are denied.**[4]

Are such fears unfounded? Many theologians do not think that they are. They see a real possibility that the Father and the Holy Ghost will be swallowed up in the conception of the Son. Levi Leonard Paine insists that this has already happened in the doctrines of many ministers.

> But what is the new wine that is being dispensed out of the old flask with its old trinitarian label? This: that God is one only both in person and in essence, but is manifested in different forms, and especially in triune form, and that this triune form has become incarnate in Jesus Christ, who is thus God manifest in the flesh, so that the whole Godhead is in Christ, and that **there is none other beside him.** What, no Father? No, except as in him. No Holy Ghost? No, not outside of Christ. Christ is the whole God; Fatherhood, Sonhood and Spirithood are simply forms of Christ's one Godhood.[5]

Others have even discarded the designation of Jesus. To them, the Trinity is simply God. Therefore, they have little patience with any discussions about the nature of the Father, Son, and Holy Ghost. Professor Josiah Royce states that he is only concerned with the "absolute" or the one God.

> So far, we have what may be called a trinity of Selves (if one is fond of the traditional but, to my mind, essentially trivial amusement of counting the "persons" in the Absolute)...As I say, I care nothing for a mere count of the "persons" of the Godhead. Three or twenty—it matters little or nothing to philosophy.[6]

In fact, many theologians are now arguing that the whole Trinitarian question has become largely irrelevant to worshippers. They worship one god. The question of how the Father, Son, and Holy Ghost are related is not a matter with which the average person concerns himself.

> For too many Christians, the doctrine of the Trinity is only a matter of intellectual curiosity, on the one hand, or a somewhat arbitrary test of faith, on the other...Accordingly, the mystery and doctrine of the Trinity is often relegated to an entirely marginal place in the total Christian scheme. Even theologians as sober as Karl Rahner have suggested that, as far as many Church members are concerned, **the doctrine could be erased completely from the Christian treasury of faith** and that many spiritual writings, sermons, pious exercises, and even theological treatises could remain in place with little more than minor verbal adjustments.[7]

The theories under which these people are operating are fallacious. The Father, Son, and Holy Ghost are not the same being nor have they ever claimed that they are. Instead, the Savior has consistently declared that the three are not the same being. For example, Jesus said:

> For God so loved the world, that he gave his only begotten Son, that whosoever believeth in him should not perish, but have everlasting life.
> For God sent not his Son into the world to condemn the world; but that the world through him might be saved.[8]

We must note that the cited passage does not state that God (the Father) came into the world, but that he sent his son. The meaning is clear: two persons are spoken of. The Son is not the same person as the Father.

Jesus made use of the distinction between the two persons. A Jewish law existed which specified that at least two or three witnesses were required to establish the testimony of anyone as a fact. Critics accused Jesus of being the only witness of his professed calling and stated that his message was not true.

Jesus stated that John the Baptist had borne witness that Jesus was the Christ. Then the Savior said that God the Father was another witness. This would have meaning only if the Father was a different being than the Son. Otherwise, the Son would merely have been bearing witness of himself. Jesus said, "And the Father himself, which hath sent me, hath borne witness of me. **Ye have neither heard his voice at any time, nor seen his shape.**"[9]

Jesus was standing in the midst of the Jews when he said this. They had heard him on many occasions. Yet they were told that they had neither heard nor seen the Father. This would only be true if the Father were a different person than the Son.

The members of the Godhead are not interchangeable. Each has his own identity and purpose. For example, the Father is a judge of those who have committed sins. The Son intercedes with the Father on our behalf (Romans 8:34; Hebrews 7:25). If the two are part of the same substance, then Christ is interceding with himself.

Robbed of an intercessor, mankind set up a new substitute. This new hope consisted of Mary and the rest of the Saints. They prayed not to these individuals, but relied upon their good deeds in order to receive forgiveness for their sins.

> [They] so confounded Christ with God the Father that instead of making him the expression and representation of Divine mercy and intercession, as the earlier intercession had always done, it made him rather a representative of Divine justice and punishment. Medieval art is in this point a true and telling witness. The face of Christ, which in early art was benignant and compassionate becomes hard and severe, and in the frequent judgment scenes he is pictured on the throne wrathful and vengeful, and in the act of punishing the guilty. No wonder that the cult of the Virgin Mary became so popular. Its growth, with all the superstitions involved, was the protest of heavy-laden souls, longing for some way of access to the mercy of God, when the old and living way through Christ had been closed.[10]

Early Christianity puzzled over the mathematical impossibility of having three persons only equal one god. A heresy known as Sabellianism arose because certain people concluded that the Father, Son, and Holy Ghost must be merely names that were descriptive of the different roles which the one God performed, notes Moltmann.

Are They The Same Being?

It was Sabellius who gave modalism its theological formulation, and it was he who later gave his name to this whole trend. The basic ideas are not at all complicated. In the history of his revelation and his communication of salvation, **the one God takes on three forms**: in the Form of the Father he appears to us as the Creator and law-giver; in the form of the Son he appears as the redeemer; in the form of the Holy Spirit he appears as the giver of life. Father, Son and Spirit are the three manifestations or modes of appearance of the One God. But this One God himself is as unknowable, unnamable and ineffable as the "One" itself.

Sabellius called the three modes of appearance of the One God not merely manifestations, but also something in God, something indwelling in him.[11]

Why was Sabellianism found to be so offensive? Because it was intimated that the Father, Son, and the Holy Ghost were not actually real beings. They were only "something in God." The opponents of this heresy argued that all three existed on an individual basis as separate beings. Novatian, who was one of the elected bishops of Rome, gave this answer to the Sabellianists:

And I should have enough to do were I to endeavor to gather together all the passages whatever on this side since the divine scripture...everywhere shows Him to be born of the Father, by whom all things were made and without whom nothing was made, who has always obeyed and obeys the Father, that He always has power over all things, but as delivered, as granted, as by the Father himself permitted to him.[12]

Novatian did not stop with this declaration. In order that none might misunderstand, he elaborated upon the differentiation between the Father and the Son by saying "the distinction however remaining, that He is not the Father who is the Son, because He is not the Son who is the Father."[13]

The renowned Roman Catholic scholar, J. Tixeront, notes that the early Fathers insisted that the Father and the Son could be numerically differentiated. This is the same as saying *1* (the Father) + *1* (the Son) = 2.

The Word, who later will be Jesus Christ, is the Son of God...Hence and by virtue of this generation, **the Son is distinct from the Father**. The distinction is placed more or less in relief by the Apologists: Saint Justin strongly insists on it. In relation to God, the Creator, the Son is another, **another as to number**, although in accord with him. He is not distinguished from him by name only, as the light is distinguished from the sun, but **he is numerically something else**...Tatian and Athenagoras use equivalent expressions...[14]

The Nicene Council of 325 A.D. also held that the Father and the Son could be numerically differentiated. But Augustine (354–430 A.D.) claimed that the laws of mathematics do not apply to the substance of God. This is essentially the same as stating *1* (the Father) + *1* (the Son) = *1*. Joseph Priestley comments on this comparison (which was incorporated into the Athanasian Creed).

> The doctrine of Transubstantiation implies a physical impossibility, whereas that of the Trinity, as unfolded in the Athanasian Creed, implies a mathematical one; and to this only we usually give the name of contradiction...
>
> Now I ask, Wherein does the Athanasian doctrine of the Trinity differ from a contradiction? It asserts, in effect, that nothing is wanting to either the Father, the Son or the Spirit, to constitute each of them truly and properly God; each being equal in eternity and all divine perfections; and yet that these three are not three Gods, but only one God. They are, therefore, both *one* and *many* in the same respect, viz., in each being *perfect God*. This is certainly as much of a contradiction as to say that Peter, James and John, having each of them everything that is requisite to constitute a complete man, are yet, all together, not *three men*, but only *one man*. For the ideas annexed to the words *god* or *man* cannot make any difference in the nature of the two propositions.[15]

Is it reasonable to affirm that God is one and three in the same respect? William Cunningham writes that "[To] affirm, directly or by plain implication, that God is one in the same respect in which he is three, would also amount to a plain contradiction, and, of course, **could not rationally be believed.**"[16]

Since the Sabellians have been declared to be heretics by the leading councils of Christianity, we must conclude that the Father, Son, and Holy Ghost have real and separate identities. Since they are separate beings, they must be physically equivalent to three Gods. Hans Kung states that when Christians concentrate upon any of the three in isolation, they think of that person as having his own identity or personality. That is really the same as picturing them as three gods, although, of course, the people do not call them that. Kung further notes that "the Trinity is largely understood in a tritheistic sense. Three 'persons' are understood in modern psychological terms as three 'self-consciousnesses,' three 'subjects,' that is to say, essentially three Gods."[17]

Sabellianism is not the only heresy which is inextricably interwoven into Trinitarianism. Patripassionism is the belief that all three members of the Godhead participated in all of the lifetime experiences of Christ, including the virgin birth and crucifixion.

This heresy is still denounced by Trinitarians, but its incorporation into its theories is inescapable. If the Father, Son, and Holy Ghost were in the universal substance and the substance cannot be divided, then all three would have taken part in the same events and felt the same pain.

Tertullian, who was the first Christian writer to use the word "trinity," also thought of the three as individuals. H. A. Wolfson makes the following point about Tertullian's theology: "In number, the Father and the Son are two and not one, and by the same token, **the Father and the Son and the Holy Spirit are three and not one.**"[18]

The idea that the Father, Son, and Holy Ghost are really individuals is very repugnant to most theologians. In fact, they go to great lengths to deny that the three can really be individuals.

They are described as relations, processions, essence, thoughts, names, modes of existence, and manifestations of the one God. The effect of this play on words is to deprive the Father, Son, and Holy Ghost of their existence as real beings. Instead, they are reduced to the role of abstractions.

Such an exercise of logic changes many doctrines and negates the whole message of the Scriptures. Jesus is the son of God the Father. To deny the separation of these two beings is to intimate that Jesus is his own Father. This robs the Father of his paternal identity. It also means that Jesus is not the son of God.

> Strict monotheism has to be theocratically conceived, and implemented, as Islam proves. But once it is introduced into the doctrine and worship of the Christian church, **faith in Christ is threatened**: Christ must either recede into the series of the prophets, giving way to the One God, or he must disappear into the One God as one of his manifestations. The strict notion of the One God really makes theological christology impossible, for the one can neither be parted or imparted. It is ineffable. The Christian church was therefore right **to see monotheism as the severest inner danger**, even though it tried on the other hand to take over the monarchical notion of the divine lordship.[19]

Can you see the contradictions which are inherent in the Trinitarian theory? Origen did and commented upon the false doctrines which are introduced into Christianity because people were afraid to acknowledge two gods, writing "'Hence,' says he, 'we may solve the scruple of many pious persons, who, through fear lest they should make two gods, fall into false and wicked notions.'"[20]

Faced with this logic, Arius concluded that Jesus could not be a god. The Unitarian churches of our day have come to the same conclusion by utilizing the idea that there is only one god. Yet they are in error. Jesus is also divine, as is the Holy Ghost. The Scriptures bear witness that the Savior is a god. This is why Matthew applied the prophecy of Isaiah to Jesus as "Behold, a virgin shall be with child, and shall bring forth a son, and they shall call his name Emmanuel, which being interpreted is, God with us."[21]

Why is Jesus called a god? Because he *is* a god. John bore witness of this fact, writing that "In the beginning was the Word [Jesus], and the Word was with God [the Father], and the Word was [a] God. The same was in the beginning with God."[22]

Many will disagree with this doctrine because it affirms the existence of at least two gods. However, we did not invent the idea. It was alive in the early Christian church. They taught that Jesus was a second god who subordinated his wishes to those of his Father. Thus the Christians worshipped the Father as God, but acknowledged the divinity of Jesus as *a* god. Eusebius, the church historian at the time of the Council of Nicea, writes:

> "If," says he, "this makes them apprehensive lest we seem to introduce two Gods, let them know that though we do indeed acknowledge the Son to be God, yet there is (absolutely) but one God, even he who alone is without original and unbegotten, who has his divinity properly of himself, and is the cause even to the Son himself, both of his being, and of his being such as he is; by whom the Son himself confesses that he lives (declaring expressly, *I live by the Father*)...and declares to be greater than himself," and "to be even his God."[23]

Many other Christians believed that Jesus was a god who had an identity which was different than that of the Father.

> Irenaeus' writings echoed the letters of Ignatius, bishop of Antioch, who was martyred in Rome under Trajan...in his letters he did not equate the Son of God and God the Father. Nor had the apologists like Justin Martyr taught such a doctrine. They taught that the Son of God was divine, as was commonly believed by the earliest Christians, but **they viewed him as a separate being altogether. They did not believe that God himself had appeared on Earth. It was only the Son, the Christ,** who was born of a virgin, although Justin admitted that not all Christians in the second century accepted the tradition about Mary.[24]

Later Fathers would declare such ideas to be inconsistent and Tritheistic. However, the Fathers of this era considered their ideas

Are They The Same Being?

to contain the express meaning of the Scriptures.

As we have noted, these early Tritheists also taught that the Father and the Son were not strictly equal. The later theologians chide them for this, and accuse the apologists of heterodoxy of failing to make the persons in the Trinity equal. The idea that the deities in the Godhead are unequal is known as Subordinationism. As we will note, Jesus Christ was a Subordinationist.

> Wherever in the New Testament the relationship of Jesus to God, the Father, is brought into consideration, whether with reference to his appearance as a man or to his Messianic status, it is conceived of and represented categorically as subordination *and the most decisive subordinationist of the New Testament, according to the synoptic record, was Jesus Himself* (cf. for example Mk. x, 18; xiii, 32; xiv, 36). This original position, firm and manifest as it was, was able to maintain itself for a long time. All the great pre-Nicene theologians represented the subordination of the Logos (Jesus) to God. The Trinitarian problem first emerged when the church in its theology was constrained for certain reasons, which were connected with the process of de-eschatologising, to abandon the concept of subordination for that of co-ordination. *Almost insoluble difficulties then inevitably produced themselves*, which in turn necessarily provoked great strife. They concerned, on the one side, the concept of God, and, on the other, the relationship of the new theology to the New Testament as the canon of dogma.[25]

We will now refer to the writings of Dr. Priestley for more evidences that the early Fathers considered the Father to be superior to the Son. Since it is impossible for a person to be superior to himself, the two must be separate and distinct beings.

> The great object of the orthodox in the second century, was to make a God of Christ, but a far inferior God, and also a God of or out of God the Father, lest he be thought to be another God, and be independent of the Father. On the other hand the great object of the orthodoxy of a later period, was to exalt the Son to a perfect equality with the Father...
>
> Novatian, whose orthodoxy, with respect to the doctrine of the Trinity, was never questioned, says..."Though he was in the form of God, he did not attempt the robbery of being equal with God. For, though he knew he was God of God the Father, he never compared himself with God the Father; remembering that he was of the Father, and that he had what the Father gave him"...
>
> Arnobius says, that "the Omnipotent, and only God, sent Christ." And again, "Christ, a God, spake by the order of the principal God."[26]

Jesus Christ is the god Jehovah of the Old Testament. However, he acted under the direction of his Father, Elohim. All of the worship which the Son received was accepted on behalf of his Father. Paul tells us that the day will come when Jesus will deliver up the kingdom to his Father.

> Then cometh the end, when he shall have delivered up the kingdom to God, even the Father; when he shall have put down all rule and all authority and power.
> And when all things shall be subdued unto him, then shall the Son also himself be subject unto him that put all things under him, that God may be all in all.[27]

As we have observed, the early Christian church taught that the Father and the Son were both gods. This same observation could be made for the Holy Ghost. These three are real beings who have their own identities. This is the true doctrine which Jesus taught.

During the apostasy, mankind puzzled over such ideas. They noted that the Bible taught that Jesus and the Father are one (John 10:30). They could see two possible explanations for this oneness. These were (1) that the three have a unity of purpose or (2) that the three are physically the same being. The theologians chose the second explanation and built the doctrines of the Trinity around it.

The Nicene Creed was built around the idea that all three are part of the same substance. Athanasius argued that this made them one god. This one substance unit is known as the Economic Trinity.

However, Augustine recognized that the Economic Trinity still was essentially three gods. As a result, he decided to institute what is called the Immanent Trinity. That this was a major overhaul and not a minor revision can be proven by the fact that it took fifteen years to put together his system. Augustine "knew that the Trinity was a stumbling block to the intellect, **for fifteen years he worked on his systematic production—*De Trinitae*—struggling to find analogies in human experience for three persons in one God.**"[28]

Writers of his day criticized the new doctrines, arguing that the church should follow doctrines that were ancient in origin. Kurt Aland states that "the famous and continually cited word of Vincent of Lerins [for which he was sainted], that 'catholic' is that which is taught always and everywhere, came out of this controversy and **was intended to be an attack on Augustine. It was directed against the new things Augustine had introduced, because that which Augustine proclaimed had not been taught always and everywhere.**"[29]

Are They The Same Being?

But what was the theology which Augustine created? Many feel that it was merely another version of Sabellianism. Note that the results of the two approaches are almost identical.

Doctrine	Sabellius	Augustine	Similarities
1. Numbers of God	One god and one substance	One god and one substance	Same
2. Tri-Unity in God	Certain amount of three-person activity in the substance	Certain amount of three-person activity in the substance	Difference is one of the duration of the activity
3. Innerdwelling	God present in heart of man	God present in heart of man	Same
4. Personality, Consciousness and Identity	Essentially one	Essentially one	Same

Was Augustine aware that he was preaching Sabellianism? He was not and preached against that heresy. However, both taught the same principles. Each said that God could only be numbered as one while the earlier Fathers had taught that the Godhead must be numbered as three. Both Augustine and Sabellius thought that the Trinity consisted of modes or relations. Paine explains why this comparison is valid.

> Here Augustine plainly sides with Sabellius. A remarkable passage in his "Tractae on the Fourth Gospel" brings out his position clearly: "The Trinity is one God: three, but not three Gods. Three what, then? I reply: "The Father, and the Son, and the Holy Spirit." But can the three be numbered, as three men can be? Here Augustine wavers. "If you ask: three what? number ceases. When you have numbered, you cannot tell what you have numbered. **Only in their relations to each other do they suggest number, not in their essential existence.** I have no name to give the three, save the Father, the Son, and the Holy Spirit, one God, one Almighty, and so one beginning." Here the monism of Augustine fully appears. The only numbering, he declares, that can apply to God is that of his essence, which is one. When the Trinity is spoken of, "number fails." This must mean that **Augustine did not figure the "three" as real** and distinct existences or individuals which, of course, can be numbered, **but only as modes or relations,** in triple form, of one existence or individual.[30]

Such observations are not limited to Paine. Others have noted that the two doctrines are incredibly close. In fact, Adolf Harnack observes that Augustine only escapes being called a Sabellianist by (1) saying that he does not want to be called one, and (2) by the clever wording that he uses. Fortman says "It was noted above that the Augustinian approach was open to the danger of Modalism, and

Harnack maintained that 'Augustine only gets beyond Modalism by the mere assertion that he does not wish to be a Modalist, and by the aid of ingenious distinctions between different ideas.'"[31]

In fact, one gets the impression that the entire Trinitarian system is built around the use of clever wordings. Few of its ideas will stand if they are expressed by themselves. Those who state one of the ideas by itself are judged to be heretics. Newman reports that "The Catholic Truth in question is made up of a number of separate propositions, each of which, if maintained to the exclusion of the rest, is a heresy."[32]

The Athanasian Creed expresses the viewpoint of Augustine very eloquently. However, the Creed contains so many contradictions, and is so complex, that even the most learned theologians have difficulty in avoiding a heresy of one kind or another. Note how a declaration of fact is made and then it is affirmed that the opposite proposition is also true. Why is this done? To maintain the scriptural proposition that there are three persons in the Godhead while also stating that you are really only talking about one metaphysical individual.

THE ATHANASIAN CREED
"Whoever will be saved: before all things it is necessary that he hold the Catholic Faith. Unless he keep this Faith whole and undefiled, without doubt he shall perish everlastingly.
And the Catholic Faith is this: we worship one God in Trinity, and Trinity in Unity, neither confounding the Persons, nor dividing the Substance..."[33]

What does it mean to confound the Persons? It means to mix up our concept of each individual so that we begin to ascribe the accomplishments and attributes of one to another.

What does it mean that the substance cannot be divided? This is the guiding premise of pantheism, the worship of nature. They thought that there was a divine substance which comprised the entire universe. In this substance were a number of divine persons.

This pagan theory was modified and adopted into Christianity. They said that Jesus Christ had been generated from the Father and that the Holy Ghost was breathed by the Father. However, this doctrine stated that the person of the Father was not decreased (of substance) in the least. This is equivalent to saying that the mass of the Father $= x$ and the mass of Jesus $= x$ and the mass of the Holy Ghost $= x$, but that the mass of the entire Trinity also $= x$. This is, of course, a mathematical contradiction.

Not dividing the substance also means that the Father, Son, and

Are They The Same Being?

Holy Ghost could never be separated. For example, the premise that Jesus left the presence of God the Father to be born is diametrically opposed to the idea that the substance cannot be divided. Let us now return to the text of the Athanasian Creed.

> For there is one Person of the Father, another of the Son, another of the Holy Ghost. But the Godhead of the Father, of the Son, and of the Holy Ghost is all one: the Glory co-eternal, the Majesty co-eternal. Such as the Father is, such is the Son, and such is the Holy Ghost...[34]

This part of the Creed begins by stating that there are three individuals in the Godhead. It clearly implies that each has his own identity and attributes. Yet the language which follows clearly contradicts this idea. We are told that the three are physically one and that each is exactly like the other two. Moreover, we are even told that all are of the same age and have the same glory. Which of these contradictory statements is considered to be true? Why, they both are!

> The Father uncreated, the Son uncreated, and the Holy Ghost uncreated. The Father incomprehensible, the Son incomprehensible, and the Holy Ghost incomprehensible. The Father eternal, the Son eternal, and the Holy Ghost is eternal. And yet they are not three eternals, but one Eternal. As also there are not three incomprehensible, nor three Uncreated, but one Uncreated and one Incomprehensible. So likewise the Father is almighty, the Son is almighty, and the Holy Ghost is almighty; and yet they are not three almighties, but one Almighty. So the Father is God, the Son is God, and the Holy Ghost is God; and yet they are not three gods, but one God. So likewise the Father is Lord, the Son Lord, and the Holy Ghost Lord; and yet not three lords, but one Lord. **For like as we are compelled by the Christian truth to acknowledge every person by himself to be God and Lord, so are we forbidden by the Catholic religion to say, there are three gods or three lords.**[35]

Each member of the Godhead is designated by the same title, yet the Athanasian Creed refuses to admit that there are three uncreateds, incomprehensibles, almighties, gods, and lords. The reader is forbidden to picture them as anything but one. Yet the same titles are granted to each on an individual basis. We cannot, then, fail to number them on a collective basis.

> The Father is made of none, neither created nor begotten. The Son is of the Father alone, not made, nor created, but begotten. The Holy Ghost is of the Father and the Son, neither made, nor

created nor begotten, but proceeding. So there is one Father, not three Fathers, one Son, not three Sons, one Holy Ghost, not three Holy Ghosts.

And in this Trinity none is before or after the other; none is the greater or less than another; but the whole three Persons are co-eternal together, and co-equal; so that in all things the Unity in Trinity, and the Trinity in Unity is to be worshipped. He therefore that will be saved must think of the Trinity.[36]

This section of the Creed declares that the Son and the Holy Ghost have been taken from the substance of the Father. Yet we are informed that all three are of the same age. To utter either statement without the other is a heresy. To utter both at the same time is considered devout. All are pronounced equal but a hierarchy is very evident. There must be a unity (one God) and yet a trinity at the same time. All of these statements must be uttered with its twin or a heresy has been committed.

How could Augustine, the writer of the Athanasian Creed, and the later Fathers use such terms in conjunction with each other? They did so because they did not think that the words would be taken seriously. They were, in effect, philosophers, and philosophers were expected to say something about the nature of God even if they did not understand it. Augustine himself admitted that he did not take any descriptions of God to be accurate (even his own).

> "God must not," he says, "even be described as unspeakable (ineffabilis), since by the very use of this term, something is spoken...Yet God, since nothing can be worthily spoken of Him, accepts the service of the human voice, and wills us to rejoice in praising Him with words of our own." And again; "Our thoughts of God are truer than our words, and His existence is truer than our thoughts."...And again: We say three persons, not as being satisfied with this expression, **but because we must use some expression.**[37]

Since Augustine did not know what the Father, Son, and Holy Ghost were, his ideas cannot be viewed as an actual portrayal of the nature of deity. To illustrate, let us suppose that someone claimed to be a mechanic and wanted to fix your automobile. The person in question, however, said that he did not know what an automatic transmission or a carburetor or brakes were. Would you allow him to repair your car? You would be extremely foolish if you did.

The same principle applies to the teachings of Augustine and the later Fathers. They admit that they do not know what God is like. This admission shows that they are unqualified to teach us about the nature of God. Using them as our spiritual guides would be equivalent to following the teachings of the Pharisees at the time of the Savior. We read:

> Then came his disciples, and said unto [Jesus], Knowest thou that the Pharisees were offended, after they heard this saying?
> But he answered and said, Every plant, which my heavenly Father hath not planted, shall be rooted up.
> Let them alone: they be blind leaders of the blind. And if the blind lead the blind, both shall fall into the ditch.[38]

Spiritually speaking, Augustine and the later Fathers are blind because they do not know what God is like. They are attempting to convey to others what they do not know themselves. And both they and those who follow their teachings fall into the deep ditch of false teachings.

Many of our modern clerics have examined the present-day doctrines of the Trinity and found them to be wanting. Many of these individuals are presently demanding that new doctrines on the subject be formulated. Why? Because they do not believe the old ones.

> The basic trinitarian dogmas are still substantially in possession today, and always will be. **But some Catholic theologians feel they are in need of a reappraisal. They see problems everywhere...**
> There is to us little doubt that Catholic theology **at present is at a critical juncture**, so that the contemporary task of assimilating the fruits both of religious studies and of the new philosophies, of handling the problems of demythologization and of the possibility of objective religious statements, **imposes on theology the task of recasting its notion of the theological method in the most thorough-going and profound fashion.**[39]

What form will the new sectarian doctrines take? As we have observed, many theologians are moving toward dissolving the Trinity and merely acknowledging one god. Why is there this movement? Because some religionists have been largely functioning without the Trinity for years and merely teach about one transcendent god. Karl Rahner observes:

> ...despite their orthodox confessions of the Trinity, Christians are, in their practical life, almost merely monotheists. We must be willing to admit that, should the doctrine of the Trinity have to be dropped as false, the major part of religious literature could well remain virtually unchanged...No wonder, since starting from Augustine, and as opposed to the older tradition, it has been among theologians a more or less forgone conclusion that **each of the divine persons** (if God freely so decided) **could have become**

man, so that the incarnation of precisely this person can tell us nothing about the particular features of this person within the divinity.[40]

As Rahner points out, the persons in this Trinity have become so much alike that there is no difference between them. And, under those circumstances, one can work as well as three.

All of these developments have happened because mankind made the wrong decision. They thought that statements like "the Father and I are one" meant that the two had the same identity. They were wrong. The Father, the Son, and the Holy Ghost are one—not in substance, but in purpose. The next chapter will document this premise.

CHAPTER 2 REFERENCES

1. Matthew 16:13–15
2. Matthew 16:16–17
3. McGiffert, *History in Christian Thought* as cited in Welch, *The Trinity in Contemporary Theology*, 49–50
4. Niebuhr, *The Purpose of the Church and its Ministry*, 44–45
5. Paine, *A Critical History of the Evolution of Trinitarianism*, 167
6. Royce, *The Conception of God*, 1:300–301
7. McBrien, *Catholicism*, 2:356
8. John 3:16–17
9. John 5:37
10. Paine, *A Critical History of the Evolution of Trinitarianism*, 34–35
11. Moltmann, *The Trinity and the Kingdom*, 135
12. Novatian, *Concerning the Trinity*, XXVI
13. Ibid., XXVII
14. Tixeront, *Histoire des Dogma dans l'Antiquite Chretienne*, 1:267 as cited in Barker, *Apostasy From the Divine Church*, 43
15. Priestley, *A History of the Corruptions of Christianity*, 321
16. Cunningham, *Historical Theology*, 2:208
17. Kung, *On Being A Christian*, 174
18. Wolfson, *The Philosophy of the Church Fathers*, 318–319
19. Moltmann, *The Trinity and the Kingdom*, 131
20. Priestley, *A History of the Corruptions of Christianity*, 19
21. Matthew 1:23
22. John 1:1–2
23. Clarke's Script. Doc., 343 as cited in Priestley, *A History of the Corruptions of Christianity*, 22
24. Hooper, *Roman Realities*, 500
25. Werner, *The Formation of Christian Dogma*, 125
26. Priestley, *A History of the Corruptions of Christianity*, 323–324
27. 1 Corinthians 15:24, 28
28. Durant, *The Age of Faith*, 68
29. Aland, *A History of Christianity*, 1:210–211
30. Paine, *A Critical History of the Evolution of Trinitarianism*, 74–75
31. Fortman, *The Triune God*, 143
32. Newman, *An Essay on the Development of Christian Doctrine*, 14

33. Brantl, *Catholicism*, 70–71
34. Ibid., 70–71
35. Ibid., 70–71
36. Ibid., 70–71
37. Illingworth, *The Doctrine of the Trinity*, 107–108
38. Matthew 15:12–14
39. Fortman, *The Triune God*, 316
40. Rahner, *The Trinity*, 10–11

3
The Unity of God

In the last chapter I mentioned that the sectarian world had erred in their interpretation of John 10:30. This passage reads "I and the Father are one." The usual interpretation of this scripture has been that Jesus and the Father are physically the same being. This is not what the Savior meant. The unity which is spoken of is that of purpose.

On what basis can we make such a determination? The first evidence which we shall cite is that of grammatical usage. John used the word *unum* when he recorded the words of Jesus. This is a neuter word and means "one thing". There was another word which was masculine and meant "one person". What does this mean? It means that John felt that Jesus was saying that the Father and the Son are one (*unum*) in purpose.

> Notwithstanding the supposed derivation of the Son from the Father, and therefore their being of the same substance, most of the early Christian writers thought the text "I and my Father are one," was to be understood of an unity or harmony of disposition only. Thus Tertullian observes that the expression is *unum*—one thing—not one person; and he explains it to mean unity, likeness, conjunction, and of the love that the Father bore to the Son. Origen says, let him consider the text, "All that believe were of one (*unum*) heart and of one (*unum*) soul," and then he will understand this, "I and my Father are one," (*unum*). Novatian says. "One thing (*unum*) being in the neuter gender, signifies an agreement of society, **not a unity of person**," and he explains it by this passage in Paul: "He that planteth and he that watereth are both one" (*unum*).[1]

Novatian found another indication of the Savior's intent in John 10:30. Jesus used the plural word "are" rather than the singular word "is." Novatian stated that this would never have been done if the Father and the Son were not distinct from one another.

> Finally, He adds, and says, "We are," not I am, so as to show, by the fact of His saying "I and the Father are," that they are two persons. Moreover, that he says one, has reference to the agreement, and to the identity of judgment, and to the loving association itself, as reasonably the Father and Son are one in agreement, in love, and in affection; and because He is of the Father, whatsoever He is, He is the Son; the distinction however remaining, that **He is not the Father who is the Son, because he is not the Son who is the Father.** For He would not have added "We are," if He had it in mind that He, the only and sole Father, had become the Son.[2]

Jesus taught that the Father, Son, and Holy Ghost are three distinct beings. Note the distinction of each when Jesus said, "But the Comforter, which is the Holy Ghost, whom the Father will send in my name, he shall teach you all things, and bring all things to your remembrance, whatsoever I have said unto you."[3]

Experts agree that the early Fathers (those who lived closest to the time of Christ) thought that the three could be distinguished numerically from one another. Origen, for example, became very upset with anyone who suggested otherwise.

> Following the custom of the Apologists and in conformity also with his own view that the Holy Ghost proceeded from the Father through the Son and is not equal with God, though it is worthy of honors and dignity, Origen takes only the Father and the Son as the subject of his discussion of distinction and unity in the Trinity. Still what he says of the Son would be true also of the Holy Spirit.
>
> Like Justin Martyr, he maintains that God and the Logos are real beings and **argues against those who believe that the distinction between them is not in number but only according to certain thoughts. This criticism of those who deny that god and the logos were numerically distinct means, of course, that he himself believes that they are numerically distinct and many, so that each one of them is numerically one.**[4]

This usage, of course, promotes a plurality of Persons. If each is one, then the total of these Persons has to be more than one. Such a formula would read 1 (the Father) + 1 (the Son) + 1 (the Holy Ghost) = 3 (the Godhead). The Fathers, in consistency with this logic, declared that the unity of the three was that of purpose (rule) and not of physical oneness.

> This conception of the relative unity of God is expressed by the Apologists in the term monarchy, that is, unity of rule, which they use as a description of the unity of God. Thus Justin Martyr, wishing to say that the philosophers are engaged in the investiga-

tion of the problem of the unity of God, says that questions continually arise for them about "the monarchy" of God. And so also Tatian, contrasting the polytheism of the Greeks with the monotheism of the Christians, describes the former as acknowledging "the dominion of many rather than the rule of one" (God the Father), the implication being that the Christian monotheism consists in the unity of rule. Similarly Theophilus describes the scriptural principle of the unity of God as the "monarchy of God" and when he wishes to say that many heathen writers at last recognized the unity of God, he says that those "who spoke of the multiplicity of gods came at length to the doctrine of the monarchy of God." The same view is expressed by Athenagoras in his statement that God, the Logos, and the Holy Spirit are "united in power," that is, in rule. The term "monarchy" and the expression "united in power" which they use as a description of the unity of God mean that, according to them, the unity of God is only a relative unity, a unity of rule.[5]

The other scripture which is often cited by Trinitarians to establish a case for physical oneness is John 14:6–9. Let us consider this passage.

> Jesus saith unto him, I am the way, the truth, and the life: no man cometh unto the Father, but by me.
> If ye had known me, ye should have known my Father also: and from henceforth ye know him, and have seen him.
> Phillip saith unto him, Lord. shew us the Father, and it sufficeth us.
> Jesus saith unto him, Have I been so long a time with you, and yet hast thou not known me, Phillip? he that hath seen me hath seen the Father; and how sayest thou then, Shew us the Father?[6]

How is it possible that Phillip could see the Father? The Trinitarians contend that it is because Jesus and the Father are the same Person. Yet we have already established that early Christians did not espouse such a doctrine. Then what is the answer? Jesus is testifying that there is a very close physical resemblance.

People often use such metaphors. For example, we say that we can see the earthly father in his son. What we really mean is that they look alike or share certain physical characteristics. Certainly one might be tempted to use the phrase if one were talking about identical twins.

Is there such a physical resemblance between God the Father and his son Jesus Christ? The Scriptures state that there is.

> Giving thanks unto the Father, which hath made us meet to be partakers of the inheritance of the saints in light;
> Who hath delivered us from the power of darkness, and hath

translated us into the kingdom of his dear Son:
   In whom we have redemption through his blood, even the forgiveness of sins:
   Who is the image of the invisible God, the firstborn of every creature.[7]

In whom the god of this world hath blinded the minds of them which believe not, lest the light of the glorious gospel of **Christ, who is the image of God,** should shine unto them.[8]

An image of anything is, according to *Webster's New Collegiate Dictionary,* "an exact likeness or a person strikingly like another person." Therefore, the response of Jesus makes perfect sense. He was explaining that the Father is like the Son and vice versa. Elder Bruce R. McConkie explains that:

> ...the Son appears and is in all respects like his Father; and conversely, the Father looks and acts like the Son. Their physical appearance is the same, both possess the attributes of godliness in their fullness and perfection; each would do and say precisely the same thing under the same circumstances. (*Mormon Doctrine,* pp. 294–295.) Hence the enigmatic and epigrammatic statement: 'He that hath seen me hath seen the Father.[9]

There are essentially three ways in which the unity of the Godhead has been explained. T.B. Strong explains these viewpoints with excellent clarity:

> We must now turn to the history of Trinitarian Theology, and see how the Church was led to define its faith as to the nature of God. Roughly speaking there are three ways in which the relation of the three Persons may be described. The difference between each person may be accentuated in a crude and careless way; this will virtually result in Tritheism—a belief in three Gods. Or, secondly, the difference may be regarded merely as a difference of mode of self-revelation. It may be held that there is an ultimate, unknowable, Divine substance, which reveals itself successively as Father, Son, and Holy Spirit, in no one of which forms is the revelation complete or permanent. Or, lastly, attention may be fixed upon the process apparently involved in the generation of the Son and the procession of the Holy Ghost; and then the Holy Trinity will be understood on the analogy of the Gnostic aeons as a process by which the absolutely unknown and unknowable Deity is brought into contact with the material world. We shall have, therefore, various interpretations of the unity and Divinity of the three Persons according to the modes of thought current in various ages.[10]

The first viewpoint which was mentioned was that of the Tritheists. They affirmed that the Son was not the Father and the Father was not the Son. In other words, they did recognize the Godhood of all three Persons, but acknowledged the primacy of the Father by worshipping him as "the only true God." I must take issue with Mr. Strong on one point: the idea of Tritheism does not necessarily need to be put together in "a crude and careless way." As we demonstrated earlier, most of the early Fathers were Tritheists. Furthermore, as W.N. Clarke notes, the apostles understood the Godhead in a Tritheistic way. The idea that the three might be physically one is not even mentioned in the Biblical writings.

> There is no mystery about their oneness and no attempt to show that there are three in one, or even a statement that the three are one. The word Trinity is never used, and there is no indication that the idea of Trinity had taken form. It has long been a common practice to read the New Testament as if the ideas of a later age upon this subject were in it, but they are not. In the days of the apostles the doctrine of the Trinity was yet to be created.[11]

That the apostles believed in three divine beings can be illustrated from Bible passages. Great care was taken to differentiate between the Father, Jesus Christ, and the Holy Ghost. This indicates a belief that each has his own identity. Such measures would not have been necessary if they were the same being.

Let us illustrate this point. Many humans use more than one name. For example, it is very common for an author to use a pen name. Samuel Langhorne Clemens used the pen name of Mark Twain. Who was he really? Using either is technically correct, because both names belong to him. However, both would not be used at the same time. There was only one man, even if he was known by two different names. We would not say that we had met Samuel Langhorne Clemens and Mark Twain. To do so would be to indicate that two men existed, not one man with two names.

The Bible differentiates between the three members of the Godhead by separating their names with the connecting word "and." This indicates three different individuals. In fact, the Savior himself used this construction in saying "Go ye therefore, and teach all nations, baptizing them in the name of the Father, and of the Son, and of the Holy Ghost."[12]

Some might argue that occasions exist when it is necessary to list both names of a person in the same sentence. When this happens, they are separated by the word "or." This does indicate that both names refer to the same individual. Since Jesus used the word "and," he was stating that each of the three was a separate being with its own identity. The apostles followed this same pattern:

> Paul, an apostle, (not of men, neither by man, but by Jesus Christ, and God the Father, who raised him from the dead).[13]

> Grace be to you, and peace, from God our Father, and from the Lord Jesus Christ.[14]

> Grace be with you, mercy, and peace, from God the Father, and from the Lord Jesus Christ, the Son of the Father, in truth and love.[15]

This separation was more than merely different identities. They had different responsibilities and perform different functions.

> Who is he that condemneth? It is Christ that died, yea rather, that is risen again, who is even at the right hand of God, who also maketh intercession for us.[16]

> But when the Comforter is come, whom I will send unto you from the Father, even the Spirit of truth, which proceedeth from the Father, he shall testify of me.[17]

As we have mentioned, the original Christian theology was Tritheistic in nature. However, many of the early Christian Fathers decided that such views were a mistake. They regarded such views to be crude (just as Mr. Strong does) and decided that such a concept was anthropomorphic. Since they decided that the Scriptures portrayer a misleading set of definitions, they decided to formulate new ones.

Such a plan is remarkably simple and efficient. Augustine and his contemporaries merely established a set of definitions which transformed the Godhead of the Bible (Father, Jesus Christ, and the Holy Ghost = three gods) into the Trinity (Father, Son, and Holy Ghost = one god). This theory was proposed in Augustine's works on the Trinity and was canonized into the Athanasian Creed. This creed begins with a series of preparatory clauses in which the reader is informed that the Father, Son, and the Holy Ghost equal one god and vice versa, the trap is sprung. We then told that the three Persons of the Godhead are to be conceived of as one god.

> And in this Trinity none is before or after the other; none is the greater or less than another; but the whole three Persons are co-eternal together, and co-equal; so that in all things the Unity in Trinity, and the Trinity in Unity is to be worshipped. **He therefore that will be saved must think of the Trinity.**[18]

The Unity of God

This tactic was very effective. A purge was undertaken in which the followers of Origen were driven from the church. These people (who had previously been considered to be very orthodox Christians) believed that the Godhead could only be numbered as three Persons. Once this was done, the new set of definitions was secure. Future generations would accept the new dogmas as if they had always existed.

This strategy worked so well that even the reformers did not see through the strategy. When they read the Bible, they interpreted the passages according to the definitions that they had been taught. Many people of today do the same thing. Gordon Kaufman states:

> Of course no individual human mind constructs the idea of God from scratch. All thinking about God and all devotion to God take place within a cultural and linguistic context in which the notion of God has already been highly developed through the imaginative work of many preceding generations. So the idea of God with which any particular individual works is always a qualification and development of notions inherited from earlier worshippers and prophets, poets and thinkers.[19]

The new definitions could not be harmonized with the scriptural message without a great deal of doctrinal development, however. Many theories were proposed in an attempt to fine-tune the emerging dogmas. Some of the new ideas were judged to be practical and were adopted in the canons of the councils which met in that day. Others were rejected and the authors were pronounced heretics. Religious histories of that day show that there were an incredible number of heresies (people who were trying to show how three persons could actually be one).

One of these heresies is mentioned by Strong. This idea is Sabellianism. It says that the Father, Son, and Holy Ghost are successive manifestations of God's substance. The leading councils of the Christian Church denounced the idea as false.

The third way of visualizing God which Strong mentioned is harder to understand. This is the system that Augustine and Thomas Aquinas installed. The Father, Son, and Holy Ghost occur as the result of certain processes. The statements of this theory are recognized as the orthodox dogmas of the Trinity.

1. There are two *processions* and only two processions in God: generation and spiration (breathing).
2. There are four *relations*, (paternity, filiation, active spiration, passive spiration), but only three *subsistent relations*, i.e., three relations which are mutually opposed and, therefore, distinct

> from one another (without, however, being distinct from the very being of God): paternity, filiation, and passive spiration. Active spiration (which involves Father and Son) is not opposed to either paternity or filiation, and, thus, does not constitute a fourth subsistent relation.
> 3. In God all things are one except what is opposed by the opposition of relations. Those relations which are opposed and, therefore, distinct one from the other are called, as noted above, subsistent relations, or *hypostases*. They give rise, in turn, to the trinity of *persons* within the Godhead: Father, Son and Holy Spirit.
> 4. Because of the unity of the divine essence, of the processions and of the relative oppositions, which constitute the Persons, there is a *mutual indwelling* (circumincession) of the Persons, one in the other two, the other two in the one, so that the Son is for all eternity in the Father, and the Father from all eternity in the Son, and so on.[20]

How does this complicated theory work? Imagine a divine substance. The Trinitarians tell us that within this substance is an entity who is known as God the Father. The entire substance is composed of love and knowledge. In fact, there is so much love that the Father does not retain it all. Some of this love leaves the Father and generates the Person of the Son.

How does such a process occur? We are told that the Son is generated in the same way that a thought is generated in a mind. Yet the generation is an ongoing process. Once the Father generates the Son, he begins to do it again.

We are further informed that the Holy Ghost is breathed, and consists of knowledge. The Father and Son produces it (out of will, not out of love). This, too, is thought to be an ongoing process. Michael Schmaus explains that such activity causes an eternal motion and ceaseless sharing of life between the Persons.

> The life and being of God is of such abundance, so overflowing with ability to know and love, that it cannot creatively display itself in the living, knowing and loving of a single person. It requires a threefold ego. Thus the tri-personality of God is a sign of life at its highest and richest potential...three persons use God's power, life-potential and faculties of knowing and loving to the full. There is no impersonal zone in God, but rather, in the sphere of the divine being, existence, life, knowledge, and will are taken to the highest possible peak of personal existence...The three divine persons exist in closest relationship with one another. **There is continually being carried on an exchange of life between them. Indeed, it is exchange that their life consists**...In the Father's giving of himself to the Son, and the Son's to the

The Unity of God

Father, there springs into being from the mightiness of their giving, a third divine Person...Each of the divine Person finds his existence and his joy in the personalities of the other two...Each of the divine Persons continually receives from each of the others fullness of life in the eternal bloom of youth, fullness so perfect as to be incapable of any enrichment.[21]

This is an interesting theory, but does it not have certain unpleasant ramifications? T.B. Strong objected to the ideas of Sabellianism, finding fault with the motion produced by the procession of the manifestations of God in reasoning: "Not only do the three Persons lose all reality and all true being, but God himself, the ultimate substance, of which these are partial manifestations, passes into the form of a blind force aimlessly repeating merely mechanical activities."[22]

Does not the theory of processions make all three Persons partial manifestations of the whole? If each of the three are constantly transmitting something to another throughout eternity, has not the substance of God been transformed into a "blind force aimlessly repeating mechanical activities?" Furthermore, the three Persons do lose all reality and are not true beings. Since all of these premises are encompassed in the idea of Processions, what is the difference between Sabellianism and Trinitarianism? How can we be sure that the three Persons are not real beings according to the Trinitarian doctrines? We can be sure because theologians plainly state that they are not.

Daniel Waterland mentions, "The Being of the Son **is an improper expression; because it supposes the Son to be a being,** [properly so called] that is, a separate being, **which he is not.**"[23]

When a cleric crosses this line and makes the Father too real, he is soundly ridiculed. Phillip Schaff tells about the case of William Sherlock:

> In the English Church the error of Tritheism was revived by Dean Sherlock in his "Vindication of the Doctrine of the Holy and Ever Blessed Trinity." He maintained that, with the exception of a mutual consciousness of each other, which no created spirits can have, the three divine persons are "three distinct infinite minds" or "three intelligent beings." He was opposed by South, Wallis, and others.[24]

As we have illustrated, the Father, Jesus Christ, and the Holy Ghost are not considered to be real beings in the doctrines of the Trinity. What are they then? Are they parts of the Trinity? They cannot even be that according to the creeds. Schaff quotes the

Westminster Confession, that, "there is but one only living and true God, who is, infinite in being and perfection, a most pure spirit invisible, **without body, parts or passions,** immutable, immense, eternal, incomprehensible, etc."[25]

The creeds of today specifically preclude any construction of God. We are told that he is a simple absolute being. This means, as G. L. Prestige points out, that there can be no compound relationships within him. He says that, "the doctrines of divine unity and self-consistency are clearly taught, the first to guard against polytheism (hence the insistence that the being of God is not susceptible of compound relationships), the second to preserve His absolute perfection."[26]

This simple being who is not capable of compound relationships has been designated as God. It has also been identified by Thomas Aquinas (who borrowed his ideas from Moslem interpretations of Aristotle) as the First Cause. Yet a First Cause cannot have anything in it that it is dependent upon. Herbert Spencer expounds:

> But to think of the First Cause as totally independent is to think of it as that which existed in the absence of all other existence; seeing that if the presence of any other existence is necessary, it must be partially dependent on that other existence, and so not be the First Cause. Not only, however, must the First Cause be a form of being which has no necessary relation to any other being, but **it can have no necessary relation within itself.** There can be nothing in it which determines change, and yet nothing which prevents change. For if it contains something which imposes such necessities or restraints, this something must be a cause higher than the First Cause, which is absurd. Thus the First Cause must be in every sense perfect, complete, "total; including within itself all power, and transcending all law. Or to use the established, it must be absolute."[27]

The Reverend Van Der Donckt followed this line of logic. He wrote an article on the Trinity and requested that it be published in the *Era.* They acceded to his wishes, with the understanding that the publishers were free to make editorial comments. In his exposition, the Roman Catholic theologian argues that there could not be any other beings inside the substance of God.

> If God were an aggregate of parts, these parts would be either necessary beings or contingent (that do not necessarily exist); or some would be necessary and some contingent. None of these suppositions are tenable, therefore, God is not an aggregate of parts.
> First supposition: If the parts of God were necessary beings

The Unity of God

> there would be several independent beings, which the infinity of God precludes. God would not be infinite, if there were even one other being independent of him, as his power, etc., would not reach that being.
> Second supposition: The Necessary Being would be the aggregate of several contingent beings. An unreasonable supposition: contingent beings cannot by their addition or collection lose their essential predicate of contingency; in other words, the nature of the parts clings to the whole.
> The third supposition is equally absurd, for if some parts exist necessarily, it must be infinite in every perfection; therefore, it would of itself be sufficient to constitute God, and could not be improved by the addition of other parts.[28]

But if the Father, Son, and Holy Ghost are not considered to be real beings and are not parts of the whole, then how are they to be understood? The framers of the Trinity thought of them as abstractions.

For example, we know that feelings such as love and hate are abstractions. They do not exist unless a person feels them. Similarly, knowledge and wisdom exist in the brain of a person. They also have no independent existence. Yet Plato considered these things to be real and to have their own existence, according to Weber, who asked, "Does this mean that because his god is an Idea he is not a reality? On the contrary, because he is an Idea, and nothing but an Idea, he is the highest reality; for, from Plato's point of view, the idea only is real."[29]

The Fathers borrowed this theory of Plato and began to personify the feelings and attributes of deity. For example, Joseph Priestley explains that Theophilus said Jesus was the wisdom of God.

> Thus Theophilus, who was contemporary with Justin, though a later writer, says, that when God said let us make man, **he spoke to nothing but his own logos, or wisdom**; and, according to Origen, **Christ was the eternal person, or wisdom of God**...Also, explaining John 1:3, he says, "God can do nothing without reason, i.e., without himself."[30]

There is no doubt that the original references to Jesus as the wisdom of God were figurative. However, the Greek element chose to interpret such passages literally.

Similarly, they came to interpret Jesus as the voice of God. John had called Jesus the Word. Priestley notes that Lactanius interpreted this in a literal sense. This brings to mind the words of Augustine (cited in a previous chapter) that Lactanius was one of those who had brought pagan teachings into the church. Was this concept (which we are considering) the one that Augustine was speaking of?

> For Lactanius, who was tutor to the son of Constantine, gives us the same account of the business...The Sacred Scriptures inform us that the Son of God is the sermo ratio (the speech or reason) of God...But he being also a **breathing** (spiritus), yet proceeding from the mouth of God with voice and sound, is the **word**; for this reason, because he was to be a teacher of the knowledge of God...[31]

Athanasius also used these beliefs in his debates with the Arians. Alfred Weber summarizes some of the logic which the bishop of Alexandria used as, "What do you mean, he (Athanasius) demands of the Arians, by assuming that the Son created the world at the command of the Father? Do you thereby assert that God the Father did not create the world, but simply ordered a demurrage to create it? **What is the Son if not the Word of God, and what is a command if not an act of speech?** Hence God commanded the Son through the Son to create the world."[32]

We must not lose sight of the fact that depriving each of the persons of their right to individuality is really making them into metaphors. In short, we cease to talk about the god of Abraham, Isaac, and Jacob who appeared in Biblical times. Gone is the Father who loved us so much that he gave his son for us. Instead, a god is instituted who is transcendent and unknowable. This god the theologians profess to know—but the three beings who are described in the Bible are now to be depicted in terms which are "shadowy."

> While modern theology an the whole wishes to retain the Trinitarian symbolism, it generally understands "Father, Son and Spirit" as symbols in the sense of metaphors expressing the inexpressible and infinite complexity in God, the infinite depth as well as the creative ground and source of all existence. John Macquarrie says "person" is inappropriate when used nonsymbolically because it then connotes separateness and "inevitable privacy and impenetrability." If the word is used, "the wisest course is to leave the meaning shadowy."[33]

But does the Bible not make the meaning of the Son of God clear? Did not Jesus tell us that his Father in Heaven had sent him to earth? Did he not talk to his disciples about the nature of the Holy Ghost? Then why should such subjects be shadowy?

As we have established, the reason for leaving the meaning

The Unity of God

shadowy is that the Trinitarians do not know what they are talking about. They are really playing with words. The Father, for example, is described as a person, a relation, a name, a mode or a manifestation of the one God. The definitions of those words are also vague. In fact, Augustine referred to the Father, Son, and Holy Ghost as three "somewhats." Anselm called them "three I know not what."

On the other hand, we do know what the word "god" means. The creeds agree that the Father is God, the Son is God, and the Holy Spirit is God. Is God an intelligent being? To argue in the negative is blasphemy. Then each of the three members of the Godhead must be an intelligent being. Not only are they divine beings, but each of them must possess all of the powers and attributes that a god possesses. William Sherlock writes:

> It is plain that the Persons are perfectly distinct, for they are Three distinct and infinite Minds, and therefore Three distinct Persons; **for a person is an intelligent being**, and to say, they are Three Divine Persons, and not three distinct Minds, is both heresy and Nonsense: The Scripture, I'm sure, **represents Father, Son, and Holy Ghost as three intelligent beings, not as three powers or faculties of the same being, which is downright Sabellianism**; for faculties are not Persons, no more than memory, will and understanding [all used by Augustine in his explanations of how the Trinity worked] are Three Persons in one Man...[34]
>
> **We must allow the divine persons to be real substantial beings,** if we allow each Person to be God, unless we will call anything a God, which has no real Being...[35]

What is a real being? A real being has a brain to control all of its actions. It has some means of implementing the wishes of that brain. This usually is accomplished by the use of arms, legs, etc., so that the entity in question can alter to suit its wishes. Any being worthy of being referred to as God must have the ability to do this. Such an entity is a stand-alone system. It is able to act on its own without need of outside intervention. Every animal has this ability. Are we to believe that a God is unable to do what we can?

A member of the Trinity does not have this ability. It is not a stand-alone system. In fact, none of the three can exist or function without the others.

For example, Trinitarians insist that God is a substance which fills the entire universe. Since, according to the theories, deity is not capable of division, the Father occupies the whole of this substance. When the Son begotten as a spiritual entity, the Father placed all of this substance in the Son. Yet in some mystical way, the Father did not lose any of his substance. Then the Father and the Son breathed the Holy Ghost and gave him all of this substance. However, the Father and the Son still retained the substance for themselves.

The message is clear: the Father, Son, and Holy Ghost have ceased to be real beings. Worse yet, they have been wholly assimilated. If we could use a powerful enough microscope to peer inside, we would not be able to discern any of the three. We are told that this is because each of them occupies the whole substance.

Let us make a comparison to something which we can comprehend. Let us suppose that I show you a chocolate rabbit which I call Bunny. I then show you this same confection and introduce it as Harvey. Then, in close succession, I introduce it twice more as Bugs and Peter Cottontail. You ask me how this confection can be all three. I inform you that the names are dictated by its origin. The original rabbit was refined from plants and then poured into a mold which gave it its shape. This rabbit is called Bunny. Then the rabbit was melted, and every last drop (all of the substance) was poured back into the mold. The second rabbit is called Harvey. The same process was repeated and the third rabbit is called Bugs. However, all three rabbits are referred to by the name of Peter Cottontail, which really is the identity of all of them. I next inform you that Bunny, Harvey, and Bugs all still exist, for all of the chocolate exists and none of it was divided from the rest.

Would you not point out that I have merely applied four different names to the same quantity of chocolate? To my protests that each identity still existed because the chocolate still exists, you say nonsense. When one rabbit was melted and all of its contents poured into the mold, the previous rabbit ceased to exist. Furthermore, no matter what name I choose to give the confection or how many times it is remolded, it is still a chocolate rabbit. Bunny, Harvey, Bugs, and Peter Cottontail are just names which I applied to it.

Regardless of whether someone chooses to call the Trinity the Father, the Son or the Holy Ghost, they are still talking about substance. The only difference lies in the names used and the modes (actions) which are associated with this substance. This is the central premise of Sabellianism. Modern Trinitarian doctrines often are remodeled Sabellianism. Consider, for example, the ideas of Horace Bushnell:

> In *God in Christ* (1849) Bushnell contends that the Trinity is instrumental or modal, a method of revelation: Father, Son and Spirit are "incidental to revelation," though they "may be and

The Unity of God

probably are from eternity," since God may have three modes of personal action through which God discloses himself, but never of three Persons in God, **for God's personality is really incomprehensible to us.**[36]

The Trinity of Reinhold Seeberg is also related to the activities which the persons engage in.

> **The Trinity, therefore, refers to differentiations in the divine universal activity,** to the "threefold will of God in relation to nature, history and personality": as Father, God is lord of nature (the entire created world); as Son, he is lord of history (and Church); as Holy Spirit, he becomes effective in and through individuals.[37]

We have reviewed some of the theories concerning the unity of God. As we have observed, they differ in some particulars, but agree in others. Those which make the Father, Son, and Holy Ghost to be real persons who have their own center of consciousness and personality are denounced for making three gods. Those which proclaim them to be relations, names, modes, or manifestations of the one God are deemed orthodox. Such ideas are, of course, versions of Sabellianism. But they are worse than that—they are false!

The Scriptures testify that Jesus Christ is the Son of God in an eternal way. Jesus testified that God the Father is his father. We are not speaking in an abstract sense, as some of the Fathers chose to do. Instead, the testimonies which have been borne concerning God the Father, Jesus Christ and the Holy Ghost portray things as they actually are. Thomas Torrance mentions, "What is at stake here is the question whether biblical statements about God—for example, about his Fatherhood in respect to Jesus Christ his incarnate Son—are related to what they claim to signify merely in a conventional way...or in a real way."[38]

What is the "real way" which the Scriptures portray? They portray each as a real being. The Son is described as standing on the right hand of the Father and interceding in our behalf. We are told that he actually lived as a mortal on the earth and died to pay for our sins. Three days later he arose and, after showing himself to many believers, ascended into heaven where he lives today.

He will return to rule over those who believe in him and keep his commandments. Jesus is no abstraction—he is a real being! God the Father is a real being.

Matthew records that Mary is the mother of Jesus, but that God is the Father. The voice of the Father was heard at the baptism of Jesus, on the mount of Transfiguration, and on the day of crucifixion. On all three occasions he bore witness that Jesus is his son. He loves us so much that he allowed his only begotten son to die and pay for our sins. Furthermore, the Book of Revelation informs us that the Father will actually come at the and of the world and dwell in our midst. God the Father is a real being!

The Holy Ghost is a real being. His influence has been felt on many occasions. Most Christians, of course, remember that his presence was evident on the day of Pentecost. Jesus said that he would ask the Father to send the Holy Ghost to teach the apostles. Paul testified that the saints had received gifts of the Spirit from this great personage. Nephi actually saw the Holy Ghost and bore record that he had a form like a man. He too is a real being!

It is precisely because these three are real beings that the whole Bible makes sense. It has many accounts of God appearing to mankind. It does not describe some vague, shapeless something which no one can know. Instead, it describes beings with body, parts, and passions like a man—because the Father, Son, and Holy Ghost are real!

CHAPTER 3 REFERENCES

1. Priestley, *A History of the Corruptions of Christianity* as cited in Roberts, *The "Mormon" Doctrine of Deity*, 151
2. Novatian XXVII
3. John 14:26
4. Wolfson, *The Philosophy of the Church Fathers*, 317
5. Ibid., 313
6. John 14:6–9
7. Colossians 1:12–15
8. 2 Corinthians 4:4
9. McConkie, *Doctrinal New Testament Commentary*, 1:731
10. Strong, *A Manual of Theology*, 161
11. Clarke, *The Christian Doctrine of God*, 230
12. Matthew 28:19
13. Galatians 1:1
14. Ephesians 1:2
15. 2 John 1:3
16. Romans 8:34
17. John 15:26
18. Brantl, *Catholicism*, 171
19. Kaufman, *The Theological Imagination*, 23
20. McBrien, *Catholicism*, 2:355
21. Fortman, *The Triune God*, 297
22. Strong, *A Manual of Theology*, 163
23. Waterland, *The Works of Daniel Waterland*, 4:345
24. Schaff, *History of the Christian Church*, 3:675
25. Westminister Confession, Art. 2, Sec. 1 as cited in Roberts, *The "Mormon" Doctrine of Deity*, 104
26. Prestige, *God in Patristic Thought*, xix
27. Spencer, *First Principles*, 29–30 as cited in Roberts, *The "Mormon" Doctrine of Deity*, 105–106
28. Roberts, *The "Mormon" Doctrine of Deity*, 52–53
29. Weber, *History of Philosophy*, 75
30. Origen, *Contra Celsum*, 247 as cited in Priestley, *A History of the Corruptions of Christianity*, 12
31. Ibid., 14–15
32. Weber, *History of Philosophy*, 188
33. Bloesch, *The Battle for the Trinity*, 93
34. Sherlock, *The Vindication of the Most Blessed and Holy Trinity*, 66–67
35. Ibid., 47

36. Welch, *The Trinity in Contemporary Theology*, 26
37. Ibid., 38
38. Bloesch, *The Battle For the Trinity*, 95

4
Does God Have A Body?

In the last three chapters we have been dealing with the sectarian theory that there is a generic substance called God which fills the universe and contains three Persons within it. It is the use of this theory which keeps the Father, Jesus Christ, and the Holy Ghost from being perceived as real beings. Without the idea of this universal substance, the Godhead must be recognized as three gods.

It is now time to ask the unthinkable questions: Who said that there is this universal substance? Who said that a deity does not have a form like man? How reliable are those who taught this idea? Were there not also many early Christians who believed that God does have a body? The LDS Church affirms that "The Father has a body of flesh and bones as tangible as man's; the Son also; but the Holy Ghost has not a body of flesh and bones but is a personage of Spirit. Were it not so, the Holy Spirit could not dwell in us."[1]

In contrast, here is the view which is usually expressed by the other Christian churches of the day. They scoff at the idea that God has a body.

> At this point Dr. Paden (of the Presbyterian Church) made his address (August 16, 1901) first taking up some of the standard workings on "Mormon" doctrine and reading from them the ideas of God as incorporated in the "Mormon" faith...He placed special stress on the idea that when man attempted to give God a human form he fashioned him after their own weaknesses and frailties. A carnal man, he said, had a carnal God, and a spiritual man a spiritual god. The teaching of a material god, said he, and of a plurality of gods, I think is heathenish. The material conception of God is the crudest possible conception.[2]

Which view is correct? It is that of the LDS Church. Then why do nearly all other Christian churches describe God as having neither body, parts or passions? Where do their ideas come from?

Do the "heathen" religions truly have a material god? We will attempt to answer these questions.

First of all, the Scriptures bear witness that God the Father, Jesus Christ, and the Holy Ghost do live. They really exist. They are not feelings (love) or acquired information (knowledge) as some have theorized. Nor are they ideas, relations, accidents or any of the other abstract concepts which men have invented. They are actual beings who are capable of answering our prayers. All of the prophets bear witness of this fact.

However, many people are unwilling to believe these prophets. They have considered the idea of a material god to be crude and foolish. And so they decided to change the doctrines concerning the nature of God to fit their own preconceived notions.

Those who have studied the Old Testament know that it describes a corporeal god. Theologians of all faiths agree that this is an indisputable fact. However, such a belief cannot be harmonized with the prejudices of many. Therefore, they have invented the theory of anthropomorphism.

> In the earliest parts of the Bible there are many passages which speak of God in a way which seems to us anthropomorphic, i.e., feelings and thoughts and acts are attributed to Him which belong to man and not to God; e.g., God is said to walk in the Garden of Eden in the cool of the day, Gen. 3:8; He is said to have repented that He had made man on the earth, and to have been grieved at the heart; Gen. 6:6, see also Gen. 11:5-7; 18:32; 32:24-32. As time went on men perceived that such language was metaphorical; but during the childhood of the race it was the most natural way in which to express man's beliefs about the ways and thoughts of God.[3]

Thus men set aside the message of the Scriptures and insert their own doctrines. Why have they done this? Because they found the literal meaning of the words to be offensive. Clement of Alexandria (who wrote long after the Scriptures were completed and who had never received a revelation from God) exclaims, "We must not even **think** of the Father of all as having a shape, or as moving, or as standing or sitting, or as being in some place, or as having a left and a right hand, even though the Scriptures say these things about him."[4]

Why did these individuals object to the idea that God had a shape and could do all these things? Because they had been educated in the ideas of Greek philosophers like Plato, Heraclitus, and Aristotle. These ancients had defined how a deity was constructed. Their ideas were not in harmony with the Scriptures.

Instead of accepting the scriptural witness, Clement, Athanasius, Augustine and others (who had attended the Greek schools, and who knew how a Greek god would be constructed) decided that a mistake had been made. The idea of a corporeal God appeared to be defective. But, as Origen pointed out, the Greeks knew how to correct such mistakes.

> It is very instructive to find Celsus (Origen, c. Cels. 1. 2) proceeding to say that the Greeks understood better how to judge, to investigate, and to perfect the doctrines devised by the barbarians, and to apply them to the practice of virtue. This is quite in accordance with the idea of Origen, who makes the following remarks on this point: "**When a man trained in the schools and sciences of the Greeks becomes acquainted with our faith, he will not only recognize and declare it to be true, but also by means of his scientific training and skill reduce it to a system and supplement what seems to him defective in it**, when tested by the Greek method of exposition and proof, thus at the same time demonstrating the truth of Christianity."[5]

But what would the Church of Jesus Christ be teaching that was defective? He knew who his Father was and had taught this knowledge to his disciples. The Greeks, therefore, had nothing to give that would help Christianity. The modifications which they inserted would paganize the faith of Christ rather than Christianizing these ideas.

What belief was so sacred in the minds of these Fathers that they would bring it into Christianity? It was the leading premise of pantheism. Pantheism is known as the worship of nature. Its premises are essentially very simple. They affirm that there is one divine substance which fills the universe. It is present in every blade of grass, in every tree, in every animal—in short, in everything. Within this divine substance are a number of persons.

Leonard Paine explains that, "The pantheist holds that there is but one substance in the universe, and that personality is an accident or quality or mode of existence of substance so that there may be and in fact are many persons included in the one universal substance of things."[6]

The number of divine beings within this substance were commonly represented as three and could be termed a trinity. Lord Bolingbroke cites a number of pagan sects which believed in this kind of trinity.

> What seems more peculiar to him is, that in the account he gives of the doctrine of the Trinity, he represents it as having been originally derived from the heathen theology. He says, that the heathen philosophers "affirmed a Trinity of divine hypostases in the Godhead. They held a *monad* or unity above all essence, a second proceeding eternally from the First, and a third proceeding eternally from the second, or from the first and second." That the hypothesis of the Trinity made a part of the **Egyptian** theology. "It was brought from **Egypt** into Greece by Orpheus, whosoever he was, and probably by others in that remote antiquity: And that it was in much use afterwards, and that we find the traces of it in all the theistic philosophers taught." He speaks of the **Egyptian, Pythagorean, Platonic,** and of the **Zoroastrian, Chaldaic,** and **Samothracian Trinity**. And he mentions it also as having been anciently taught among the **Chinese**, and produces a passage out of one of their ancient books to this purpose.[7]

Were these trinities similar to the modern orthodox Christian Trinity? We must insist that they are. Ralph Cudworth attempts to show the similarities in order to claim that the pagans borrowed this idea from the Hebrews. However, it seems more likely to me that the Christians borrowed this idea from the pagans.

> Now the Scholiasts upon Dionysius pretended to give a reason of this Denomination of the Persian Mithras, Triplatos, or Threefold, from the Miracle done in Hezekiah's Time, when the day was increased, and almost Triplicated; as if the Magi had thereupon given the name of Threefold, to their God Mithras, that is the Sun, and appointed an Anniversary Solemnity for a Memorial thereof. But learned men have already shewed the Foolery of this Conceit; and therefore it cannot be well otherwise concluded, but that **here is a manifest indication** of a Higher Mystery, viz., a Trinity in the Persian theology...[8]

That the Fathers adopted the pantheistic idea of one divine substance can be readily demonstrated by observing their preoccupation with the idea of substance or essence. They talked about it incessantly, even though they admitted that they had no idea what it was composed of. J.R. Illingworth refers to the statements of several fathers:

> "That God is, I know," says Basil; "but what His essence is, I hold to be above reason...faith is competent to know that God is, not what he is." "With regard to the Creator of the world," says Gregory of Nyssa, "we know that He is, but deny not that we are ignorant of the definition of his essence." John of Damascus exclaims, "Neither do we know, nor can we tell what the essence of God is..."[9]

The concept that there was a universal substance was considered to be so important that the Fathers developed their entire system of divinity around it. For example, when Arius and Athanasius stated their differences at the council of Nicea, they were both arguing about the nature of this essence. Arius stated that God could not communicate his substance, and thus Jesus could not be God. Athanasius contended that Jesus and the Father were composed of the exact same substance, and that this condition made them one God. The words which were utilized to describe this oneness were *homoousios* (one substance) and "consubstantial."

For Arius and Athanasius, the central question was whether Jesus was part of this central substance or if he was derived from something outside this essence. Both agreed that if Jesus were not made of this substance, he could not be God.

> ...the Son is begotten of the Father in a manner altogether different from that of human generation; **not only is he similar to the Father's substance, but he cannot be divided from it**...Therefore the synod [of Nicea], rightly understanding the matter, wrote that the Son is consubstantial with the Father, in order to overthrow the perversity of the heretics, and to show that the Word is different from all things that have been made. (Athanasius, De decretis Nic. Syn., 20)[10]

The Bible described God as having a form like a man. This idea was clearly not compatible with the concept of a universal substance. Therefore, the Fathers decided to construct a new image of God. As we have seen, they did not know what he is like. In order for them to construct such an image, it was necessary for them to work backwards. They would first determine what characteristics God does not have and by a process of elimination establish what characteristics God does have. Athanasius said, "Although it is impossible to comprehend what God is, yet it is possible to say what He is not."[11]

The Fathers decided to start from the premise that God was not a man. Then they began to subtract all of those characteristics which make us human. Clement of Alexandria, head of the Christian Platonic school, describes this process:

> If we abstract from all the natural qualities of a body, first from its depth, then from its breadth, and then from its length, we are left with a concept of what we might call unity with position. By abstracting, further, from position, we reach the notion of unity itself. If then, abstracting from all the qualities of bodies, and of the things we call incorporeal, we cast ourselves into the magni-

tude of Christ, and, thence, in holiness, advance into his immensity, we reach some slight understanding of the Omnipotent: not that we understand what it is, but rather what it is not. (Clement of Alexandria, *Stromata*, V, 11:71, 2, 3; MG 9, 1078; Stahlin II, 374)[12]

Is this a valid way to determine what God is like? Logic itself should show us that it is not. Our entire thought processes are human. Whatever we finished with would have some human characteristics. Dean Mansel argues that the end result of such a process of elimination would be a monstrosity.

> They may not forsooth, think of the unchangeable God as if he were their fellow man, influenced by human motives, and moved by human supplications. They want a truer, juster idea of the Deity as he is, than that under which he has been pleased to reveal himself; and they call on their reason to furnish it. Fools, to dream that man can escape from himself, that human reason can draw aught but a human portrait of God. **They do but substitute a marred and mutilated humanity for one exalted and entire: they add nothing to their conception of God as He is, but only take away part of their conception of man**...Do we ascribe to him a fixed purpose? Our conception of such a purpose is human. Do we speak of him as continuing unchanged? Our conception of continuance is human...**But our rational philosopher stops short in his reasoning. He strips off from humanity just so much as suits his purpose; and the residue thereof he maketh a god**...**Man is still the residue that is left; deprived indeed of all that is amiable in humanity, but in the darker features which remain, still man**...Better is the superstition which sees the image of God in the wonderful whole which God has fashioned, than the philosophy which would carve out for itself a deity out of the remnant which man has mutilated...to deify the emptiest of all abstractions, a something or nothing, with just enough of its human original left to form a theme for the disputation of philosophy, but not enough to furnish a single ground of appeal to the human feelings of love, of reverence, and of fear. Unmixed idolatry is more religious than this. Undisguised atheism is more logical.[13]

In fact, believing that God is without body, parts, and passions could be considered by many to be anthropomorphic. Strong points out that any human speculations on the subject of God, since they come from the mind, are open to question. No reason can really be formulated as to why a belief in a formless, invisible, immaterial god is less anthropomorphic than a belief in a corporeal god.

> And in this region we can never tell whether an anthropomorphic taint is or is not clinging to our highest and most abstract

conceptions of the Divine nature. **The most philosophical theory of God's nature may be as anthropomorphic as that of the crudest savage, for all we know**; as tightly bound, that is by human limitations...in the one case human characteristics were rashly imported into the notion of God; in the other they are simply left out, and there is no clear rule why one is better than the other...The principle of anthropomorphism covers much more than the use of the human form, it is involved in all human speculations which originate in and do not transcend the mere use of human faculties.[14]

In order to utilize the theory of a universal substance, many theologians compare it to God's spirit. They state that God is everywhere because he is a spirit and a spirit does not have a body. This is not a true statement. Paul declared that there is such a thing as a spiritual body, that "it is sown a natural body; it is raised a spiritual body. There is a natural body, and there is a spiritual body."[15]

This spiritual body has substance. Joseph Smith points out that it is composed of matter, saying, "There is no such thing as immaterial matter. All spirit is matter, but it is more fine or pure, and can only be discerned by purer eyes; We cannot see it; but when our eyes are purified we shall see that it is all matter."[16]

Such doctrines were believed by ancient Christianity and were not invented by the LDS Church. Ralph Cudworth, who wrote in 1678 (long before Joseph Smith was born), documents that such beliefs existed among Christians in the first centuries.

> However this at least is certain from hence that Origen himself took it for granted, that **humane souls** departed, were not altogether Naked or Unclothed, but Clothed with a certain **subtle body**, wherein they could also Visibly appear, and that in their pristine form.[17]

Cudworth cites several Scriptures to establish the fact that a spirit does have a body.

> Moreover, it might be here observed also, that when upon our Savior's first **apparition** to his disciples, it is said, that they were affrighted, as supposing they had seen a spirit; **our savior does not tell them, that a spirit or ghost, had no body at all**, wherein it could Visibly appear; but (as rather taking that for granted) that **a spirit had no flesh and bones**, no such **solid body**, as they might find him to have; bidding them therefore, handle him; to remove that Scruple of theirs. As if he should have said, Though Spirits, or Ghosts, and Souls Departed, have Bodies (or Vehicles) which may by them be so far condensed, as sometimes to make a Visible

appearance to the Eyes of men; yet have they not any such **solid bodies**, as those of **flesh and bone** and therefore by Feeling and Handling, may you satisfie your selves, that I am not a meer Spirit, Ghost, or Soul, Appearing; as others have frequently done, without a Miracle; but that I appear in that very same **solid body**, wherein I was crucified by the Jews, by Miraculous Divine Power, raised out of the sepulchre, and now to be found no more there...This is a place of Scripture, which as it hath been interpreted by the Generality of the Ancient Fathers, would Naturally Imply, even the **soul of our Savior Christ** himself, after his **death**, and before his *resurrection*, not to have been quite **naked** from all Body, but to have had a certain **subtle** or **spirituous clothing**, and it is this of St. Peter, which being understood by those Ancients, of our Savior Christ's descending into **Hades** or **Hell**, is accordingly thus rendered in the Vulgar Latin, **put to death in the flesh, but quickened in the spirit. In which (spirit) also, he went and preached, to those spirits, that were in prison**, So...As also the following Verse is to be understood; That our Savior Christ, went in that **spirit**, wherein he was **quickened, when he was put to death in the flesh, and therein preached to the spirits in prison.** (1 Peter 3:18–19) By which Spirits, in Prison also, would have meant, not **pure incorporeal substances or naked souls**, but **souls** Clothed with **subtle spiritous bodies**; as that word may be often understood elsewhere in Scripture. But thus much we are unquestionably certain of; from the Scripture; That not only Elias, whose **terrestrial body**, seems to have been, in part at least, Spiritualized, in his **ascent** in that **fiery chariot**, but also Moses, appeared Visibly to our Savior and his Disciples, upon the Mount (Matthew 17:1–7), and therefore (since piety will not permit us to think this is a meer Prestigious thing) in Real Bodies; which Bodies also seem to have been Luciform or Lucid, like to our Savior's then **transfigured body.**[18]

In 1777 Joseph Priestley published a book entitled *Disquisitations Relating to Matter and Spirit*, arguing that the early Christians had believed that a spirit was composed of matter.

In this book, Priestley quotes Isaac de Beausobre (*Histoire Critique de Manichee et du Manicheisme*), who states that many early Christians believed that God had a body. In fact, the idea that God did not have a body was thought to be heresy.

If the modern metaphysician be shocked at what he has heard already, what will he say of the **anthropomorphites**, who maintained that God had even a human form? and yet Beausobre says, p. 502, **that this error is so ancient, that it is hardly possible to find the origin of it.** They supposed that God had a body, subtle like light, but with organs exactly like the human body, not for necessity, but for ornament, **believing it to be the most excellent of forms.** This opinion must have been very common in the East.

Does God Have A Body?

The contrary opinion was even considered as heresy, because it was the opinion of Simon Magus.[19]

Catholics and Protestants alike proclaim that Adolph Harnack is one of the foremost authorities on early Christian beliefs. He notes that the anthropomorphists were not heretics, but were "the old *regula* of the church." Such individuals chose to believe that God had a body because the Bible described him that way. They were not subdued until the fifth century.

> ...how many shades of belief there were between the crude anthropomorphists and the spiritualists! The latter, as a rule, had reason to dread the arguments, and frequently the fists of the former; **they could not but be anxious about their own orthodoxy, for the old regula was on the side of their opponents**...[20]

One of the leading Christian authorities of the early third century was Tertullian. He was the first Christian to use the word "trinity." However, Tertullian believed that God had a body and ridiculed those who disagreed with him.

> I assert that nothing insubstantial and void could have proceeded from God, since he himself is not insubstantial and void from whom it issued...Is it conceivable that an insubstantial being should have created concrete things; a void, solids; an incorporeal, bodies?...The Scripture says (Exodus 20:7): "Thou shalt not take the name of God for nothing." (in vanum, "for a void thing," "for unreality") This is surely he "who being in the form of God, thought it not a prize to be equal with God" (Phil. 2:6). What form is this? Surely in some form, not none. For **who will deny that God is a body**, although he is a spirit?[21]

Let us return to the writings of Priestley. He quotes Beausobre who cites the sentiments of Tertullian as a proof that Christians did believe that God had a body.

> "In general," says my author, p. 474, "the idea of a substance absolutely incorporeal was not a common idea with Christians at the beginning. When I," he adds, "consider with what confidence Tertullian, who thought that God was corporeal, and **figured**, speaks of his opinion, it makes me suspect that it must I have been the general opinion of the Latin church. Who can deny," says he, "that God is a body, though he is a spirit? Every spirit is a body, and has a **form** proper to it. Melito, so much boasted of for his virtues and knowledge, composed a treatise to prove that God is corporeal."[22]

Here we must note that those who persist in believing that God is corporeal are usually referred to as "crude" and "vulgar". What is meant when these two words are applied?

The *American Dictionary of the English Language* defines "crude" as "raw, unprepared: not reduced to order form: unfinished: undigested: immature." The Greek theologians hung this label upon the anthropomorphists because they did not consider this view to be as enlightened and polished as that of the spiritualists. The word "vulgar" is defined as "pertaining to or used by the common people." In other words, the belief in a corporeal God was a common one among the rank and file Christians. Those who considered themselves to be among the spiritually elite (philosophically trained) said that God had no form.

The anthropomorphists did not believe that God had no form. To them, matter was necessary in order to sustain attributes.

> The vulgar, who consider **spirit** as a **thin genial substance**, would be exceedingly puzzled if they were to realize the modern idea of a proper **immaterial being**; since to them it would seem to have nothing **positive** in its nature, but to be only a **negation of properties**, though disguised under the positive appellation of **spirit**. To them it must appear to be the idea of **nothing at all**, and to be incapable of supporting any properties.[23]

As we have previously stated, those who were philosophically trained concluded that God was composed of a universal immaterial substance. The Scriptures do not mention any such substance.

> It will be said, that if the principle in **man** may be a property of a material substance, the **divine being** himself may be material also; whereas, it is now almost universally believed to be the doctrine of revelation, that the Deity is, in the strictest sense of the word, an immaterial substance, incapable of local presence; though it will be shown in its proper place, that the sacred writers say nothing about such a substance.[24]

The Scriptures portray a corporeal god who is often described as being like a man in form. Groups like the anthropomorphists interpreted these passages literally. As Priestley points out, if such a conception was really objectionable, the prophets and apostles would have denounced it. Since they did not, we must assume that they agreed with the idea which was being presented.

> Now, had even this opinion been a **dangerous one** (though it is not philosophically just) there would certainly have been something said to guard us against it, and prevent our entertaining a

notion so dishonorable to God, and so injurious to ourselves. But it is remarkable that nothing of this kind does occur.[25]

We have mentioned that especially in the second, third, fourth and fifth centuries, there were a great number of Christians who believed that God was a universal substance. Such individuals interpreted the Bible allegorically. They had learned that the Bible would not sustain their speculations. In order to justify these beliefs, one had to read between the lines.

Let us consider the case of Augustine. His mother had enrolled him as a catechumen as soon as he was born. His father, Petricius, was a pagan and made sure that his son was trained in the Greek religions. Augustine, who possessed one of the most brilliant minds that the world has ever known, did not believe the doctrines of Christianity as a youth. Hugh Nibley writes:

> For twenty years at least, Augustine was never able to find out just what the Christian church believed. He tells how he went to school as a boy and made fun of the things his mother believed, how he joined a strange Christian sect, the Manichaeans, which enjoyed enormous popularity at the time, and for once in his life thought he knew certainty; when he left the Manichaeans, he says the bottom of his world fell out, and he spent the ensuing years in dark despair; He joined a group calling themselves the sancti, large numbers of whom were living secretly in Rome; and all the time his mother kept after him to return to the church of his birth, but this he could not do because their arguments could not stand up to those of the Manichaeans, from whom in a vague way he still hoped for light; when he finally became a catechumen (again) upon the urging of his mother and St. Ambrose, easily the most important leader in the church of the time, he still did not know what to believe but was "doubting everything, tossed back and forth in it all." In listening to Ambrose, he says, he gradually came to the conviction that "if the Catholic Church did not teach the truth, **at least it did not teach the kind of error I formerly attributed to it.**"[26]

What was the error which Augustine had previously thought that the Christians believed? It was that God had a body like man. Where did he get this idea? He learned it from his mother and the other members of the church with whom he associated.

> Very instructive is Augustine's confession (*Confess.* V. fin.; VI.) that it was the sermons of Ambrose that first delivered him from **the prejudice that the Catholic Church taught that the deity was fashioned like man.** If we reflect how much Augustine had mingled with Catholic Christians before his conversion, and how

much he had heard of the Church, we cannot suppose that he was the only one guilty of this prejudice.[27]

How did Ambrose deliver Augustine from this prejudice? He said that one had to read between the lines in the Scriptures and interpret the passages allegorically. Augustine was so elated by this news that he was baptized shortly thereafter.

> Ambrose was another man with a thoroughly non-Christian education who had joined the church by compulsion late in life; it was he, says Augustine, who "drew aside the mystic veil, laying open spiritually those things which if taken literally seemed to teach perversity." Perversity to whom? to Augustine and his fellow skeptics in the schools. Ambrose taught them that it was not necessary to believe all that childish literal-minded stuff in order to be a Christian. But why had he not known that from the first? He was born and reared a Christian by a singularly devout parent; now he was over thirty years old and had studied Christianity all his life—he was anything but stupid: why then had he been so thoroughly convinced that the church accepted the Scriptures literally, as he and the other intellectuals never could? Simply because the Christians did accept them that way. Augustine says he could never accept the Bible until he realized that it was a double back, "so that it might receive all in its open bosom, and through narrow passages waft over to thee some few."[28]

Why was the idea that God had a form like man so outrageous to Augustine? Because his pagan father had taught him that God was a substance that filled the universe. Those who had a Greek education regarded any idea that God had a body to be impious. Clement of Alexandria wrote, "Let no one, then, think that the Hebrews really attributed hands and feet and eyes and a mouth to God, or that they thought of him as really coming in and going out, or being angry and issuing threats. It is more pious to believe that some of these words are being used allegorically."[29]

Is it really pious to believe that God is a substance? How does it help us to have a stronger assurance that he lives?

Joseph Priestley states that, "For my part, I do not see how this notion of immateriality, in the strict metaphysical sense of the word, is at all calculated to heighten our veneration for the Divine Being."[30]

Nor is a belief in a corporeal deity going to cause any lack of devotion on the part of the worshippers. Beausobre points out that such beliefs still allow God to have all of his characteristics and attributes.

Does God Have A Body?

...whatever be the error of believing God to be corporeal, religion suffers nothing by it. Adoration, the love of God, and obedience to his sovereign will, remain entire. He is not the less the most holy, the most high, the almighty, and the immortal. Were Tertullian, Melito, etc., who believed God to be corporeal, on that account, the less good Christians (*Beausobre*, Vol. 1, p. 85)?[31]

Let us examine the Scriptures and see if there are some good reasons for us to believe that God does have a body like a man. As we do so, we shall attempt to refer to some principles which are at the heart of the Christian message.

1. Man was created in the image of God. By inverse logic, we can theorize that God has an image like man's. The account of the creation testifies of this likeness.

And God said, let us make man in our image, after our likeness: and let them have dominion over the fish of the sea, and over the fowl of the air, and over the cattle, and over all the earth, and over every creeping thing that creepeth upon the earth.

So God created man in his *own* image, in the image of God created he him; male and female created he them.[32]

As you will note, a definite impression is created by this wording. It is evident that the author (Moses) wanted to convey precisely this concept, because he uses the same phrase on other occasions in the book of Genesis.

This is the book of the generation of Adam. In that day that God created man, in the likeness of God created he him;[33]

And God blessed Noah and his sons, and said unto them, Be fruitful, and multiply, and replenish the earth.

Whoso sheddeth man's blood, by man shall his blood be shed: for in the image of God made he man.[34]

Some might argue that this anthropomorphistic idea was corrected in the New Testament. This is not the case. Instead, we find James using the same language when he says, "Therewith bless we God, even the Father; and wherewith curse we men, which are made after the similitude of God."[35]

2. A person who is a God has all of the parts which are present in a physical body on Earth. Let us begin with the description which John gave of someone whom he said looked like the resurrected Savior:

And in the midst of the seven candlesticks one like unto the Son of man, clothed with a garment down to the **foot**, and girt about the **paps** with a golden girdle.
His **head** and his **hairs** were white like wool, as white as snow; and his **eyes** were as a flame of fire;
And his **feet** like unto fine brass, as if they burned in a furnace; and his **voice** as the sound of many waters.
And he had in his **right hand** seven stars: and out of his **mouth** went a two-edged sword: and his **countenance** was as the sun shineth in his strength.[36]

Religionists differ on who this heavenly being is. Some contend that it was the Savior himself, while others state that it is an angel. We shall not debate that point here. In either case, his form is like that of the Savior, and he has a body like a man's. This is evident from the body parts which were described. Let us next consider the description which Ezekiel gave:

And above the firmament that was over their heads was the likeness of a throne, as the appearance of a sapphire stone: and upon the likeness of a throne was **the likeness as the appearance of a man above it.**
And I saw as the color of amber, as the appearance of fire round about within it, **from the appearance of his loins** even upward, and **from the appearance of his loins** even downward, I saw as it had brightness all about.
As the appearance of the bow that is in the cloud in the day of rain, so was the appearance of the brightness round about. **This was the appearance of the likeness of the glory of the Lord.** And when I saw it, I fell on my face, and I heard a voice of one that spake.
And he said unto me, son of man, stand on thy feet, that I heard him that spake unto me.[37]

The Lord was extremely angry with the Israelites upon one occasion. Moses chose this time to ask to see the "glory of the Lord". The Lord responded that no man could see him under those conditions (without protection) and survive. After these precautions had been taken, the Lord appeared to Moses.

And he said, Thou canst not see my face: for there shall no man see me and live.
And the Lord said, Behold, there is a place by me, and thou shalt stand upon a rock:
And it shall come to pass, while my glory passeth by, that I will put thee in a cleft of the rock, and I will cover thee with my **hand** while I pass by:
And I will take away my **hand**, and thou shalt see mine **back parts**: but my **face** shall not be seen.[38]

The Bible also mentions many other body parts of God. Let us consider some of these:

> And he gave unto Moses when he had made an end of communing with him upon mount Sinai, two tablets of stone, written with the **finger** of God.[39]

> Behold the name of the Lord cometh from afar, burning with his anger, and the burden thereof is heavy; his **lips** are full of indignation, and his **tongue** is as a devouring fire.[40]

> For the **eyes** of the Lord are over the righteous, and his **ears** are open unto their prayers: but the **face** of the Lord is against them that do evil.[41]

> For my **thoughts** [implying that God has a brain] are not your thoughts, neither are your ways my ways, saith the Lord.
> For as the heavens are higher than the earth, so are my ways higher than your ways, and my **thoughts** than your thoughts.[42]

All of these parts, when placed together, would be characteristic of a human body. And, since a description of all these parts is applied to God, we are left with the distinct impression that God does have a body. In fact, the Scriptures specifically testify that Jesus (who is a god) does have a body.

> For our conversation is in heaven; from whence also we look for the Savior, the Lord Jesus Christ:
> Who shall change our vile body, that it may be fashioned like unto **his glorious body**, according to the working whereby he is able even to subdue all things unto himself.[43]

3. Jesus received a physical resurrection. This means that he, as a god, has a body of flesh and bones. A body, therefore, is one of his characteristics.

As we shall see, the Greek element failed to understand this principle. They thought that possessing a physical body would be a limiting factor. In order to repair this supposed defect, they taught that Jesus had shed his body and become part of the universal substance.

This teaching has been perpetuated by Trinitarianism. In 1932 the Abbe L. Bataille wrote a course on Catholicism in which he said, "What has become of Jesus Christ? Where is he right now? He answered '*Jesus est partout comme Dieu.*' Everywhere like God."[44]

However, such theories have no basis in fact. Let us illustrate the truth of our statement by tracing what happened when Jesus died and was resurrected. All of Christianity affirms that Jesus died on the cross, as Luke writes, "And when Jesus had cried with a loud voice, he said, Father, into hands I command my spirit: and having said thus, he gave up the ghost."[45]

Joseph of Arimathaea claimed the body of Jesus and buried it in his own tomb. There the physical body dead for three days. According to Mark, "And he brought fine linen, and took him down, and wrapped him in the linen, and laid him in a sepulcher, which was hewn out of a rock, and rolled a stone unto the door of the sepulcher."[46]

What happened to the spiritual body of Jesus? Many think that it was asleep for the three days, but it was not. Instead, the spiritual body of Jesus was perfectly conscious and went to the spirit world, where the spirits of all men go when they die.

> For Christ also hath once suffered for sins, the just for the unjust, that he might bring us to God, being to death in the flesh, but quickened by the Spirit:
> By which also he went and preached unto the spirits in prison;
> Which sometime were disobedient, when once the long-suffering of God waited in the days of Noah, while the ark was a preparing, wherein few, that is, eight souls were saved by water.[47]

One of the apocryphal books which was read by early Christians is the Gospel of Nicodemus. It gives a longer description of the visit of Jesus to this place. Here is a short part:

> While David was thus speaking, there came to Hades, **in the form of a man**, the Lord of Majesty, and lighted up the eternal darkness, and burst asunder the indissoluble chains; and the aid of unconquered power visited us, sitting in the profound darkness of transgressions, and in the shadow of death of sins.[48]

After three days, Jesus rose from the dead. This means that his spiritual body reentered his physical body. They were united, never to be separated. This is why the women did not find the body in the tomb.

> And they found the stone rolled away from the sepulcher.
> And they entered in, and found not the body of the Lord Jesus.
> And it came to pass, as they were much perplexed thereabout, behold, two men stood by them in shining garments:
> And as they were afraid, and bowed down their faces to the earth, they said unto them, **why seek ye the living among the dead?**
> **He is not here** [his body] **but is risen**: remember how he spake

unto you when he was yet in Galilee,
  Saying, the Son of man must be delivered into the hands of sinful men, and be crucified, and the third day rise again.[49]

Later, Jesus appeared to all the apostles with the exception of Thomas. They were in a locked room at the time. This demonstrates that a body does not constitute a handicap to a immortal being.

  Then the same day at evening, being the first day of the week, when the doors were shut where the disciples were assembled for fear of the Jews, came Jesus and stood in the midst, and saith unto them, Peace be unto you.
  And when he had so said, he shewed unto them his hands and his side. Then were the disciples glad, when they saw the Lord.[50]

The Gospel of Luke supplies some needed details about this appearance. Jesus declared that he was not just a spirit. He had a body of flesh and bones.

  And as they thus spoke, Jesus himself stood in the midst of them, and saith unto them, Peace be unto you.
  But they were terrified and affrighted, and supposed that they had seen a spirit.
  And he said unto them, Why are ye troubled? and why, do thoughts arise in your hearts?
  Behold my hands and my feet, that it is I myself: handle me and see; for a spirit hath not flesh and bones, as ye see me have.[51]

The Savior appeared on many occasions to demonstrate, in the presence of many witnesses, that he truly had been resurrected. Then he ascended into heaven.

  And when he had spoken these things, while they beheld, he was taken up; and a cloud received him out of their sight.
  And while they looked steadfastly toward heaven as he went up, behold, two men stood by them in white apparel;
  Which also said, Ye men of Galilee, why stand ye gazing up into heaven? this same Jesus, which is taken up from you into heaven, shall so come in like manner as ye have seen him go into heaven.[52]

In what manner did Jesus ascend into heaven? He was in a physical body. How will he return? In a physical body. Elder Bruce A. McConkie states:

  In his ascension, as in all else, our Lord chose to dramatize and teach a gospel truth in such a way that it could not be misunderstood. Here he is teaching the literal nature of his Second Coming. He stands on the Mount of Olivet and ascends visibly;

angels attend; they reveal that his going establishes the pattern for his return. Thus that Jesus whom the apostles knew intimately, whose immortal body they had felt and handled, that same resurrected personage who had eaten fish and an honeycomb before them now ascends personally, literally as they behold. And **so shall he come again**, on the Mount of Olivet, **literally, personally**, in the flesh, as a glorified man, as a personage of tabernacle.[53]

Did Jesus shed his body after he ascended into Heaven? We affirm that he did not. The prophet Zechariah states that Jesus will show the wounds in his hands and feet to the Jews when he comes again, prophesying that "And one shall say unto him, What are these wounds in thine hands? Then he shall answer, Those with which I was wounded in the house of my friends."[54]

This same belief was taught in early Christianity. Ignatius, who was the first Christian to apply the word "catholic" to the Christian Church, wrote:

> And I know that He was possessed of a body not only in His being born and crucified, but I also know that He was so after His resurrection, and **believe that He is so now**. When, for instance, He came to those who were with Peter, He said to them, "Lay hold, handle Me, and see that I am not an incorporeal spirit. For a spirit hath not flesh and bones, as ye see Me have." And he says to Thomas, "Reach hither thy finger into the print of the nails, and reach hither thy hand, and thrust it into My side;" and immediately they believed that he was Christ. Wherefore Thomas also says to Him, "My Lord and my God." And on this account also did they despise death, for it were too little to say, indignities and stripes. Nor was this all; but also after He had shown Himself to them, that He had risen indeed, and not in appearance only, He both ate and drank with them during forty entire days. And thus was he, with the flesh, received up in their sight unto him that sent him, being with that same flesh to come again, accompanied by glory and power. For, say the (holy) oracles, "This same Jesus, who is taken up from you into heaven, shall so come, in like manner as ye have seen Him go unto heaven."[55]

Since Jesus does have a body of flesh and bones today, he is not part of a generic god who has neither body, parts, and passions. He is a real being. And since Jesus is not a part of that shapeless entity, it cannot be a trinity. However, the Savior is not the only one who is banished from the Trinity by this line of logic. God the Father is also excluded from the substance, for Jesus is the perfect reflection of his Father.

And now I ask, as I did in my discourse, **is Jesus God?** Is he a manifestation of God—a revelation of him? If so, there must be in him an and of controversy; **for whatever Jesus Christ was and is God must be, or Jesus Christ is no manifestation, no revelation of God.** Is Jesus Christ in form like man? Is he possessed of a body of flesh and bone which is eternally united to him—and now an integral part of him? Does he possess body, parts and passions? There can be but one answer to all these questions, and that is, "Yes; he possessed and now possesses all these things." **Then God also possesses them;** for even according to both Catholic and orthodox Protestant Christian doctrine, Jesus Christ was and is God, **and the complete manifestation and revelation of God the Father.**[56]

4. **The Scriptures portray a deity as occupying a certain amount of space.** This means that none of the Godhead can be spoken of as being physically present everywhere at the same time. Instead, God is portrayed as leaving one place and going to another. The Book of Genesis reports: "And **the Lord went his way,** as soon as he had left communicating with Abraham: and Abraham returned unto his place."[57]

The Greek element attacked this conception, for it was not compatible with the idea of a universal substance. They thought that God was omnipresent by way of an infinite extension of his substance. William Sherlock examined this premise and found the idea to be false.

> Omnipresence is a great and unquestionable Perfection, but to be present by infinite Extension (if such a thing could be) would be no perfection at all; for this would be Perfect only by parts; as if a body might be which is infinitely extended, and a Body is as capable of infinite Extension, as any Man can conceive a Spirit to be; and yet if a Spirit be Omnipresent only by infinite Extension, the whole Substance of that Spirit is not present everywhere, but part of it in one place, and part of it in another, as many Miles from each other as the places are, where such parts of the Omnipresent Spirit are. This all man will confess to be absurd; and yet if the whole mind and Spirit be present every where, it is certain it is not by way of Extension; for the whole Extension of an infinitely Extended Spirit is not present every where; And if Omnipotence itself cannot be owing to infinite Extension, no Man can tell me, why an infinite Mind should be Extended at all: for Extension is no Perfection.[58]

Why then did the Fathers adopt the idea of the infinite extension? It was the only way that they could explain how God could see whatever we did and answer all of our prayers. They could not understand how a corporeal being could do this.

However, technology of our present day demonstrates that it is possible for even mortals to monitor the actions of a number of individuals at the same time. Some large companies place a surveillance camera in each room. The pictures which these units take are then relayed to a room where there is a large wall of television monitors. Thus one man can monitor the efforts of literally hundreds of people at the same time without being physically present with any of them.

Can man do anything that God cannot? If mankind can do this, is it not reasonable to believe that our supreme deity can monitor our efforts without being physically present with us?

As we have observed, the God of the Bible is not present everywhere at the same time. Instead, he travels from place to place. Here are some other scriptures which demonstrate this principle.

> **And the Lord came down on Mount Sinai,** an the top of the mount: and the Lord called Moses up to the top of the mount; and Moses went up.[59]

> And all the people stood afar off, and **Moses drew near unto the thick darkness where God was.**[60]

> **And the Lord went before them** by day in the pillar of a cloud to lead them the way and by night in a pillar of fire, to give them light: to go by day and by night.[61]

There are many other scriptures that convey this same message. Elder James E. Talmage explains why the premise that God is not everywhere is so reasonable.

> There is no part of creation, however remote, into which God cannot penetrate; through the medium of the Spirit the Godhead is in direct communication with all things at all times. It has been said, therefore, that God is everywhere present; but this does not mean that the actual person of any one member of the Godhead can be physically present in more than one place at one time. The senses of each of the Trinity are of infinite power; His mind is of unlimited capacity; His powers of transferring Himself from place to place are infinite; plainly, however, His person cannot be in more than one place at any one time. Admitting the personality of God, we are compelled to accept the fact of his materiality; indeed, an immaterial being, under which meaningless name some have sought to designate the condition of God, cannot exist, for the very expression is a contradiction in terms. If God possesses a form, that form is of necessity of definite proportions and therefore of limited extension in space. It is impossible for

Does God Have A Body?

Him to occupy at one time more than one space of such limits; and it is not surprising, therefore, to learn from the scriptures that He moves from place to place.[62]

As we have demonstrated, the Scriptures bear witness that God has a body which is in form like a man's. Many of the early Fathers also believed and taught this truth. Whatever knowledge which we have of the nature of deity is based upon what God has revealed to us. Does it make sense to set aside the revelations of God in order to cling to the idea of an immaterial universal substance? I do not think that it does. The *New Bible Commentary* reads:

> God makes Himself known to man so that man may attain the end of his creation, which is to know, love and worship Him. The transcendent Creator is inaccessible to His creatures until He discloses Himself, and man's knowledge of God, where it exists, is correlative to and consequent on God's prior self-revelation.[63]

We therefore choose to believe the witness of the Bible that the members of the Godhead do have bodies like men. In fact, as we shall see in the next chapter, the alternative is to know little or nothing about God at all.

CHAPTER 4 REFERENCES

1. Doctrine & Covenants 130:22
2. Roberts, *The "Mormon" Doctrine of Deity*, 10–11
3. The Syndics of the Cambridge University Press, *A Concise BibleDictionary*, 65
4. Stromata, V. 4 as cited in Lonergan, *The Way to Nicea*, 116
5. Harnack, *History of Dogma*, 2:176
6. Paine, *A Critical History of the Evolution of Trinitarianism*, 117
7. Leland, *A View of the Principal Deistical Writers*, 2:218–219
8. Cudworth, *The True Intellectual System of the Universe*, 1:288
9. Illingworth, *The Doctrine of the Trinity*, 105
10. Lonergan, *The Way to Nicea*, 99
11. Illingworth, *The Doctrine of the Trinity*, 105
12. Lonergan, *The Way to Nicea*, 122
13. Mansel, *Limits of Religious Thought*, 56–58
14. Strong, *A Manual of Theology*, 142–143
15. 1 Corinthians 15:44
16. Doctrine & Covenants 131:7–8
17. Cudworth, *The True Intellectual System of the Universe*, 2:804
18. Ibid., 804–805
19. Priestley, *Disquisitions Relating to Matter and Spirit*, 187–188
20. Harnack, *History of Dogma*, 3:198
21. *The Early Christian Fathers*, 143
22. Priestley, *Disquisitions Relating to Matter and Spirit*, 184–185
23. Ibid., 72
24. Ibid., 103
25. Ibid., 135
26. Nibley, *The World and the Prophets*, 92–93
27. Harnack, *History of Dogma*, 3:241
28. Nibley, *The World and the Prophets*, 93
29. Lonergan, *The Way to Nicea*, 116
30. Priestley, *Disquisitions Relating to Matter and Spirit*, 146
31. Ibid., 184–185
32. Genesis 1:26–27
33. Genesis 5:1
34. Genesis 9:1, 6
35. James 3:9

36. Revelation 1:13–16
37. Ezekiel 1:26–28; 2:1
38. Exodus 33:20–23
39. Exodus 31:18
40. Isaiah 30:27
41. 1 Peter 3:12
42. Isaiah 55:8–9
43. Phillipians 3:20–21
44. Ursenbach, *The Quest,* 172
45. Luke 23:46
46. Mark 15:46
47. 1 Peter 3:18–20
48. The Gospel of Nicodemus, Chapter 5
49. Luke 24:2–7
50. John 20:19-20
51. Luke 24:36–39
52. Acts 1:9–11
53. McConkie, *Doctrinal New Testament Commentary,* 2:28
54. Zechariah 13:6
55. *Ignatius to the Symraeans* II, iii
56. Roberts, *The "Mormon" Doctrine of Deity,* 95
57. Genesis 18:33
58. Sherlock, *Vindication of the Most Blessed and Holy Trinity,* 80
59. Exodus 19:20
60. Exodus 20:21
61. Exodus 13:21
62. Talmage, *Articles of Faith,* 42–43
63. *The New Bible Commentary*

5

The Generic God

As we have noted, the three Persons in the Trinity (Father, Son, and Holy Ghost) have been transformed by many into one being. This absolute and transcendent being is simply referred to as God. Yet, as W. Adams Brown points out, this concept is not Christian in origin. It was borrowed from the Greek philosophers.

> The contribution of Greece to the Christian conception of God is the identification of religion with the Absolute of philosophy. By the Absolute we mean the ultimate reality which lies back of phenomena and which binds the various elements in experience into a unity. In Greek thought-both in its Platonic and Aristotelian forms-this reality was often conceived in an abstract and transcendent way. This is especially true of the later development which culminated in Neo-Platonism. Here God is thought of as standing over against the universe, acting upon it through intermediate beings like the Logos (Christ), but himself without part in its finite and imperfect life. This abstract conception of God is foreign to the genius of Christianity, and historically has been the source of many errors.[1]

Gordon Kaufman notes that there is a tension between a humane God and a transcendent God. This means that the two concepts are not compatible. They function under different ground rules.

> There has always been considerable tension between the two central motifs in the symbol of God-humanness, with its tendencies toward anthropomorphism and its emphasis on human fulfillment; and transcendence or absoluteness, with its emphasis an God's radical otherness, God's mystery, God's utter inaccessibility.[2]

What is the difference between the two concepts? A humane God is very interested in others, but a transcendent is God is interested in himself. A humane god reveals himself to mankind, but a transcendent god is aloof, unknowable, and incomprehensible. In fact, a transcendent god is so absorbed in his own self that he derives his enjoyment from being with himself.

> It is peculiar to God alone, to be essentially blessed in himself, **even in the contemplation and fruition of his own perfections from everlasting to everlasting.** And yet so great is the goodness of God, that he hath made man capable of the same blessedness with himself; to enjoy not another, but the same felicity **which God enjoys in the enjoyment of Himself.**[3]

The Scriptures declare that both God the Father and his son Jesus Christ love us. However, many of the Fathers were not comfortable with this concept. They felt that man was too insignificant for God to be interested in him. As a result, clerics began to try to find another way in which God might love man. For example, Augustine declared that this meant God *used* mankind.

> For God loves us, and Holy Scripture frequently sets before us the love He has towards us. In what way then does He love us? As objects of use or as objects of enjoyment? If He enjoys us, He must be in need of good from us, and no sane man will say that; for all the good we enjoy is either Himself or what comes from Himself. And no man can be ignorant or in doubt as to the fact that the light stands in no need of the glitter of the things it has itself lit up. The Psalmist says most plainly, "I said to the Lord, Thou art my God, for Thou needest not my goodness." He does not enjoy us then, but makes use of us. For if He neither enjoys nor uses us, I am at a loss to discover in what way He can love us.[4]

Can one build a conception of God using the powers of human speculation, as the Fathers and the philosphers did? The Greeks thought that they could rid the true God of all imperfections. However, as Peter Browne points out, they actually succeeded in introducing many imperfections into the concept of God.

> By the term Infinite when applyed to God, is commonly meant that He is infinite in Expansion, Duration, and Perfection. Now to conceive God actually infinite in Extension or Expansion, is most absurdly attributing to Him our Idea of Matter or Space stretched out as far or farther than our Imagination can reach; so that in this respect that Term when applied to God can mean nothing but a Negation of his being bounded by Matter or Space. To think of him infinite in Duration; is no other than adding to his existence as many Hours, and Days, and Years backward and forward as exceed our Power of reckoning: So that there is a

The Generic God

> Negation only of his Existence being bounded by Time or duration. To say that he is infinite in Perfection, means nothing Real and Positive in him, unless we say in a Kind of Perfection altogether inconceivable to us as it is in it self: For the multiplying or magnifying the greatest Perfections whereof we have any direct Conception or Idea, and adding our gross Notion only of Indefinite to them; is no other than heaping up together a number of imperfections to form a Chimera of our imagination; which is so far supposed to become the more worthy Object of divine Worship, the more it is swelled up beyond the stated Dimensions of Nature, and exceeds all human Size and Proportion.[5]

You will observe that Peter Browne treats the idea of God as though he is a mystery about which we can know nothing. This attitude is common among many modern ministers. According to Gordon Kaufman, the idea that God is incomprehensible has turned the Christian deity into an x. One may enjoy philosophizing about what an unknown is like, but it is impossible to feel any allegiance to such an entity. Many people feel perfectly safe in ignoring him altogether.

> On the other hand, the motif of God's absoluteness and transcendence may be developed so as to emphasize God's wholly-otherness, God's transcendent mysteriousness and unknowability. This has also occurred in modern times, with the consequence that for many God has become simply an unknown "X," the ultimate Mystery which is the horizon bounding all our experience and knowledge but which we can never penetrate or comprehend. Such a God has become empty of content and meaning and thus ultimately irrelevant to the day-to-day concerns of human life, one who can safely be ignored or neglected. Much modern agnosticism and religious indifference is an expression of this loss of meaning and significance in the symbol of God. "God" has become something of which we need no longer need take serious account.[6]

But is God mysterious and unknowable? He is not. The early Christians did not think that he was, either, as Joseph Priestley establishes:

> For it must be understood that when the doctrine of the divinity of Christ was first started, it was not pretended, except by Irenaeus in the passage above quoted (who was writing against persons who pretended to more knowledge of this mysterious business than himself), **that there was anything unintelligible in it, or that could not be explained.** Everything, indeed, in that age, was called a mystery that was reputed sacred, and the knowledge of which was confined to a few; but **the idea of unintelligible, or**

inexplicable, was not then affixed to the word mystery. The heathen mysteries, from which the Christians borrowed the term, were things perfectly well known and understood by those who were initiated, though concealed from the vulgar (common people).[7]

In fact, the idea that God is unknowable is not a Christian concept. The annals of the early Fathers show that the pagans of that day were making fun of them because they taught that man could understand God. Hugh Nibley cites some evidences that early Christians did not think that God was incomprehensible:

> The thought that the Apostles might be searching for God is simply laughable. Yet that was one of the first danger signals to appear in the church-the predicted activity of those intellectuals who would be "ever seeking and never coming to a knowledge of the truth (2 Timothy 3:7)." Already, at the end of the first century, Ignatius of Antioch, writes to the Trallians: "There are some Christ-betrayers, bearing about the name of Christ in deceit, and corrupting the word of the Gospel...They do not believe in his resurrection. **They introduce God as unknown** (Ignatius, *Epistle to the Trallians*, VI)" and to the Smyrnaeans he says: "Go ye, therefore, mark those who preach other doctrines, how they affirm that the Father of Christ cannot be known (Ignatius, *Epistle to the Smyrnaeans* IV–VI)."...Irenaeus's first charge against the Gnostics is that "they say the Father cannot be known (Irenaeus, *Contra Haereses* I, 2)."
> On the other hand, nothing shocked or scandalized the pagans more then the Christian insistence in knowing God; Celsus is outraged at such a presumption, and to his charge, Origen replies that God is indeed unknown to bad men (Origen, *Contra Celsum* IV–VI). The fountain of all error in the world, according to Melito of Sardis, "is that man does not know God, and accordingly adores something in his place that is not God" (Melito, Fragmentum)...The first principle of the law which God has given to all men, says Lactanius, is to know God himself, **and not to know him is the greatest of all faults** (Lactanius Devero Cultu 9)...And we have also noted Tertullian remark that it is all right for philosophers to grope around for answers to the great questions of the universe, but that such behavior is unpardonable in a Christian, **who is supposed to have the answers given to him direct from Heaven**.[8]

Many of the Fathers were converted pagans who had a very difficult time accepting the revelations of the Bible. The Greeks received omens from their gods by cutting up birds and looking at their entrails. To such individuals, God was a shadowy being about whom little was known. Philosophers like Heraclitus, Plato, and Aristotle theorized that this lack of knowledge was caused because

The Generic God

the nature of God could not be comprehended by mortals. As a result, we soon find theologians stating that they do not know what God is.

John Wesley said, "I know that there is a God. But who will show me what that God is? The more I reflect the more convinced I am, that it is not possible for any or all of the creatures to take off the veil which is on my heart, that I might discern the unknown God..."[9]

Let us ask which of the Godhead theologians such as those whom have been quoted classify as unknown and unknowable. Is it God the Father, who loved us so much that he sent his son, Jesus Christ? Is it the Son, who loved us so much that he laid down his life for our sakes? Or is it the Holy Ghost, who is a messenger from the presence of the Father, to bear witness of the Son? Do not the Scriptures tell us a great deal about each of these three?

If these are not known, it is because we are not in possession of the spirit of God. According to the Scriptures, the spirit reveals the deep things of God. Let's look at 1 Corinthians 2:10–14:

> But God hath revealed them unto us by his Spirit: for the Spirit searcheth all things, yea, the deep things of God.
> But what man knoweth the things of a man, save the spirit of man which is in him? even so the things of God knoweth no man, but the Spirit of God.
> Now we have received, not the spirit of the world, but the spirit which is of God; that we might know the things that are freely given to us of God.
> Which things also we speak, not in the words which man's wisdom teacheth, but which the Holy Ghost teacheth; comparing spiritual things with spiritual.
> But the natural man receiveth not the things of the Spirit of God: for they are foolishness unto him: neither can he know them, because they are spiritually discerned.

The philosophers were very adroit at speculation. Since they denied that mankind could have any specific information about deity, they dressed up their words with superlatives to hide their ignorance. The supreme deity was referred to as the Absolute and the Infinite and the Ultimate Substance (a concession to pantheism). The methods of these people are transparent. They attempted to visualize the grandest entity and then said that God was better then those words.

At the same time, the Fathers sought to remove any limiting factors from their concept of God. To them, this meant that the First Cause must be free of such factors on both an internal and an external basis. One factor which they felt would limit the First Cause was the possession of attributes. According to *Webster's New Collegiate Dictionary*, an attribute is "an inherent characteristic or quality." Yet, according to the orthodox theologians, attributes are incompatible with the nature of God.

> The rational conception of God is that **he is, nothing more**. To give him an attribute is to make him a relative God...We cannot attribute to him any quality, for qualities are inconceivable apart from matter. (S. Baring-Gould, *Origin and Development of Religious Beliefs—Christianity*, p. 112).[10]

Denying that God has attributes strips him of any unique identity. This is a very dangerous thing. It soon leaves us with nothing at all. Similarly, attempting to make him the sum of everything which we can conceive of produces the same result. For if he is one thing, he is excluded from being another. Attempting to make him all things will, as Dean Mansel explains, eventually relegate him to a state of nothingness.

> But the Infinite, if it is to be conceived at all, must be conceived as potentially everything and **actually nothing**; for if there is anything in general which it cannot become, it is thereby limited; and if there is anything in particular which it actually is, it is thereby excluded from being any other thing. But again, it must also be conceived as actually everything and potentially nothing; for an unrealized potentiality is likewise a limitation. If the infinite can be that which it is not, it is by that very possibility marked out as incomplete, and capable of a higher perfection. If it is actually everything, it possesses no characteristic feature, by which it can be distinguished from anything else, and discerned as an object of consciousness.
> This contradiction, which is utterly inexplicable an the supposition that the infinite is a positive object of human thought, is at once accounted for, when it is regarded as the mere negation of thought....Existence itself, that so-called highest category of thought, is only conceivable in the form of existence modified in some particular manner. Strip off its modification, and the apparent paradox of the German philosopher becomes literally true;—**pure being is pure nothing**.[11]

Is this statement true? It is. Depriving God of his attributes also deprives him of his personality. Doing that means that he has nothing which makes him different from anything else. Royce, in his book *The Conception of God*, writes that, "The individual is not merely **this**, but **such a this** that its place can be taken by no other."[12]

A god which has no unique characteristics is not really anything.

The insistence that God is not a being robs him of any identity. McBrien agrees, stating, "Is God a person? No and yes. **No, because God is not an anything. God is not even a being.** Yes, in an analogical sense. God is **like a person** in that God is loving, caring, compassionate, faithful, forgiving. It is better to attribute personality than to deny it to God."[13]

This highly abstract concept of God did not come from the Bible. It was borrowed from the pagan religions. B.H. Roberts writes:

> It is conceded by Christiun writers that Christian doctrine of God is not expressed in New Testament terms, but in the terms of Greek and Roman metaphysics, as witness the following from the very able article in the Encyclopedia Britannica on Theism, by the Rev. Dr. Flint, Professor of Divinity, University of Edinburgh: "The proposition constitutive of the dogma of the Trinity—the propositions in the symbols of Nice, Constantinople and Toledo, relative to the immanent distinctions and relations in the Godhead **were not drawn directly from the New Testament**, and could not be expressed in New Testament terms. They were the product of reason speculating on a revelation to faith—the New Testament representation of God as a Father, a Redeemer and a Sanctifier—with a view to conserve and to vindicate, explain and comprehend it. **They were only formed through centuries of effort**, only elaborated by the aid of the conceptions, and **formulated in the terms of Greek and Roman metaphysics.**"[14]

Nor are the premises upon which orthodox Trinitarianism is built based upon Greek and Roman religion alone. As Hans Kung points out, they have much in common with the Hindu and Buddhist religions as well:

> We should not therefore quarrel about words, either with Hindus and Buddhists or with modern agnostics or even with Christians. God is certainly not person as man is person: the All-embracing and All-pervading is never an object from which man can dissociate himself in order to make statements about it. The primal reason, primal support and primal meaning of all reality, who determines every individual existence is not one individual person among other persons, is not simply a superman or a superego. And he is certainly not an infinite, still less a finite, alongside or above finite things. He is the infinite in all that is finite, being itself in all that is. **Out of reverence for the divine mystery, the Eastern religions** and a number of recent thinkers **insist on this fact against all-too-Human "theistic" ideas of God.** Christian theologians too recognize it when they speak of God as the divinity, the supreme good, truth, goodness, love itself, sun, ocean.[15]

This is why Jesus and God the Father appeared to Joseph Smith. The Savior said that the creeds of that day were abominations. What is an abomination? In scriptural terms, an abomination is anything which is connected with idols or the worship of pagan gods. Can anyone think of a more literal fulfillment of these words? The pagan gods have no power to answer prayers. Those who have studied the concepts of pagans like Aristotle—upon whom Thomas Aquinas based his ideas about God as the First Cause—comment that his god was not available to help the worshipper.

Although Aristotle frequently calls this prime mover "God" and sometimes refers to his first philosophy as a theology, later critics have often pointed out that this is not the sort of god that religious believers worship. It is more like a scientific principle of actuality, than a religious god.

> Whitehead, SMW, opens his chapter on God with a discussion of Aristotle, and finds the latter's God "not very available" for religious purposes. (See also Ross, *Aristotle*, pp. 179-186).[16]

In contrast to the god of Aristotle, the god of Abraham, Isaac and Jacob has always been very available to his worshippers. The Old Testament is filled with instances where he interceded in behalf of his worshippers. O.F. Ursenbach lists a few of these instances:

> ...let us recall the wanderous events of divine power under Moses, Joshua, Elijah, Elisha, and numerous other prophets, wherein the very mandate of power was obeyed. The Red Sea was divided; the wells of Jerico fell; armies were smitten; water supplied to famishing armies of Moab; the dead were raised; then the wonderous event at Mount Carmel under Elijah; men immunized from the heat of the fiery furnace; Daniel freed from the den of ferocious lions...[17]

God does not change the way in which he operates. In the New Testament era, he was also accessible. On three separate occasions, the voice of the Father bore record of the Son. Stephen saw the Father and the Son before he was stoned. Paul was not converted through contemplation concerning an invisible deity, but actually had Jesus manifest himself to him. He would also see the Savior on at least two more occasions before his death. Clearly, deity was very accessible in the New Testament. This is because the Father and the Son actually exist.

On the other hand, the pagan gods do not exist. Therefore, changing the doctrines of the Bible in order to conform to the teachings of the philosophers does not make sense. It should be the other way around.

> [Christianity] was based on the conviction that in the person of the Christ there was given a full revelation of God—he was the truth—and so salvation consisted essentially in the knowledge of God, as **contrasted with the errors of heathendom** and the defective conceptions of even the chosen people...[18]

We need not blindly follow the theories of pagans like, Plato and Aristotle any more. The true nature of deity has been revealed. Joseph Smith testified:

> And now, after the many testimonies which have been given to him, this is the testimony, last of all, which we give of him: That he lives!
> For we saw him, even on the right hand of God; and we heard the voice bearing record that he is the Only Begotten of the Father.[19]

It therefore makes perfect sense that Jesus would appear in our day to repudiate the doctrines which men are teaching about him. The nature of God is not unknown or incomprehensible. There is no generic god that has a universal substance. Instead, there are the Father, the Son, and the Holy Ghost.

CHAPTER 5 REFERENCES

1. Brown, *Outline of Christian Theology*, 5
2. Kaufman, *The Theological Imagination*, 41
3. Sherlock, *The Practical Christian*, 3
4. Augustine, *On Christian Doctrine*, i, 31
5. Browne, *Things Divine and Supernatural*, 270–271
6. Kaufman, *The Theological Imagination*, 43
7. Priestley, *A History of the Corruptions of Christianity*, 13
8. Nibley, *The World and the Prophets*, 54–56
9. Wesley, *A Further Appeal to Men of Reason and Religion*, as cited in White, *The Search for God*, 82
10. Roberts, *The "Mormon" Doctrine of Deity*, 110–111
11. Mansel, *Limits of Religious Thought Examined*, 94–95
12. Royce, *The Conception of God*, 304
13. McBrien, *Catholicism*, 2:341
14. Roberts, *The "Mormon" Doctrine of Deity*, 116–117
15. Kung, *On Being a Christian*, 302–303
16. Brumbaugh, *The Philisophers of Greece*, 194, 251
17. Ursenbach, *The Quest*, 20
18. Bethune-Baker, *An Introduction to the Early History of Christian Doctrine*, 68
19. Doctrine & Covenants 76:22–23

6
Who Is Christ?

Who hath believed our report? and to whom is the arm of the Lord revealed?
For he shall grow up before him as a tender plant, and as a root out of a dry ground: he hath no form or comeliness; and when we shall see him, there is no beauty that we should desire him.
He is despised and rejected of men; a man a sorrows, and acquainted with grief: and we hid as it were our faces from him; he was despised, and **we esteemed him not**.[1]

Most people recognize that the preceeding prophecy of Isaiah refers to our Savior. What many people do not understand, however, is that the prophecy is still being fulfilled. Many have rejected the true nature of Jesus and have inserted their own idea of Jesus as they would like him to be.

Many Christians of today believe that Jesus Christ has two natures. One of these is, according to the theories, human, while the other is divine. John O'Brien summarizes the Roman Catholic version of this doctrine:

> Our Christian religion teaches that Jesus Christ is divine in his personality and **possesses two distinct natures, human and divine**. "He is God of the substance of the Father, begotten before time," says the Athanasian Creed formulated in the fourth century, and He is Man of the substance of his mother, born in time.[2]

What does this statement mean? The *New American Webster Handy College Dictionary* defines "nature" as "the essential character of a person or thing." The same dictionary defines "character" as "the aggregate of properties and qualities that distinguishes one person or thing from another." The meaning of O'Brien's statement, therefore, is that there are actually two Christs: one divine and one human.

This is an important question. Christianity fought over its implications for hundreds of years. Indeed, one cannot understand what happened in Christian history unless he grasps what various individuals were teaching concerning the two natures of Christ.

Jesus Christ does not have two natures; he only has one. One cannot have two aggregates of properties or qualities in an individual without having two different identities. In short, there would be two Christs. And, because of the doctrine of the resurrection, both Christ beings would be eternal. How did these false teachings start? Let us review the historical record to discover the beginnings of the heresy.

A review of the annals of Christianity reveals that most of the disputes with heretics were really disputes between Christians concerning who and what Christ was. Most of them could easily accept the idea that Jesus was God. After all, their former (pagan) religions had trinities. Why would they object if Christianity had one too? In fact, many pagans had already begun to worship Jesus.

> On the pagan side there are signs at this time of a desire to absorb Christ into the Establishment, as so many earlier gods had been absorbed, or at any rate to state the terms on which peaceful coexistence could be considered. It may well have been with some such purpose in mind that Julia Mamaea, the Empress Mother, invited Origen to her court; we are told that her son, the Emperor Alexander Severus, kept in his private chapel statues of Abraham, Orpheus, Christ and Apollonius of Tyana, four mighty prophetai to all of whom he paid the same reverence. He was not alone in adopting this attitude: about the same date the Gnostic Carpocrates was preaching a similar comprehensive cult—if we can believe Irenaeus and Augustine, his followers worshipped images of Homer, Pythagoras, Plato, Aristotle, Christ and St. Paul.[3]

However, the pagans did not understand how Jesus, a god, could become a man. Such an occurrence was without parallel in their religions. They began to search for some way to explain the Incarnation. You see, they thought that a god was composed of a universal substance while humans were created out of nothing. Therefore, they could not understand how God could become a man.

Christians argued for seven centuries over what the true nature of Jesus was. Joseph Priestley explains two heresies that flourished during this time:

> Almost all the ancient writers who speak of what they call the heresies of the two first centuries, say, that they were of two

kinds; the first were those that thought that Christ "was man in appearance only," and the other that he was "no more then a man." Tertullian calls the former Docatoe, and the latter Ebionites. Austin, speaking of the same two sects, says, that the former believed Christ to be God, **but denied that he was a man**, whereas the latter believed him to be man, **but denied that he was God**.[4]

Such doctrinal developments existed during the times of the apostles. They objected to both, insisting that Jesus was a man. He still had the powers and characteristics of a God, but was a man.

> Hereby know ye the Spirit of God: Every Spirit that confesseth that Jesus Christ is come in the flesh [author's note: that Jesus truly is a man] is of God.
> And every spirit that confesseth not that Jesus Christ is come in the flesh is not of God: and this is that spirit of antichrist, whereof ye have heard that it should come; and even now already is it in the world.[5]

This is not an isolated text. The Scriptures abound with passages which testify that Jesus was a man.

> For there is one God, and one mediator between God and men, the man Christ Jesus.[6]

> For as in Adam all die, even so in Christ shall all be made alive.
> But every man in his own order: **Christ the first fruits**; afterward they that are Christ's at his coming.[7]

> But not as the offence, so also is the free gift.
> For if through the offence of one [Adam] many be dead, much more the grace of God, and the gift by grace, which is by one man, Jesus Christ, hath abounded unto many.[8]

As we have pointed out, many heretical groups rejected this idea and preached that Jesus was not human. The body of Jesus was rejected by some as a deception.

> Educated in the school of Plato, accustomed to the sublime idea of the logos, they readily conceived that the brightest Aeon, or Emanation of the Deity, might assume the outward shape and visible appearances of a mortal; but they vainly pretended that the imperfections of matter are incompatible with the purity of a celestial substance. While the blood of Christ yet smoked on Mount Calvary, the Docetes invented the impious and extravagant hypothesis, that, instead of issuing forth from the womb of the Virgin, he had descended on the banks of the Jordan in the form of perfect manhood; that he had imposed on the senses of his enemies and of his disciples; and that the ministers of Pilate

had wasted their impotent rage on an airy phantom, who **seemed** to expire on the cross, and, after three days, to rise from the dead.⁹

This idea was, of course, denounced as a heresy. Jesus was human. The Scriptures bear witness of this fact. Those who objected to this idea soon came up with another theory. They said that there were two spirits (natures) inside the Savior's body. One was the human Jesus and the other was the divine Christ. Joseph Priestley quotes some of the Fathers who taught this idea:

> This confusion of ideas and inconsistensy appears to have been soon perceived. For we presently find that all those who are called orthodox, **ran into the very error of the Docetae**, maintaining that it **only was the human nature of Christ that suffered**, while another part of his nature, which was no less essential to his being Christ, **was incapable of suffering**; and to this day all who maintain the proper divinity of Christ, are in the same dilemna. They must either flatly contradict the Scriptures, and say, with the Docetae, that Christ did not suffer, or that the divine nature itself may feel pain. This being deemed manifest impiety, they generally adopted the former opinion, viz. that the human nature of Christ only suffered, and contended themselves with asserting some inexplicable mixture of the two natures; notwithstanding the idea of **one part of the same person (and of the intellectual part too) not feeling pain, while the other did, is evidently inconsistent with any idea of proper union or mixture.**
>
> The very next writer we meet with, after Irenaeus, viz. Tertullian, asserts, contrary to him, that it was not Christ, but **only the human nature of Christ, that suffered**. "This voice," says he, "My God, my God, why hast thou forsaken me?" was from the **flesh** and **soul**, that is, the **man**, and not the **word** or **spirit**, that is, it was not of the God, who is impassible, and who left the Son while he gave up his man to death. (*Adv. Praxeam*, C. xxx. 518.) What could any of the Docetae have said more?
>
> Arnobius expresses himself to the same purpose. Speaking of the death of Christ, with which the Christians were continually reproached, "That death," says he, "which you speak of, was the death **of the man** that he had put on, not of himself, of the burden, not of the bearer. (*Adversus Gentes*, L. x. p. 244)."¹⁰

Where did these Fathers get the idea that Jesus had two spirits in his body? They had borrowed this theory from the teachings of Aristotle. He taught that all men had two souls or spirits.

> For Aristotle there were two souls, the animal soul and the rational soul. The animal soul determined the functions of growth and reproduction and was manifested in the perceptions of the senses and impulsive movement. The rational soul was the thinking soul of man. Animals had an animal soul, but not a

thinking soul. Man had both an animal and a thinking soul. (Ernest von Aster, *Historia de la Filiosofia*, p. 104).[11]

The Fathers decided that if a human body could accomodate two spirits, it could also accomodate the divine spirit of Christ. However, using the teachings of the philosophers to define the nature of Christ was extremely foolish. Many of the precepts which they taught have since been proven to be false. James L. Barker explains:

> The part of Greek philosophy which concerns the subject matter of modern science has long since been outgrown; for example, the philosophical teaching that the heavenly spheres move eternally "in circular orbits" while the earthly elements "move in a straight line" and that there are "four elements, fire, air, water and earth."
>
> These ideas are no longer received, because they are contradicted by observation and experimentation, On the other hand, though unconfirmed by revelation, the philosophical ideas that were incorporated into religious dogma, and which could not be tested by ordinary experience or by observation, are still largely believed.
>
> "There is nothing so foolish but it may be found in the pages of the philosophers." (Will Durrant, *The Age of Faith*, p. 2–7)
>
> Just as the "scientific" teachings of that day are often absurd in the light of experience (observation and experimentation) today, so the dogmas of the councils are usually incomprehensibly contradictory, and, in the light of experience (modern revelation confirmed by the testimony of the Spirit) today, are far from the truth as revealed at any time.
>
> The church, "orthodox" in its acceptance of the canons of the Council of Nicea, split up again into factions as different answers were given to these questions; some affirmed as at an earlier period that Jesus did not have two natures, He had only a divine nature, and He only appeared to have a human body (the Docetists); others, He was not divine, but only a man; others, He had two natures after the incarnation; others, He had two natures, but only one "energy," only one will; others, He had two natures and two wills.[12]

Why was there such a diversity of opinion concerning the nature of Christ? Because a whole host of doctrines had been repudiated which the original Christian Church believed in, like:

1. That all of mankind are the sons and daughters of God.
2. That all spirits are immortal by nature.
3. That there is only one spirit in any man.
4. That all of those who are faithful can become like our Father in Heaven.

5. That all humans lived as spirits in heaven prior to their mortal existence.

It was the rejection of these and other scriptural ideas which threw the ancient Christian Church into turmoil. After all, it takes time to evolve new doctrines. As we shall see, the seven centuries of Christological debate make sense only if new doctrines were being formulated.

As we have mentioned, many of the Fathers taught that all life (except for God) was created out of nothing. This viewpoint contains a whole series of false doctrines.

In the first place, God does not make anything out of nothing. *Webster's New American Dictionary* defines "nothing" as "that which does not exist." Therefore, to assert that God created everything out of nothing does not make any sense. It involves a contradiction of terms. As soon as you use the phrase "he created it out of," you imply that something was used for building materials. To say that building materials were used that do not exist does not make any sense. It is nonsense.

In reality, the true meaning of the word "create" is to organize existing components. Joseph Smith explains that this is the meaning that the word "create" is given in the Bible.

> You ask the learned doctors why they say the world was made out of nothing; and they will answer, "Doesn't the Bible say He **created** the world?" And they infer, from the word create, that it must have, been made from nothing. Now, the word create came from the word baurau, which does not mean to create out of nothing; **it means to organize**; the same as a man would organize materials and build a ship. Hence we infer that **God had materials to organize the world out of chaos**—chaotic matter, which is element, and in which dwells all the glory. **Element had an existence from the time He had. The pure principles of element are principles which can never be destroyed; they may be organized and reorganized, but not destroyed. They have no beginning and can have no end.** (*Teachings of the Prophet Joseph Smith*, pp. 350–352)[13]

This same principle applies to life itself. Spirits are composed of matter. This spirit element is, in and of itself, a living entity. It has always existed. Smith said:

> All learned men, and doctors of divinity, say that God created it in the beginning; but it was not so; the very idea lessens man in my estimation. I do not believe the doctrine. I know better. Hear it, all ye ends of the world, **for God has told me so**. If you don't

believe me it will not make the truth without effect. We say that God himself is a self-existent being. Who told you so? It is correct enough, but who told you that man did not exist in like manner upon the same principle? God made a tabernacle and put his (man's) spirit into it, and it became a living soul. How does it read in Hebrew? It does not say in Hebrew that God created the spirit of man. It says, God made man out of the earth and put in him Adam's spirit, and so became a living body. The mind, or the intelligence which man possesses is co-eternal with God himself.

I am dwelling on the immortality of the spirit of man. Is it logical to say that the intelligence of spirits is immortal, and yet that it had a beginning? The intelligence of spirits had no beginning, neither will it have an end. That is good logic. **That which has a beginning may have an end.** There never was a time when there were not spirits, for they are co-eternal with our Father in Heaven. I want to reason more on the spirit of man; for I am dwelling on the body and the spirit of man—on the subject of the dead. I take my ring from my finger and liken it unto the mind of man—the immortal part, because it has no beginning. Suppose you cut it in two; then it has a beginning and an end; but join it again, and it continues one eternal round. So with the spirit of man. As the Lord liveth, if it has a beginning it will have an end. All the fools and learned and wise men from the beginning of creation, who say that the spirit of man had a beginning, prove that it must have an end: and if that doctrine is true, then the doctrines of annihilation would be true. But if I am right, I might with boldness proclaim from the house tops that God never had the power to create the spirit of man at all. God himself could not create himself. Intelligence is eternal, and exists upon a self-existent principle. It is a spirit from age to age, and there is no creation about it. The spirit of man is not a created being; it existed from eternity, and will exist to eternity. Anything created cannot be eternal: and earth, water, etc., had their existence in an elementary state, from eternity.[14]

Some have argued that the majesty of the creation (and of God himself) is demeaned unless everything is created from nothing. This is not necessarily so. We ascribe great creative achievements to many earthly things where the artist works with existing materials. For example, we do not insist that the painter manufacture the paints and paintbrushes that he works with. Similarly, the sculptor is not required to extract the stone from the quarry. In both cases, the artist uses existing materials to produce his masterpiece. How do we describe the result? In both cases we say that he created a work of art. Why? Because a change in form was accomplished. Instead of individual paint colors, people see the Mona Lisa, and instead of a slab of rock, they see the statue of David.

Would the creative work of God be any less wonderful if he had used pre-existing materials? It would not. We now know what elements are utilized in the construction of the human body. Scientists have studied the way that the human body works for years, and yet we cannot duplicate the miracle. We can only marvel at the wonderful working unit which God has constructed. And thus we see that it is not necessary for God to have created everything out of nothing. Instead, we were created out of existing spirit element.

This spirit element is co-eternal with God and is known as intelligence. However, a change must take place before an intelligence can be properly designated as a spirit. Intelligences have always existed, and can be neither created nor destroyed. The Doctrine & Covenants reports that, "Man was in the beginning with God. Intelligence, or the light of truth, was not created, nor indeed can be."[15]

This does not mean that all intelligences are equal. No two spirits are equally intelligent. God the Father is superior to all of us.

> Howbeit that he made the greater star; as, also, if there be two spirits, and one shall be more intelligent than the other, yet these two spirits, notwithstanding one is more intelligent than the other, have no beginning; they existed before, they shall have no end, they shall exist after, for they are gnolaum, or eternal.
>
> And the Lord said unto me: These two facts do exist, that there are two spirits, one being more intelligent than the other; there shall be another more intelligent than they; I am the Lord thy God, I am more intelligent than they all.[16]

This is why Jesus can be the Son of God and yet also be eternal in nature. Jesus became the Son at a certain time, but his elements have always existed. Men also have always existed.

The Fathers applied the name of creature to those forms of life that were created. They considered mortal man to be a creature, but said that Jesus was not a creature.

But was Jesus truly a creature? As we have previously explained, Jesus was a man; therefore, he had to be a creature. In speaking of Jesus, Paul said, "Who is the image of the invisible God, **the firstborn of every creature.**"[17]

Many of the early Fathers agreed with Paul. Paine points out that several individuals plainly taught that Jesus was a creature.

> But his (Arius') polemic led him to take a step further in the direction toward which Origen had pointed, and which already had been anticipated by such Origenists as Dionysius of Alexandria and Eusebius of Caesarea, that the Son of God, **must be a**

creature, though the highest creature in the universe, and the creator himself, as the Logos or mediation principle, of all other creatures.[18]

The Scriptures clearly testify that Jesus existed prior to his birth as a mortal. Here are some passages that convey this message:

> And now, O Father, glorify thou me with thine own self with the glory which I had with thee before the world was.[19]

> When Jesus knew in himself that his disciples murmured at it, he said unto them, Doth this offend you?
> What and if ye shall see the Son of man ascend up where he was before?[20]

> In the beginning was the Word, and the Word was with God, and the Word was God. The same was in the beginning with God.[21]

A furious battle was waged in the early Christian Church concerning the age of the Son. Many argued that there must have been a time when Jesus was not the Son, and that he could not be co-eternal with the Father. In response, the councils of the day pronounced an anathema against anyone who said that there was a time when the Son was not. Dionysius preached a sermon against those who argued that there was a time when the Son was not.

> It is therefore not a trifling, but a very great irreverence to say that the Son was made in some way. For if the Son was made, **there was a time when He did not exist**; and yet He always was, if He undoubtedly is, as He himself declares, in the Father. (John 14:10)[22]

A lack of knowledge is a dangerous thing. The Fathers were attempting to answer questions about the nature of Christ and his relationship to the Father and man. Yet they did not know what they were talking about and they admit it. Henri Mansel quotes from the writings of Gregory of Nyssa:

> "**We live in ignorance of all things. Of ourselves first of all**, and then of other things. For who is there, that has come to a comprehension of his own soul? Who has a knowledge of its essence? Whether it be material or immaterial? Whether purely incorporeal, or whether there be something corporeal in it? How it comes into being, how it is regulated? Whence it enters the body, how it departs?" etc. (Opera, Paris, 1615, Vol. II, p. 321.) Of body as distinguished from its attributes, he says; "For if any one were to analyze into its component parts, what appears to the senses, and, having stripped the subject of its attributes, should

strive to get a knowledge of it, as it is in itself, I do not see what would be left for the mind to contemplate at all. For once we take away color, figure, weight, size, motion, relativity, each one of which is not of itself the body, and yet all of them belong to the body—what will be left to stand for the body? **Whoever, therefore, is ignorant of himself, how is he to have knowledge of things above himself?**" (Ibid., p. 332).[23]

However, people expected their religious leaders to have the answers. So the Fathers decided to reason their way to the truth.

Nowhere is the fact that the Fathers are improvising clearer than in their explanations of how Jesus can be the son of God and still be eternal in nature. They speculated that if he were really begotten, there would be a time when he was not. Therefore, they invented the doctrine that Jesus was being eternally generated.

These Scriptures testify that Jesus is begotten of the Father in a real sense. This implies that it happened at a specific time. Following this train of logic, they reasoned that Jesus would not have existed before that moment in history. But what if they could somehow make this begetting act an ongoing process? If the Father were constantly begetting the Son, then there would be no moment in history when Christ would not have existed.

However, this did not appear to be physically possible. How could the Father constantly beget the Son? Such an arrangement was clearly impossible if one used the idea of begetting in a literal sense. But what if the word really meant something else? The Fathers searched for some other way that the Son might have been produced by the Father. They found a plausible idea in Greek metaphysics.

Many of the philosophers had theorized that God was a mind. A mind creates or generates ideas. What if Jesus had been generated by the Father in this way? But, in order for the theory to be credible, the process had to be continuous. In other words, the Father was always generating the Son. When he completed the generating action, he started over. Phillip Schaff explains:

> Generation and creation are therefore entirely different ideas. Generation is an immanent, necessary, and perpetual process in the essence of God himself, the Father's eternal communication of essence or self to the Son; creation, on the contrary, is an outwardly directed, free, single act of the will of God bringing forth a different and temporal substance out of nothing.[24]

A premise of this type may be very satisfying to one who is schooled in metaphysics, but does not really have any significance

Who Is Christ?

to Christians. One does not love an idea.

A Christian loves Jesus, who, as a real being, died to pay for the sins of his fellow mortals and who, because he was a god, rose from the dead so that we might live forever.

As we have mentioned, the Fathers were greatly confused concerning the nature of Christ. This same confusion extended to the nature of man (as Gregory of Nyssa pointed out) and of angels. In their ignorance, the Fathers made angels into another species which was neither God nor man. This is a false idea. Angels are messengers of God. That name (angel) is a generic description. Angels may be beings who have not yet been born, or they may be resurrected beings—but they are men! John saw an angel an the isle of Patmos and attempted to worship him, writing, "And I fell at his feet to worship him. And he said unto me, See thou do it not: I am thy fellowservant, **and of thy brethren** that have the testimony of Jesus: worship God: for the testimony of Jesus is the spirit of prophecy."[25]

This angel stated that he was of the brethren of John. This means that he either had been a mortal or would be in the future. Joseph Smith explained that there were two kinds of angels.

> There are two kinds of beings in heaven, namely: Angels, who are resurrected personages, having bodies of flesh and bones—
> For instance, Jesus said: **Handle me and see, for a spirit hath not flesh and bones, as ye see me have.**
> Secondly, the spirits of just men made perfect, they who are not resurrected, but inherit the same glory.[26]

While the Christians of Jesus' day understood the role of angels, the Fathers of Augustine's day had no understanding of the subject. Tixeront points out the latter point, but admits that many theologians believed that angels had a body.

> Aside from the probation of the angels and the fall of a number of them, and the beneficient functions of the good angels and the malignity of demons, the Latin theologians of the 4th century, including St. Augustine, had left Christian angelology in a state of uncertainty and confusion. When were the angels created? What is their nature? Is there an order, a hierarchy among them, and what is their character? All of these problems had not received a satisfactory answer. The theologians of subsequent centuries strove to clear up some of them; but in order to do this, they simply transported the speculations of the Pseudo-Areopagite to the West.
> What is their nature? Are they pure spirits or composed of spirit

and body? St. Augustine thought it more probable that they had bodies. Cassian calls them spirits, but believes that they have bodies that are more subtle than ours. This is also the view of Faustus, Claudian Mimertus, and Gennadius. St. Fulgentius observes the magni et docti viri ascribe to the good angels a body of fire, and to the devils a body of air. However, from St. Gregory onward, the contrary opinion gained ground, although it did not obtain universal acceptance.[27]

In reality, God the Father, Jesus Christ, and the Holy Ghost are all members of the same species. Angels and mankind also belong to this same species but are at different stages of development from their superiors. All of them existed prior to this earth life. Hugh Nibley cites the evidence set forth in the *Clementine Recognitions*:

> In the Clementine Recognitions, Clement, recalling what Peter has taught him, says, "After these things when you were explaining the creation of the world, you said something about God's plan or decree, which he presented as his own will in the presence of all the first angels, and which laid down an eternal law for everyone; and you said that it provided two kingdoms, that is, the present and the future, and fixed the time for each, setting up a future day of judgement, which he himself determined, in which all things and spirits would be judged and sent to their proper place." Clement, paraphrasing Peter, then goes on to describe the creation of the earth, and concludes: "Then after he had commanded these living things to come forth from the earth and the waters, he made paradise, which he called a place of delights. And finally after all these things he made man, in whose behalf all had been prepared by him, and **whose real nature** (interna species) **is more ancient** (than they, and for his sake all were made and turned over to his supervision and for use as his habitation." (*Clementine Recognitions* I, 24, in PG 1:1220 and I, 28, in PG 1:1222.) Our Patrologia editor notes in a note to this passage that Justin is here referring to the belief of the early Fathers that the spirit of man is older than his body. **This doctrine is very old in the Church.** According to the Apostolic Constitutions, one of the greatest errors common to the heretics is that "they do not believe that the spirit is immortal by nature," a position in which the churchmen of a latter day were to concur wholeheartedly with the heretics.[28]

Since both Jesus and mankind existed prior to mortality, they have a common bond. Jesus declared that all were the sons of God.

> Jesus saith unto her [Mary Magdelene], Touch me not, for I am not yet ascended to my Father but go to my brethren, and say unto them, I ascend unto my Father, and your Father; and to My God, and your God.[29]

Be ye therefore perfect, even as your Father which is in heaven is perfect.[30]

Take heed that ye do not your alms before men, to be seen of them: otherwise ye have no reward of your Father which is in heaven...
  That thine alms may be in secret: and thy Father which seeth in secret himself shall reward thee openly...
  Be not ye therefore like unto them: for your Father knoweth what things ye have need of, before ye ask him...
  After this manner therefore pray ye: Our Father which art in heaven, Hallowed be thy name...
  But if ye forgive not men their trespasses, neither will your Father forgive your trespasses...
  That thou appear not unto men to fast, but unto thy Father which is in secret: and thy Father, which seeth in secret, shall reward thee openly...
  Behold, the fowls of the air; for they sow not, neither do they reap, nor gather into barns; yet your heavenly Father feedeth them. Are ye not better than they?...
  (For after all these things do the Gentiles seek:) for your heavenly Father knoweth that ye have need of all these things.[31]

The Bible indicates that many of us lived with God before we were born in the flesh. While we lived there, many of us were ordained to perform certain tasks. One of these individuals was Jeremiah.

Then the word of the Lord came unto me, saying,
  Before I formed thee in the belly I knew thee; and before thou camest forth out of the womb I sanctified thee, and I ordained thee a prophet unto the nations.[32]

Tixeront points out that the Jews believed in the pre-existence of many of the Old Testament prophets.

...in the Mischna, composed about 200 A.D., the immediate subject of theophanies is the Metatron, the first of spirits, though we cannot determine at what precise time these conceptions were first framed.
  But an important idea appearing then is that of the preexistence of some considerable persons or objects which are only manifested and externally revealed when they appear in the world...this much is certain: at the time of which we are speaking, we find that the notion applied to Jerusalem, to the Temple, to the Law, and also to some personages, Moses, Abraham, Isaac and Jacob. We shall see that it was applied, quite naturally indeed, to the Messias.[33]

Why is the author spending so much time and effort to establish that both Jesus and all men existed prior to the creation of this earth? It is because the orthodox Christology was based upon the supposition that the spirit of a man and the spirit of a God were two different things. It was because of this theory that the Fathers endowed Jesus with both a human nature and a divine nature. They did not think that Jesus could suffer and die if he were a God.

But what if they were wrong? Suppose, if you will, that there is only one kind of spirit. We are told that God is a spirit. John says, "God is a spirit: and they that worship him must worship him in spirit and in truth."[34]

Man is also a spirit. You will note that the Bible does not try to differentiate between a divine spirit and a human spirit—a spirit is a spirit.

> To the general assembly and church of the firstborn, which are written in heaven, and to God the Judge of all, and to the spirits of just men made perfect.[35]

> The Spirit beareth witness with our spirit, that we are the children of God.[36]

Therefore, there were not two spirits inside the body of Jesus, but only one. When Jesus died, there was no mention of two spirits being involved, but only one. According to Mark, "And Jesus cried with a loud voice, and gave up the ghost."[37]

This process is not limited to Jesus himself. When the spirit leaves the body, it dies. Note that there is no mention of an animal spirit to keep the body functioning. Instead, only one spirit is mentioned. The Book of James mentions that, "For as the body without the spirit is dead, so faith without works is dead also."[38]

After Jesus died, his body was laid in the tomb. His spirit went into the spirit world, the place where the spirits of all men go when they die.

> For Christ hath also once suffered for sins, the just for the unjust, that he might bring us to God, being put to death in the flesh, but quickened by the Spirit.
> By which also he went and preached unto the spirits in prison.[39]

The quoted scripture does not speak about two spirits in Christ, but only one. A fuller account of Christ's visit to the spirit world is given in the gospel of Nicodemus. In this account, many of the ancient prophets celebrate when they hear that Jesus is coming.

Jesus then appears and, after subduing Satan, leads many of the saints out of Hades so that all can be resurrected. In this story there is only one entity mentioned for each person.

> And all the multitude of the saints, hearing this, said to Hades, with the voice of reproach: Open thy gates, that the King of glory may come in. And David cried cut, saying: Did I not, when I was alive upon earth, prophesy to you: Let them confess to the Lord His tender mercies and His wonderful works to the children of men: for He has shattered the brazen gates, and burst the iron bars; He has taken them up out of the way of their iniquity (Psalms 107: 15–17 according to the LXX and the Vulgate)? And when I was alive upon earth, prophesy to you: The dead shall rise up, and those who are in their tombs shall rise again, and those who are upon earth shall exult; because the dew, which is from the Lord, is their health (Isaiah 26:19, according to the LXX)? And again I said, Where, O Death, is thy sting? where, O Hades, is thy victory (Hos. 13:14; 1 Cor. 15:55)?...
>
> While David was thus speaking, there came to Hades, **in the form of a man**, the Lord of majesty, and lighted up the eternal darkness, and burst asunder the indissoluble chains; and that aid of unconquered power visited us, sitting in the profound darkness of transgressions, and in the shadow of death of sins...
>
> Then we all went forth thence along with the Lord, leaving Satan and Hades in Tartarus. And to us and many others it was commanded that we should rise in the body, giving in the world a testimony of the resurrection of our Lord Jesus Christ, and of those things which have been done in the lower world.[40]

When the Fathers attempted to place two natures in Christ, many heresies developed. Two of these were Nestorianism and Eutychienism. Joseph McSorley writes:

> The Church teaches that Christ possesses two natures (divine and human) united in one Person, but not fused nor absorbed; and that in Christ there are two wills (divine and human). The Catholic doctrine is thus midway between heretical extremes: Nestorianism, which exaggerates Christ's humanity, making it an independent person; and Eutychianism, which suppresses Christ's humanity, making it less then a real nature.[41]

In other words, there was a great battle in the Catholic Church concerning what the true nature of Christ really was. Two contradictory statements were being made, and the statement of one (to the exclusion of the other) was deemed to be a heresy. The early Christians had examined the modern orthodox Christological theories and stated that the mechanics were impossible.

The outward juxtaposition of the two natures does not help to overcome the difficulties. It is impossible to make the divinity and the humanity combine in their entirety into one person [de inc. pp. 384, 388, 389, 400). Two persons would be the necessary result (ib. 387, 392). "That two complete things should become one is not possible" (Athan. c. Apol. 12).[42]

Introducing the theory of two natures into theology is fraught with difficulties. That would mean that the human nature of Jesus would also be a part of the Trinity. It was for this reason that Apollinaris objected to the idea of the two natures.

> In the 4th century the debate about the teaching of Apollinaris of Laodicea had also a very similar result...According to Apollinaris, the whole of Christianity would be ruined, if it were not recognised that the body of the earthly Christ also belonged to the Trinity. For, if one now distinguished in the earthly Christ two Persons, the divine and the human (which was bound to the former and in the Resurrection of Jesus was raised with it), then there must be added to the divine Trias a new entity, a fourth: hence the Trias became the Tetras. But this Tetras was much worse than the Gnostic one of Valentinus; for in it figured a man, united with one of the three divine persons.[43]

In order to keep this from happening, it was necessary for both natures to become highly abstract. We have already seen how difficult it is to find a definition of the Persons in the. Trinity. Any definition which portrays the Father, Son, and Holy Ghost as real beings is thought to be heretical. Even today most theologians have not settled on a mutually acceptable definition. And the definition of a nature is even more elusive than that of a person.

> ...the attempt to examine the relations existing between the two natures in the incarnate Son was attended by no less serious troubles. The uncertainty as to what constituted a nature, was as great as the uncertainty in regard to a "person".[44]

The problem of defining what a nature consists of is shown by the fact that two of them would need to be equal to one person. If two natures combined to be more than one person, then Christ would be greater now than he was before he was born to Mary. Yet if the two natures are equal to one person, is definitely greater now for he (according to the theory) has two natures, while he had only one prior to his birth.

Moreover, the mechanics of having two natures creates problems with the idea of a universal substance. The human nature of

Christ must, according to the theories of the day, have been created out of nothing. This would make part of Jesus to be made of something other than the universal substance. But this would mean that part of God himself was human. This is a possibility that most of the clergy find repugnant, but it cannot be avoided.

If we did not follow this line of reasoning, then the nature of the Father and the Holy Ghost would be different than the human nature of Christ. That would mean that Jesus was not the exact manifestation of the Father, but was only half like his Father.

Also, part of Jesus would have a beginning in time. It would mean that the Trinity had been expanded by the resurrection. The entire unit would have been changed by the addition. As Fortman says, this is contrary to the idea of a universal substance:

> It is clear that the Council did not explicitly affirm that the Son, as "consubstantial with the Father" had the one same identical divine substance as the Father, and hence this was not its specific or formal teaching. But when it said the Son was "consubstantial with the Father" it meant at least that He is "utterly like the Father in substance, utterly unlike creatures in substance," that He is "of the Father's substance" and "**of no other substance.**"[45]

As we have observed, the theories of Christology are full of problems. Is this the function of true religion? Should it not answer controversies instead of creating them?

We began this chapter by stating that the theories of Christology represented a repudiation of the true nature of Jesus Christ. Hugh Nibley illustrates that there are those who restructure this nature to meet their own ideas:

> Both Harnack and Schweitzer laid great emphasis on the claim that virtually nothing is or can be known about a historical Jesus. This freed them to work out a kind of Jesus that pleased them. "We are thankful," wrote Schweitzer, "that we have handed down to us only gospels, not biographies of Jesus." When new discoveries come out, they receive, to say the least, a very cold reception. If the real Jesus walked in on them, they would invite him to leave. They have the Jesus they want, and they do not want more. The scholars made their own Jesus: Kierkegaard and Oilthey decided that if we must take history we can at least make it into a thing expressive of our own experience; this led to the existentialism of today, in which the individual rejects as myth anything he does not feel inclined to accept.[46]

This, of course, did apply to those of the Greek educations. They were ashamed of Christ because he had been crucified.

> All the early heresies arose from men who wished well to the gospel, and who meant to recommend it to the Heathens, and especially to philosophers among them, whose prejudices they found great difficulty in conquering. Now we learn from the writings of the apostles themselves, as well as from the testimony of later writers, that the circumstance at which mankind in general, and especially the more philosophical part of them, stumbled the most, was the doctrine of a **crucified saviour**. They could not submit to become the disciples of a man who had been exposed upon a cross, like the vilest malefactor. Of this objection to Christianity we find traces in all the early writers, who wrote in defence of the gospel against the unbelievers of their age, to the time of Lactanius; and probably it may be found much later. He says, "I know that many fly from the truth out of their abhorrence of the cross" (*Lactantii Epitome*).
>
> The apostle Paul speaks of the crucifixion of Christ as the great obstacle to the reception of the gospel in his time; and yet, with true magnanimity, he does not go about to palliate the matter, but says to the Corinthians (some of the politest people among the Greeks, and fond of their philosophy), that he was determined to know nothing among them but "Jesus Christ and him crucified:" for though this circumstance was "unto the Jews a stumbling-block, and unto the Greeks foolishness," it was to others "the power of God and the wisdom of God." (I Cor. i. 23, 24).[47]

The result of this inquiry is inescapable. There is only one Jesus Christ (I Cor. 8:6). Christ cannot be divided (I Cor. 1:13). Therefore, the human spirit of Jesus and the divine spirit of Christ are the same spirit. This immortal being, who is a god, had his spirit placed in a mortal body. Jesus, by virtue of the fact that he was born of Mary, was a man. He inherited from her the ability to be tempted, to suffer, and to die. All of this was possible because he was like us.

> For we have not an high priest which cannot be touched with the feeling of our infirmities; but was in all points tempted like as we were, yet without sin.[48]
>
> For verily he took not in him the nature of angels; but he took on him the seed of Abraham.
> Wherefore in all things it behooved him to be made like unto his brethren, that he might be a merciful and faithful high priest in things pertaining to God, to make reconciliation for the sins of the people.[49]

This, then, is the crucial point. Orthodox Christianity insists that the divine Christ cannot be a man. The Unitarians insist that Jesus, being a man, cannot be a god. In fact, both of these positions are wrong. They are built upon the premise that all of God's creations are the same. For this reason, the fathers persisted in calling both men and the animals creatures. But they are not the same. Jesus made this clear. When the Jews accused him of blasphemy because he claimed to be the Son of God:

> Jesus answered them, Is it not written in your law, I said, Ye are gods [Psalms 82:6]?
> If he called them gods, unto whom the word of God came, and the scripture cannot be broken;
> Say Ye of him, whom the Father hath sanctified, and sent into the world, Thou blasphemst; because I said, I am the Son of God?[50]

All of mankind are the children of God. Paul testified in his sermon on Mars' Hill:

> Forasmuch then as we are the offspring of God, we ought not to think that the Godhead is like unto gold, or silver, or stone, graven by art and man's devices.
> And the times of this ignorance God winked at; but now commandeth all men every where to repent:[51]

What should we think that the Godhead is like then? The Son bears the image of the Father, so the Father is like his Son. And we also shall bear the image of the Father if we are faithful.

> Behold, what manner of love the Father hath bestowed upon us, that we should be called the sons of God: therefore the world knoweth us not, because it knew him not.
> Beloved, now are we the sons of God, and it doth not yet appear what we shall be: but we know that, when he shall appear, we shall be like him; for we shall see him as he is.[52]

CHAPTER 6 REFERENCES

1. Isaiah 53:1–3
2. O'Brien, *The Faith of Millions*, 17
3. Dodds, *Pagan and Christian in an Age of Anxiety*, 107
4. Lardner's *History of Heretics*, 17 as cited in Priestley, *A History of the Corruptions of Christianity*, 4
5. John 4:2–3
6. 1 Timothy 2:5
7. 1 Corinthians 15:22–23
8. Romans 5:15
9. Gibbon, *The Decline and Fall of the Roman Empire*, 678–679
10. Priestley, *A History of the Corruptions of Christianity*, 23
11. Barker, *Apostasy From the Divine Church*, 335
12. Ibid., 337–338
13. McConkie, *Mormon Doctrine*, 169
14. Roberts, *The "Mormon" Doctrine of Deity*, 100–101
15. Doctrine & Covenants 93:29
16. Abraham 3:16–17
17. Colossians 1:15
18. Paine, *A Critical History of the Evolution of Trinitarianism*, 36
19. John 17:5
20. John 6:61–62
21. John 1:1–2
22. Denzinger, *The Sources of Catholic Dogma*, 23
23. Mansel, *Limits of Religious Thought Examined*, p. 306
24. Schaff, *History of the Christian Church*, 3:658–659
25. Revelation 19:10
26. Doctrine & Covenants 129:1–3
27. Tixeront, *History of Dogmas*, 3:328–329
28. Nibley, *The World and the Prophets*, 227–228
29. John 20:17
30. Matthew 5:48
31. Matthew 6:1, 4, 8, 9, 15, 18, 26, 32
32. Jeremiah 1:4–5
33. Tixeront, *History of Dogmas*, 1:34–35
34. John 4:24
35. Hebrews 12:23
36. Romans 8:16
37. Mark 15:32
38. James 2:26

39. 1 Peter 3:18–19
40. The Gospel of Nicodemus, 5, 10
41. McSorley, *An Outline History of the Church by Centuries*, 125
42. Seeberg, *Textbook of the History of Doctrines*, 1:244
43. Werner, *The Formation of Christian Dogma*, 254
44. Bethune-Baker, *An Introduction to the Early History of Christian Doctrine*, 240
45. Fortman, *The Triune God*, 67
46. Nibley, *Old Testament and Religious Studies*, 4–5
47. Priestley, *A History of the Corruptions of Christianity*, 8
48. Hebrews 4:15
49. Hebrews 2:16–17
50. John 10:34–36
51. Acts 17:29–30
52. 1 John 3:1–2

7
The Offspring of God

We are the offspring of God. We lived with him before we were born as mortals, and we will dwell with him after this life if we are faithful. The Church of Jesus Christ of Latter-Day Saints proclaims these truths.

But not all churches share this view. Many Christian sects proclaim that man did not live before he was created on the earth. Furthermore, they state that God created us out of nothing.

However, these premises (now accepted by the orthodox as true) were not believed by early Christianity. Indeed, the early Christians believed in a continuing purpose for life. They thought that God always created worlds and peopled them with his children. Tertullian wrote:

> God cannot be called "omnipotent" without the existance of subjects aver which he may exercise his power; and therefore in order that God may be displayed as "omnipotent" it is essential that everything should subsist...Since "all-sovereign" entails "subjects" it follows of necessity that God created these subjects in the beginning, and that there was no time when they did not exist. If there were such a time...it would follow that the unchangeable and, unalterable God would be altered and changed. For if he made everything later on it is clear that he would change from not-making to making.
> (To the question, what was God doing before this world began, if this world had a beginning in time?) We reply...that God does not begin his activity with the creation of this visible world, but just as after the dissolution of this world there will be another world, so also before this world there were, we believe, other worlds.[1]

Many have accused Joseph Smith of making this doctrine up. He did not. It is an established doctrine that appears everywhere in early church doctrines.

When one begins to talk about the pre-existence, one also talks about a council in heaven. It is in this council that the plans for creating the earth were discussed. It was during this council that it was established that Jesus would be crucified for our sins. John referred to this event by observing, "And all that dwell upon the earth shall worship him, whose names are not written in the book of life of the lamb [Jesus] slain from the foundation of the world."[2]

All of the children of God who would live on this earth took place in this council. The apocryphal Gospel of Phillip points out that God has many more sons than have ever lived on the earth.

> Worlds come and go; only progeny [sonship] is eternal (Gospel of Phillip 123:6–12); "The man of heaven, many are his Sons, more then the man of earth. If the sons of Adam are many but die, how many more the sons of the perfect man [God the Father], they who do not die but are begotten at all times" (ibid. 106:17).[3]

Joseph Smith translated the Book of Abraham from some ancient records which were discovered in Egypt. In this book, the Lord tells Abraham about those spirits that were present.

> Now the Lord had shown unto me, Abraham, the intelligences that were organized before the world was; and among all these there were many of the noble and great ones;
> And God saw these souls that they were good, and he stood in the midst of them, and he said: These I will make my rulers; for he stood among those that were spirits, and he saw that they were good; and he said unto me: Abraham, thou art one of them; thou wast chosen before thou wast born.[4]

Many will object to the use of apocryphal sources and LDS Scriptures to establish the points that we are making. We will not apologize for using them. We believe that the LDS Scriptures were given by revelation from God. The apocryphal books are cited because they indicate what the Christians of that particular period believed.

The Book of Enoch (which is quoted in Jude) speaks about many spirits who live in the presence of the Father.

> And after that, I saw a hundred thousand times a hundred thousand, ten million times ten million, an innumerable and uncountable [multitude] who stand before the glory of the Lord of Spirits.[5]

What is the significance of all these spirits? Since the resurrection had not yet occurred, these spirits can only be those who who

The Offspring of God

were waiting to be born on earth. The Book of Job speaks about sons of God who were present when the earth was created.

> Where wast thou when I laid the foundations of earth? declare, if thou hast understanding.
> Who hath laid the measures thereof, if thou knowest? or who hath stretched the lines upon it?
> Whereupon are the foundations thereof fastened? or who laid the corner stone thereof?
> When the morning stars sang together, and all the sons of God shouted for joy?[6]

Who were the sons of God who were mentioned here? All of mankind are. Many passages in the Scriptures declare that we are the children of God.

> **Ye are the children of the Lord your God**: ye shall not cut yourselves, nor make any baldness between your eyes for the dead.[7]

> Yet the number of the children of Israel shall be as the sand of the sea, which cannot be measured nor numbered; and it shall come to pass, that in the place where it was said unto them, Ye are not my people, there it shall be said unto them, **ye are the sons of the living God**.[8]

> And will be a Father unto you, and **ye shall be my sons and daughters**, saith the Lord Almighty.[9]

> And because ye are sons, God hath sent forth the Spirit of his Son into your hearts, crying, Abba, Father.
> Wherefore thou art no more a servant, but a son; and if a son, then an heir of God through Christ.[10]

Jesus told the story of the prodigal son. It is the parable about a man who has two sons (Luke 15:11–32). The first runs away, spends his life in riotous living, and then returns. He is received with rejoicing by his loving father. Who are these characters really? Clearly the prodigal son must be wayward mankind. But who is the loving father? It is our Father in Heaven. We truly are his children.

What would someone who is a child of God be like? He would be like God. After all, "A horse sires a horse, a man begets man, a god brings forth a god."[11]

This brings us to the doctrine of the council in heaven. The children of God met to discuss the plans for the creation of the earth.

> And there stood one among them that was like unto God, and he said unto those who were with him: We will go down, for there is space there, and we will take of these materials, and we will make an earth wherein these may dwell; And we will prove them herewith, to see if they will do all things whatsoever the Lord their God shall command them; And they who keep their first estate [the pre-existence] shall be added upon; and they who keep not their first estate shall not have glory in the same kingdom with those who keep their first estate; and they who keep their second estate shall have glory added upon their heads for ever and ever.[12]

What was the second estate? It was our mortal existence upon earth. The manner of government was discussed in this great body. Two plans were presented. The first was Satan's and the second was from Jesus.

> And I, the Lord God, spake unto Moses, saying: That Satan, whom thou hast commanded in the name of mine Only Begotten, is the same which was From the beginning, and he came before me, saying Behold, here am I, send me, I will be thy son, and I will redeem mankind, that one soul shall not be lost, and surely I will do it; wherefore give me thine honor.
> But, behold, my Beloved Son, which was my Beloved and chosen from the beginning, said unto me Father, thy will be done, And the glory be thine forever.
> Wherefore, because that Satan rebelled against me, and sought to destroy the agency of man, which I, the Lord God, had given him, and also, that I should give unto him mine own power; by the power of mine Only Begotten, I caused that he should be cast down;
> And he became Satan, yea, even the devil, the Father of all lies, to deceive and to blind men, and to, lead them captive at his will, even as many as would not hearken unto my voice.[13]

Why was the plan of Satan so enticing? Remember, the plan which had been presented was that the children of God would go down to earth in order to determine who would obey the commandments of the Lord. Some would fail to keep either their first or second state. This would be their choice. Nevertheless, it was a foregone conclusion that many would fail to return to the presence of the Father. Satan promised to force everyone to do good so that all would return. Cleon Skousen explains:

> Knowing, therefore, the tremendous risk involved and the fact that there would be many casualties, the Father took every precaution to make certain that all those who entered the Second Estate of mortal probation did so voluntarily and on their own initiative. That was why the entire matter was presented to us for

discussion and our sustaining vote in the pre-existence; and reflect for a moment upon the fact that even though we were told that it was the next step in the plan of eternal progression, nevertheless, one third of the hosts in the spirit world were afraid to go forward. The risk was too great.

Lucifer rallied these around him and gained their support for a plan which **would not entail any risk.** He proposed to prevent any spirits from falling short of salvation by simply forcing them to live throughout the Second Estate or mortal estate in strict compliance with celestial law. He would have to admit that his plan involved a violation of personal free agency—a principle on which God had evolved the entire cosmic universe, but undoubtedly he justified himself on the ground that it was for a good end. When the Father said he would not accept the plan, Lucifer whipped his followers into an open rebellion against God, and so violent did the dispute become that it finally resulted in the complete ejection of Lucifer and his hosts from the presence of the Father.[14]

There was no doubt as to the motives of Lucifer, however. He was doing this so that he could become more powerful than the Father. Isaiah mentioned the confrontation in heaven and compared Lucifer to the king of Babylon.

> How art thou fallen from heaven, O Lucifer [day star, son of dawn], son of the morning! how art thou cut down to the ground, which didst weaken the nations!
> For thou hast said in thine heart, I will ascend into heaven, I will exalt my throne above the stars of God; I will also sit upon the mount of the congregation, in the sides of the north;
> I will ascend above the heights of the clouds; **I will be like the most high.**
> Yet thou shalt be brought down to hell, to the sides of the pit.[15]

The confrontation between Satan and the Father is recorded in the Bible. It is called the War in Heaven.

> And there was war in heaven: Michael and his angels fought against the dragon; and the dragon fought and his angels,
> And prevailed not; neither was their place found any more in heaven.
> And the great dragon was cast out, that old serpent, called the Devil, and Satan, which deceiveth the whole world: he was cast out into the earth, and his angels were cast out with him.[16]

How many people followed Satan? It was one-third of all the spirit children of God. The Bible records: "And his [the dragon's] tail drew the third part of the stars of heaven, and did cast them to the earth."[17]

These followers of Satan were mentioned in the New Testament as well. Both Jude and Peter mentioned them.

> And the angels which kept not their first estate, but left their own habitation, he hath reserved in everlasting chains under darkness unto the judgement of the great day.[18]

> For if God spared not the angels that sinned, but cast them down to hell, and delivered them into chains of darkness, to be reserved unto judgment;[19]

It was during this council in heaven that Jesus was chosen and ordained to be our Savior.

> Forasmuch as ye know that ye were not redeemed with corruptible things, as silver and gold, from your vain conversation received by tradition from your fathers;
> But with the precious blood of Christ, as of a lamb without blemish and without spot:
> Who verily was foreordained before the foundation of the world, but was manifest in these last times for you.[20]

Many of us were chosen to be leaders at this same time. Paul declarerd this truth:

> Blessed be the God and Father of our Lord Jesus Christ who hath blessed us with all spiritual blessings in heavenly places in Christ.
> According as he hath chosen us in him before the foundation of the world, that we should be holy and without blame before him in love:[21]

This council in heaven is mentioned in the apocryphal books. Hugh Nibley cites the Apocalypse of Abraham as an evidence that early Christians believed in this doctrine.

> And he tells Abraham how "I explained my will to those who stood before me in this form that I am showing you in the spirit world before they came into existence." Abraham is shown the council of heaven in the spirit world in the preexistence. It is plain enough what is meant by "coming into existence."[22]

As we have mentioned, God ordained many to be leaders on earth. Ancient sources mention this belief.

> ...what interests us here is the teaching of "the Elders" that "to some of them, that is, those angels who had been faithful to God (lit. Gods) in former times, he gave supervision over the government of the earth, trusting or commissioning them to rule

well...And nothing has occurred (since) to put an end to their order."[23]

Just because a person is foreordained does not mean that they are predestined to do something. They still have their free agency and can choose not to obey.

> The mightiest and greatest spirits were foreordained to stand as prophets and spiritual leaders, giving to the people such portion of the Lord's word as was designed for the day and age involved. Other spirits, such as those who laid the foundations of the American nation, were appointed beforehand to perform great works in political and governmental fields. In all this there is not the slightest hint of compulsion; persons foreordained to fill special missions in mortality are as abundantly endowed with free agency as are any other persons. By their foreordination the Lord merely gives them the opportunity to serve him and his purposes if they will choose to measure up to the standard he knows they are capable of attaining.[24]

As we have noted, there is a vast number of sources that, testify about a pre-existence. Hugh Nibley mentions some more quotations:

> "I'll came from the house of my Father," says the Psalm of Thomas, "in a far land, and I shall mount up until I return to that land of the pure." There is a moving scene at the end of the Pearl, the most moving of all the early Christian Syriac writings, where the hero finally returns to his home, his mission accomplished. He's met at the gate of greeting and honor by his entire family. He bows and worships his Father and the Christ of the Father "who has sent me the garments and given the orders while I was on the earth." All the princes of the house were gathered at the gate. They embraced him with tears of joy as the organ plays and they all walk back to the house together.
> And Gregory of Nyssa, one of the three great Cappodocians, writing about this, says that in his time, the Fourth Century, the church was very confused about these teachings. They were being rapidly lost. He says, "Christians are all confused about the preexistence. Some say we lived in families there, and in tribes just as we do here, and that we lost our wings when we came down here and will get them back again upon earth." So they mix up tenable and un-tenable things; all sorts of strange ideas get in the picture. Regardless of what the true picture is, we know that the early Christians did believe very strongly in the preexistence. The mysterious word propators, which they used a lot, is now recognized as not meaning the Father who was before our Heavenly Father as our forefather, our propator—"the father of our preexistent spirit," says a quotation from a newly found

work. "When they ask who you are," says the Apocryphon of James, "say I am a son and I come from the Father." And when they ask you what sort of son and from what father, answer, "From the pre-existent Father and I am a son of the Preexistence."[25]

Catholics accept certain Deuterocanonical books as part of the Bible. One of these books is the Wisdom of Solomon. This book points out that spirits exist before they enter the body: "I was, indeed, a child well-endowed, having had a noble soul fall to my lot; or rather being noble I entered an undefiled body."[26]

The body is actually designed to bear the resemblance to the spirit. This is verified by the Testament of Naphtali.

> For just as a potter knows the pot, how much it holds, and brings clay for it accordingly, so also the Lord forms the body in correspondence to the spirit, and instills the spirit corresponding to the power of the body. And from one to the other there is no discrepancy, not so much as a third of a hair, for all the creation of the Most High was according to height, measure, and standard.[27]

Joseph Smith also bore witness of this principle. The spiritual body bears the likeness of the physical body, and vice versa. He said, "...that which is spiritual being in the likeness of that which is temporal; and that which is temporal in the likeness of that which is spiritual; the spirit of man in the likeness of his person, as also the spirit of the beast, and every other creature which God has created."[28]

The early Jewish church also believed that the soul existed prior to mortality. A late midrash reads:

> The angel immediately fetches the soul before the Holy One blessed be He, and when she arrives she bows forthwith before the King of Kings, whereupon the Holy One blessed be He commands the soul to enter into the drop of semen contained in so and so;...The Holy One blessed be He answers, "The world into which I am about to place you will be more lovely for you than the world in which you have dwelt hitherto, and when I created you, it was only for this seminal drop that I created you."[29]

The early Christian church taught that there was a pre-existence. One of the most famous advocates of this idea was Origen, who "...writes that evil was introduced into the world by the freedom that had been created and that sins had been committed by human souls before the present order of things."[30]

How can we be sure that the opinion of Origen was shared by the church of that day? Because Origen was honored by the theologians of that day, not denounced. Cardinal John Henry Newman points out that no action was taken against Origen for hundreds of years thereafter.

> The great Origen after his many labours died in peace; his immediate pupils were saints and rulers in the Church; he has the praise of St. Athanasius, St. Basil, and St. Gregory Nazianzen, and furnishes materials to St. Ambrose and St. Hilary; yet, as time proceeded, a definite heterodoxy was the crowing result of his theology, and at length, three hundred years after his death, he was condemned, and, as has generally been considered, in an Ecumenical Council.[31]

Jesus is the Son of the Father in an eternal sense, and so are the rest of mankind. It naturally follows that Jesus is our brother.

> But we see Jesus, who was made a little lower than the angels for the suffering of death, crowned with glory and honour; that he by the grace of God should taste death for every man.
> For it became him, for whom are all things, and by whom are all things, in bringing many sons unto glory, to make the captain of their salvation perfect through sufferings.
> For he that sanctifieth and they who are sanctified are all of one; for which cause **he is not ashamed to call them brethren**.[32]

> For whom he did foreknow, he also did predestinate to be conformed to the image of his Son, that he might be the firstborn among many brethren.[33]

Jesus is not merely the son of God. Because of all that he has done, he also has the status of a god. This means that if we are faithful, we can have the same privilege. This is what Paul meant in the cited scripture in Romans by our being conformed to the image of "his son."

It was a doctrine of the early Christian Church that man could become like our Father in Heaven. For example, Irenaeus writes: "...but following the only true and steadfast teacher, the Word of God, our Lord Jesus Christ, who did, through his transcendent love, become what we are, that he might bring us to be even what He is Himself."[34]

Athanasius, who argued what would later become the orthodox views concerning the Nicene Creed, taught that mankind could become like God. Here are several passages that indicate this belief:

> Therefore, if, even before the world was made, the Son had that glory, and was Lord of glory and the Highest, and descended from heaven, and is ever to be worshipped, it follows that He had not promotion from His descent, but rather Himself promoted the things which needed promotion; and if He descended to effect their promotion, therefore He did not receive in reward the name of the Son and God, but rather He Himself has made us sons of the Father, and deified men by becoming Himself man.
> Therefore He was not man, and then became God, but He was God, and then became man, and that to deify us.[35]
>
> Specially striking is what he says de synod 51: Christ could not make others gods if He himself had, to begin with, been made God; if He possessed His godhood merely as something bestowed upon Him, He could not bestow it, for it would not be in His own power, and He would not have more than He needed Himself.[36]
>
> And how can there be deifying apart from the Word and before him? yet, saith He to their brethren the Jews, "If He called them gods, unto whom the Word of God came." And if all that are called sons and gods, whether in earth or in heaven, were adopted and deified through the Word, and the Son Himself is the Word...[37]
>
> For He was made man that we might be made God...[38]

Paul taught that we are the offspring of God. What should the offspring of God be like? Paul says, "Forasmuch then as we are the offspring of God, we ought not to think that the Godhead is like unto gold, or silver, or stone, graven by art and man's device."[39]

The offspring of God grow up to be like their parents. Around 1300 A.D., the Dominican Meister Eckhart preached the doctrine that "The seed of God is in us. Given an intelligent farmer and a diligent farmhand, it will thrive and grow up to God whose seed it is, and accordingly, its fruit will be God-nature. Pear seeds grow into pear trees; nut seeds grow into nut trees, and God-seed into God."[40]

Mortals receive an inheritance from their parents. This may come as a result of death, or it may be awarded at some specific time. We also receive an inheritance from our Heavenly Father. What shall this award be? It shall an inheritance like Jesus received.

> For as many as are led by the Spirit of God, they are the sons of God.
> For ye have not received the spirit of bondage again to fear; but ye have received the Spirit of adoption, whereby we cry, Abba, Father.

The Offspring of God

> The Spirit itself beareth witness with our spirit, that we are the children of God:
> And if children, then heirs; heirs of God, and joint-heirs with Christ; if so be that we suffer with him, that we may be also glorified together.
> For I reckon that the sufferings of this present time are not worthy to be compared **with the glory which shall be revealed in us.**
> For the earnest expectation of the creature waiteth **for the manifestation of the sons of God.**[41]

> And the glory which thou gavest me I have given them; that they may be one, even as we are one:[42]

> Wherefore thou art no more a servant, but a son; and if a son, then an heir of God through Christ.[43]

In other words, if we are faithful we can become like our Father in Heaven. He will share with us all that he has. Remember the promise which the father gave to his faithful son in the parable of the prodigal son? The Bible records: "And he said unto him, Son, thou art ever with me, and **all that I have is thine.**"[44]

This promise will be literally fulfilled. Those who are faithful will receive an inheritance from our Father. We will receive all that the Father has. We will be crowned with glory and rule in His behalf.

> And when the chief Shepherd shall appear, ye shall receive a crown of glory that fadeth not away.[45]

> **He that overcometh shall inherit all things**; and I will be his God, and he shall be my son.[46]

> To him that overcometh will I grant to sit with me in my throne, even as I also overcame, and am set down with my Father in his throne.[47]

> And hath made us kings and priests unto God and his Father; to him be glory and dominion for ever and ever. Amen.[48]

> Blessed and holy is he that hath part in the first in the first resurrection: on such the second death hath no power, but they shall be priests of God and of Christ, and shall reign with him a thousand years.[49]

Many feel that having man become God robs the Father of his own status in same way. This is not true. We do not extort godhood from the Father; he gives it to us willingly. Yet the Father loses none of his own power and authority by honoring us as gods. Regardless of our station, we still worship God the Father.

> And there shall be no more curse: but the throne of God and of the Lamb shall be in it; and his servants shall serve him.[50]

Let us consider the fact that those who are most intimately acquainted with the beliefs of early Christianity believed in this doctrine. This would not be so, if the idea had not been passed down from the earliest of times. Elder Milton R. Hunter cites the teachings of many of these Fathers.

> During the early Christian centuries, the Church retained as part of its doctrine the divine verity previously proclaimed by Jesus and His apostles, that "men may become Gods." The teachings on this doctrine as given by the early Christian fathers are so nearly identical with those of the Latter-day Saint prophets that one would find difficulty in trying to tell which came from which age. It is logical that these teachings should be identical, since the early Christians still retained many Gospel truths and the same verities were revealed to the Prophet Joseph Smith. For example, Methodius, the Greek father, emphatically declared that "every believer must, through participation in Christ, be born a Christ," and he also taught dogmatically that "He was made man that we might be made Gods (S. Angus, *The Mystery Religions and Christianity*, pp. 106–107)." Lactanius (about 325 A.D.) affirms that the chaste man will become "identical in all respects with God" (Cited in Ibid., p. 106). Clement of Alexandria employed a language that is well understood by John the Beloved and the Mormons alike. (John 17:3; Doctrine & Covenants 132:24) The following statement, taken from Clement's teachings, shows that he had a comprehensive understanding of the doctrine of men's becoming Gods:
> "If anyone knows himself he shall know God, and by knowing God he shall be made like unto him"; and again, "that man with whom the Logos dwells...is made like God and is beautiful...That man becomes God, for God so wills it"; and "the Logos of God became man that from man you might learn how man may become God." Further, that the true Christian Gnostic "has already become God. (Angus, op. cit., p. 106)".[51]

We have already seen how later theologians floundered about concerning the nature of God. Even the most simple questions recording deity took centuries to resolve. Often beliefs which were held to be orthodox in one century were declared to he heretical in another. It was so in this case.

In order to elevate God, the nature of man was lowered. It was decided that man could never become like God. Yet those who formulated these doctrines had never received a revelation on the subject. And the teachings of people like Augustine and Jerome were a direct reversal of the teachings of those who had come before.

Such changes are not implemented without strife and bloodshed. In order to replace the doctrine of pre-existence, Augustine taught that mankind was predestined to be either saved or damned. This caused a great strife between his followers and those of Pelagius. It was necessary to excommunicate the disciples of Origen from the church, for they taught that man did exist in a pre-existent state. In order to establish the idea that God was justified in predestination of mankind, the doctrine of original sin was invented.

The battles of the Christological period were also caused by confusion over the natures of God and man. All of these problems could have been avoided if mankind had only clung to the teachings of the Savior instead of borrowing from the teachings of the Greeks. The next chapter will establish how these teachings were changed.

CHAPTER 7 REFERENCES

1. *The Early Christian Fathers*, 261
2. Revelation 13:8
3. Nibley, *Old Testament and Related Studies*, 206
4. Abraham 3:22–23
5. 1 Enoch 40:1–2
6. Job 38:4–7
7. Deuteronomy 14:1
8. Hosea 1:10
9. 2 Corinthians 6:18
10. Galatians 4:6–7
11. The Gospel of Phillip 75:25
12. Abraham 3:24–26
13. Moses 4:1–4
14. Skousen, *The First 2,000 Years*, 47
15. Isaiah 14:12–16
16. Revelation 12:7–9
17. Revelation 12:4
18. Jude 6
19. 2 Peter 2:4
20. 1 Peter 1:18–20
21. Ephesians 1:3–4
22. Nibley, *Old Testament and Related Studies*, 157
23. Nibley, *The World and the Prophets*, 226
24. McConkie, *Mormon Doctrine*, 290
25. Nibley, *Old Testament and RelatedStudies*, 157
26. The Wisdom of Solomon 8:19–20
27. The Testament of Napthali 2:2
28. Doctrine & Covenants 77:2
29. Tanh. Pekude 3 as cited in the Anchor Bible, 43:28
30. Barker, *Apostasy From the Divine Church*, 46
31. Newman, *An Essay on the Development of Christian Doctrine*, 194
32. Hebrews 2:9–11
33. Romans 8:29
34. Irenaeus, *Against Heresies*, V, preface
35. Athanasius, *Four Discourses Against the Arians*, 1:38–39
36. Harnack, *History of Dogma*, 4:27
37. Athanasius, Four Discourses Against the Arians, 1:39
38. Athanasius, De Incarnatione Vervi Dei, 54:3
39. Acts 17:29

40. Placher, *A History of Christian Theology,* 169
41. Romans 8:14–19
42. John 17:22
43. Galatians 4:7
44. Luke 15:31
45. 1 Peter 5:4
46. Revelation 21:7
47. Revelation 3:21
48. Revelation 1:6
49. Revelation 20:6
50. Revelation 22:3
51. Hunter, *The Gospel Through the Ages,* 108–109

8
Their Hearts Are Far From Me

In 1820 Joseph Smith knelt in prayer to ask which of the existing churches was right. To his surprise, both the Father and the Son appeared. Their answer has bothered many.

> I was answered that I must join none of them, for they were all wrong; and the Personage who addressed me said that all their creeds were an abomination in his sight; that those professors were all corrupt; that: "they draw near to me with their lips, but their hearts are far from me, they teach for doctrines the commandments of men, having a form of godliness, but they deny the power thereof."[1]

What does this passage mean? The Savior was stating that an apostasy had occurred and that men had changed many of the precious truths of the Gospel. In order that we might have these truths again, the Lord would reveal them again to the prophet Joseph Smith.

One of the many doctrines that was changed was the nature of God. Mankind removed the pure and clear teachings of Jesus Christ in order that they might insert their own ideas on the subject. The Lord told Jeremiah:

> Hath a nation changed their gods, which are yet no gods? but my people have changed their glory far that which doth not profit.
> Be astonished, O ye heavens, at this, and be horribly afraid, be ye very desolate, saith the Lord.
> For my people have committed two evils; they have forsaken me the fountain of living waters, and hewn them out cisterns, broken cisterns, that can hold no water.[2]

Mankind has manufactured many gods. Of course, none of these man-made gods really exist. They cannot answer our prayers, let alone solve our problems. To use scriptural language, "they can hold no water."

The most dominant culture for many centuries was Greek. Everyone assumed that the Greek civilization was the most enlightened on the earth. The Roman Empire absorbed the Greek mythology and ideas on a wholesale basis. Other groups of that time period did likewise.

When Greece or Rome conquered another country, a concerted effort was made to convert the new subjects to the Greek religious ideas. This process is known as Hellenization. The Jews and the Christians were exposed to strong pressure in this regard.

The first attempts to exercise this influence were very heavy handed. The Greeks originally attempted to force everyone to accept their point of view. For example, they attempted to destroy the influence of the God of Israel by offering pagan sacrifices. A Jewish priest became enraged by this sacrilege and killed those who were responsible. He then led the revolt of the Maccabees which liberated Israel.

> In B.C. 175 Antiochus Epiphanes became king of Syria, and made a determined effort to stamp out the Jewish religion. He at first met with considerable success, **owing partly to a Hellenizing movement among the Jews themselves,** and altars were erected to Zeus in many parts of the Holy Land. Resistance began at Modin, a town near Bethhoren, where an aged priest named Matthias, of the Family of Asmon or Chasmon, slew the sacrificers, and also the king's officer under whose direction the altar had been erected. Mat. was the father of five sons, I Macc. 2:15-23 and with a large body of followers took refuge in the mountains.[3]

The Hellenizers learned their lesson from incidents such as this one. It is far easier to modify the religions of others than to force them to accept yours. Therefore, future attempts centered around influencing theology from the inside. One of the most successful accomplishments in this regard was translating the Old Testament into Greek. Once the translation was completed, the Jewish nation began to use it in preference to all other renditions.

The translation was accomplished by seventy elders in the city of Alexandria. This city was famous for the library which housed the wisdom of the ages. It also had a school which studied the writings of the philosopher Plato. It was, of course, understandable that philosophy should be a part of this labor. Ptolemy Philadelphus (the king) and the philosopher Menedus both consulted with the elders before they undertook the translation.

And while not the king only, but the philosopher Menedus also, admired them, and said, that all things were governed by Providence, and that it was probable that thence it was that such force or beauty was discovered in these words, they then left off asking any more questions.[4]

We must note that Ptolemy Philadelphus was not converted to the Jewish religion. He was not ready to renounce the worship of Zeus and the other pagan gods. In fact, Aristeus, one of the king's counselors, introduced the idea that Zeus and the Israelite God were the same deity.

> ...that God, who supporteth thy kingdom, was the author of their (the Jewish) laws, as I have learned by particular inquiry; for both these people and we also **worship the same God**, the framer of all things. We call him, and that truly, by the name of Znva, (or life, or Jupiter) because he breathes life into all men.[5]

A huge collection of Jewish literature was placed in the library at Alexandria. This caused religious scholars to gravitate to that location. The Jews did not merely study the Scriptures, however. They also imbibed freely of the teachings of the philosophers. One of the most famous of these scholars was Philo Judaeus.

Philo was a consistent Hellenizer. To him, many of the ideas which were expressed in the Scriptures were false. For example, many of the passages in the Old Testament conveyed the idea that God had a physical body. Philo rejected this idea, preferring to interpret by allegorical means.

> Following Aristobulus in the same kind of philosophy was Philo, the learned Jew of Alexandria, born about the year 20 B.C. He was supposed to be a descendant of Aaron, and belonged to one of the wealthiest and most influential families among the merchants of Egypt; and he is said to have united a large share of Greek learning with Jewish enthusiasm...To begin with the former: the literal sense must be wholly set aside, when it implies anything unworthy of the Deity—anything unmeaning, impossible, or contrary to reason. Manifestly this canon, if strictly applied, would do away not only with all anthropomorphisms, but cut the knot whenever difficulties seemed insuperable.[6]

In other words, Philo was rejecting the true knowledge of God, which was received by revelation, and inserting the philosophical views of the Greeks, which were developed by speculation. Philo borrowed heavily from the teachings of the Stoics.

Philo's doctrine starts from the idea that God is "being" absolutely bare of all quality. All quality in finite beings has limitation, and no limitation can be predicated of God who is eternal, unchangeable, simple substance, free, self-sufficient. To predicate any quality of God would be to reduce him to the sphere of finite existence. Of him we can only say **that he is, not what he is**, and such purely negative predictions as to his being appear to Philo...Philo is guided partly by Plato and partly by the Stoics; but at the same time he makes use of the concrete religious conceptions of heathenism and Judaism.[7]

The easiest way to control what a religion teaches is to control the clergy. Therefore, the Sanhedrin (the ruling Jewish religious body) was appointed by the government. Although this body had existed for many centuries prior to that time, the fact that the civil rulers now chose the Sanhedrin virtually guaranteed that Hellenization would occur.

> ...its nucleus probably consisted of the members of certain ancient families, to which, however, from time to time **others were added by the secular rulers**...But after the reduction of the high priesthood from a heredity office to one bestowed by the political ruler according to his pleasure, and the frequent changes in the office introduced by the new system, the high priest naturally lost his prestige.[8]

The system of Hellenization was very effective. Soon the Alexandrine interpretation was accepted by the entire Sanhedrin and the Bible was being interpreted allegorically.

As we have stated, the Jews from Alexandria were teaching that God was immaterial. Imagine their disgust when they debated with Stephen. He was teaching that Jesus (a god) had been resurrected with a physical body. In fact, the Alexandrian Jews were so outraged that they turned Stephen over to the Sanhedrin so that he could be stoned for blasphemy.

> Then there arose certain of the synagogue, which is called the synagogue of the Libertines, and Cyrenians, and Alexandrians, and of them of Cilicia and of Asia, disputing with Stephen.
> And they were not able to resist the wisdom and the spirit by which he spake.
> Then they suborned men, which said, We have heard him speak blasphemous words against Moses, and against God.
> And they stirred up the people, and the elders, and the scribes, and came upon him, and caught him, and brought him to the council.[9]

Stephen would not renounce his testimony. As a result, he was granted a vision of the Savior standing on the right hand of the Father. When he shared his testimony with the Sanhedrin, they stoned him to death.

> But he, being full of the Holy Ghost, looked up steadfastly into heaven, and saw the glory of God, and **Jesus standing on the right hand of God**,
> And said, Behold, I see the heavens opened, and the Son of man standing on the right hand of God.
> Then they cried out with a loud voice, and stopped their ears, and ran upon him with one accord.
> And cast him out of the city, and stoned him: and the witnesses laid down their clothes at a young man's feet, whose name was Saul.[10]

This was not the last time that someone would become offended because the Christians preached that Jesus was resurrected. Paul taught the same truth in Athens. The Epicureans and the Stoics labeled Jesus as a "strange god" because he had been physically resurrected. Remember that Philo had been influenced by the Stoics.

> Then certain philosophers of the Epicureans and of the Stoics, encountered him [Paul]. And some said, What will this babbler say? other some, He seemeth to be a setter forth of strange gods: because he preached unto them Jesus, and of the resurrection.[11]

Paul and the other apostles were well acquainted with the philosophies of that day. As a matter of fact, Paul and Jesus were contemporaries of Philo Judaeus.

> Philo Judaeus, born about 20 B.C. and died about A.D. 40, was a Jewish thinker and leader of the Jewish community in Alexandria, Egypt. He left many writings, mostly preserved in the original Greek, but some in Armenian translations. Philo was a contemporary of both Jesus and Paul.[12]

Since the apostles were familiar with the teachings of the philosophers, we should examine their feelings on the subject. Why? Because the apostles are our experts on what Jesus taught. If Plato or Aristotle or any other philosopher had a correct idea concerning the nature of God, the apostles could (and should) have informed us of that fact.

Paul warned, "Beware lest any man spoil you through philosophy and vain deceit, after the tradition of men, after the rudiments of the world, and not after Christ."[13]

The apostles were aware that many of the newly converted Christians still believed in the philosophers. However, they did not cater to these beliefs. Instead, following such teachers was a mark of apostasy. One of the early apocryphal sources, the Apocalypse of Peter, has Jesus state that his teachings were being supplanted by those of others.

> They will cleave to the name of a dead man, thinking that they will become pure. But they will become greatly defiled and they will fall into a name of error and into the hand of an evil, cunning man and a manifold dogma, and they will be ruled heretically. For some of them will blaspheme the truth and proclaim evil teaching. And they will say evil things against each other...But many others, who oppose the truth and are the messengers of error, will set up their error and their law against these pure thoughts of mine, as looking out from one [perspective], thinking that good and evil are from one [source]. They do business in my word...And there shall be others from outside our number who name themselves bishop and deacons, as if they have received their authority from God. They bend themselves under the judgement of the leaders. These people are dry canals.[14]

Predictions of such an apostasy are commonplace. The apostles stated that the church was about to depart from the truths which Jesus had taught. They then voiced very strong condemnations concerning those who were responsible for teaching these innovations.

> I marvel that ye are so soon removed from him that called you into the grace of Christ unto another gospel:
> Which is not another: but there be some that trouble you, and would pervert the gospel of Christ.
> But though we, or an angel from heaven, preach any other gospel unto you than that which we have preached unto you, let him be accursed.[15]

Why would these teachers appear in the church? Apostasy would occur because the people were rejecting the true teachings of Christ.

> For the time will come when they will not endure sound doctrine; but after their own lusts shall they heap to themselves teachers, having itching ears;
> And they shall turn away their ears from the truth, and shall be turned unto fables.[16]

Has Paul identified the source of this apostasy? He states that they will turn to fables. What culture was known for telling fables? The most famous fable teller was Aesop, a Greek. Paul was identifying the source of the apostasy as being the doctrines of the Greeks. The event which Paul spoke of did happen. When the apostles died, the central church collapsed. Each bishop then governed his own church, and determined what doctrines would be taught there. This new organization soon allowed the emergence of many new doctrines into the church. And, because there was no central organization to declare such idea heretical, many of the ideas from the Greek culture entered Christianity at this time.

> ...the same author [Hegesippus], relating the events of the times, also says, that the Church continued until then as a pure and uncorrupt virgin; whilst if there were any at all that attempted to pervert the sound doctrine of the saving gospel, they were yet skulking in dark retreats; but when the sacred choir of apostles became extinct, and the generation of those that had been privileged to hear their inspired wisdom had passed away, then also the combinations of impious error arose by the fraud and delusions of false teachers. These also, as there were none of the apostles left, henceforth attempted without shame to preach their false doctrine against the gospel of truth. Such is the statement of Hegesippus.[17]

Some have failed to understand why the adoption of all these Greek ideas would be so terrible. But these concepts of the philosophers were also present in the mystery religions. Joseph Lortz states that this syncretism shows that the new converts had not really changed their lives.

> The worship occupies a large place in the preoccupation of the church. The church must, in fact, adapt it to the spirit of the peoples that it had just converted. The barbarians were like children. Their naive and uncultured souls understood less that which addressed itself to the mind than that which appealed to the senses ad the imagination. They had to have then a worship full of life and pomp, of a nature to curb their barbarity and grosser instincts. The Christian life of the converted barbarians still resembled their pagan life.[18]

Martin Werner agrees, noting, "By this process ecclesiastical Chrstianity could not truly conquer the paganism of the world in which it lived; rather it absorbed it into itself and lapsed itself into it."[19]

One of the earliest Christian writers was Justin Martyr. He was born about 100 A.D. and was converted to Christianity about thirty years later. As a convert from the philosophical groups, he still believed very strongly in what they taught. One of his most famous statements illustrates his beliefs very well:

> It is unreasonable to argue, in refutation of our doctrines, that we assert Christ to have been born a hundred and fifty years ago, under Cyrenius, and to have given his teaching somewhat later, under Pontius Pilate; and to accuse us of implying that all men born before this time were not accountable. To refute this, I will dispose of the difficulty of anticipation. We are taught that Christ is the First-born of God, and we have explained above that he is the Word (reason) of whom all mankind have a share, and those who lived according to reason are Christians, even though they be classified as atheists. For example; among Greeks, Socrates and Heraclitus; among non-Greeks, Abraham, Ananias, Azarias, and Mishael, and Elias, and many others.[20]

Was Justin wise in placing the teachings of the philosophers on the same level as the Old Testament prophets? Let us consider the case of Heraclitus.

Justin Martyr declared that the philosopher Heraclitus had discovered the truth through reason. This choice illustrates our point well. Heraclitus was known as "the Obscure" because people had difficulty understanding his teachings. As a matter of fact, his conclusions are very compatible with those of Zen Buddhism.

> The revolt against essence in the interests of existence is a dominant theme in the philosophy of our own century; the paradoxical tension between time and eternity is a dominant theme in Japanese Zen Buddhist thought; and in the light of these later attempts to explore the concrete existence of finite things, Heraclitus of Ephesus might qualify as the "first Western existentialist," because of his new direction of approach to philosophy.
>
> Heraclitus was known in antiquity as "the Obscure" or "the Dark."[21]

Heraclitus did not think of God in the same sense that deity was portrayed in the Old Testament. In the Old Testament, God is an individual being who appeared to people. Heraclitus thought that deity was like fire. Moreover, this God (or *Logos*) was really cosmic order.

> And yet, from the purposeless, cyclic flow of time, there does result a logos-a-formula, word, ratio, cosmic order. There is a cycle of transformation by which the exchange of fire and earth

and wter takes place, an "upward" and a downward way. But as soon as we think that at least here we have a clear proposition of Milesian physics—odd as the choice of fire is for a basic stuff—we read that "upward and downward the way is one and the same." The logos "steers all and runs through all..."; "Hearken, not to me, but to my logos"; man can find the logos in something that is "common," not in the private worlds of opinion and dream.[22]

Another favorite of Justin's was Plato. What kind of god did he believe in? Plato had been a student of Cratylus, who was a student of Heraclitus. We should not be surprised, therefore, to learn that Plato's god is also not material in composition. In fact, Plato's ideas of reality differ substantially from ours.

> The early theologians were largely influenced by Plato; the theology of the Middle Ages will turn to Aristotle.
> For Plato, an object consists of the "form or idea" and the matter of material of which it is made. The ideas of beauty, justice, goodness, etc., which for us are abstract ideas, which do not exist apart from the object. But for Plato these abstract ideas are the realities. The objects with which they are associated are perishable, therefore the greater reality for him, is the "ideal" or "form" back of the object.
> For Plato, the Supreme Being is absolute goodness, and since matter, for him, is evil and a hindrance to the perfect expression of the idea, "God is immaterial."[23]

Plato visualized God as the ultimate idea. It will, of course, be observed that this concept is highly abstract. It does not have the concrete sense of identity which is identified with the scriptural God of Israel. In fact, the god of Plato could most accurately be described as a principle.

Like most philosophies, Platonism itself was subject to reformation. A new version which was called Neo-Platonism came into vogue. Its leader was Plotinus.

> The school which he (Plotinus) founded in that city (Rome) included men from every country and every station in life: physicians, rhetoricians, poets, senators, nay, even an emperor and an empress...
> It became the center of what remained of pagan philosophy, science and literature. Countless commentaries were written on the Attic philosophers of Athens; they were even worshipped as Jesus; the apostles, and the martyrs were worshipped by the Christian community.[24]

Plotinus also believed that God was an abstraction. His deity could not even be said to exist.

> Every being is composed of matter and form. God (the One, the Form) and matter are the constructive principles...of the universe...God produces everything; matter suffers everything.... All that we can say of God is that he transcends everything that can be conceived or said. Strictly speaking, we cannot even affirm that he exists, for he transcends existence itself. He is the highest abstraction. God is the creator of ail things.[25]

The early Christian missionaries often disputed with the philosophers. Since the teachings of the philosophers were highly revered, differing with them was considered stupid. It might be compared to having a minister debate with a scientist today. In the later case, whatever the scientist said would be accepted as authentic; in the first case, the philosopher would be revered.

In order to negate this advantage, the Christians established their own theological schools. those who attended tried to reconcile the doctrines of the church with the philosophical theories.

> Pagan Greece produced great thinkers, still revered throughout the world, Socrates, Plato, Aristotle and others.
> Greek philosophy had reached its zenith in the fourth century B.C. In the time of the apostles, philosophic ideas had long been debated; and in connection with Christianity in the fourth century, were often discussed by the common people.
> The Greek philosophers were also the scientists of their time. They enjoyed great prestige. When their ideas came in conflict with what the "unlearned and ignorant men"—the apostles of Jesus had "seen and heard," an attempt was made to interpret what had been given by revelation and to reconcile it with the accepted philosophical beliefs.
> "Until the middle of the second century, the tendency to meet the philosophers on their own ground was not pronounced. Very few Christians had philosophical training, but as men with philosophical education joined the church, what was more to be expected than that they should, in the absence of continuous revelation, make increasing use of the philosophical (geometrical) method in their defense of Christianity and organize schools in imitation of the academies of the philosophers, to teach what was sometimes called the "revealed philosophy"?[26]

Two of these schools became very influential. They were located in Alexandria and Antioch. The doctrines which were taught in these schools would soon dictate orthodox doctrines for all of Christianity. The graduates of these two schools were usually chosen as bishops of the largest and most prestigious churches. Why did this happen? Because these graduates were better educated and had training in rhetoric. As a result, their placement was a foregone conclusion. Fernand Mourret, the Roman Catholic historian, tells of the founding of the school of Alexandria:

> The city of Alexandria was...to become the center of the Christian intellectual movement.
> This great city was always the home of scientific speculations. Teachers, recruited from everywhere, discussed, before audiences the most composite, but always eager to instruct themselves, the most diverse theories, borrowed from Jewish and pagan circles...It was there that a bold Christian resolved to found a great school of religious philosophy...
> This man, whom Clement of Alexandria, his disciple, calls "the first in value of all the holy and worthy men who were his masters," was called Pantaenus. The Church honors him with the title of saint. He was by birth a Sicilian and had been, before embracing Christianity, a partisan of the Stoic doctrines. Interviews which he had with several disciples of the apostles, perhaps with Saint Polycarp...brought him to the Christian faith. He devoted himself with ardor to the study of the holy Scriptures. His reputation as a exegete, as a philosopher, and as a theologian spread afar...
> In the time of Pantaenus, the Christian school of Alexandria, of which the administration was to take an later a character, in some sort official under the direction of the bishop, had only a rudimentary organization. It had no special hall. They met in the home of the professor...seeing the enthusiasm of his auditors, one could foresee the great brilliancy, which this school was, one day to throw over the Christian world.[27]

The school of Alexandria produced many of the prominent early Fathers. Such individuals as Origen, Clement of Alexandria, Alexander, and Athanasius were students and instructors there. They were not merely studying Christian doctrines, however. They were changing existing doctrines to make them more palatable to the Greek masses. Hugh Nibley explains:

> But about the year 200 the schools start to take over everywhere in Christian society. In Asia Minor, Palestine, Edesse, and the West, important schools suddenly come into being and a strongly intellectual orientation becomes evident in the church. Incomparably the most important of these new schools was the catechetical school of Alexandria, the true home of conventional Christian theology, whose foundations were laid by the famous Clement of Alexandria and his more famous pupil, Origen.
> It was Clement's project to put the intellectual superiority of

Greek philosophy at the disposal of the church...He was all for the church; he was going to give it a break by lending to it the advantages of his training and intellect. Very patronizing, one must admit, but one can imagine how that would have gone down with the Apostles. Such a point of view, really quite. naive, was only possible, says Harnack, because Clement missed the whole point of what Christianity was all about, **"because for him the heritage of the church in its totality and in every particular**—with the exception of some utterances in the Gospels **was something foreign."** The university was his world, and his offer of assistance to the church had dangerous strings attached to it: "He submitted to its authority," writes Harnack, "but could only adapt himself to it after a specific and philosophic re-working (Bearbeitung)." He would embrace the teachings of the church, but only on **his** terms...Firmly convinced that what he had learned in school was the truth, and that **all** knowledge is revelation (following Plato), he proceeded to re-edit the gospel to something nearer to his heart's desire: "The total revamping (rejoining, Umprägung) of the Christian heritage into a Hellenic religious philosophy or a historical foundation cannot be denied," says our authority Harnack. And what remained of Christianity after that, aside from some of its practical and sentimental appeal? he asks, and gives an almost shocking answer: "Ein Phlegma—a sediment, a scum—that can under no possible circumstances be called Christian." Yet Clement was a moral and an earnest man, the first great teacher of the Catechetical School of Alexandria, the school that was to have more influence in the making of Christian doctrine than all the rest put together.[28]

By what authority could Clement and Origen decide what the true doctrines of Christianity were? They were merely teachers in a school in Alexandria. No one had ever identified the school as being the official interpreter of theology for all of Christianity, but they were acting as if it had been.

Moreover, how could any doctrine invented over a hundred years after Christ was crucified profess to encapsulate what the ture nature of God was? These men never claimed to receive a revelation upon the subject, so why would they know more than anyone else? Clearly they were speculating upon things wherein they had no knowledge.

This opinion of Clement is shared by many other scholars. One of these historians is Joseph Milner, who writes:

[Clement of Alexandria] was of the Eclectic sect, a scholar of Pantaenus, and of the same philosophical cast of mind. He ascribed too much to the wisdom of this world, and did not duly consider that "the world by wisdom knew not God."...It is not grounding our religion on the truth of Divine revelation, but on that philosophy which feeds the pride of the depraved heart, and lulls it into security in self-righteousness, by the blandishments of mere reason; vain man would be wise.[29]

Clement was followed by his pupil, Origen. He, like his teacher, sought to make Christianity respectable by incorporating the teachings of the philosophers. Indeed, Origen and others like him were trying to set up a spiritual elite in the church. These great scholars, he argued, were the only ones who could truly understand what the true doctrines of the church were.

> Clement is completely overshadowed by his pupil Origen, next to St. Augustine alone the most influential thinker of the Christian Church. "Origen created the doctrinal theology of the Church," writes Harnack. **Not Christ, not the apostles, but Origen.** "Among the ancient Greek writers of the Church," writes DeLarue in the Patrologia, "there is possibly none who has left to posterity such a reputation for learning as Origen." Jerome notes that his reputation was as great among the pagans as among the Christians. In his time, he was indisputably the foremost authority in the church on doctrine; the greatest bishops eagerly sought his counsel and instruction; his voice was the deciding one in grave disputes; requests for information poured in an him at such a rate that **we are told that he kept seven secretaries, shorthand experts, busy night and day taking down the answers he dictated to all parts of the world.**
>
> Like his teacher, Origen betrays strong Neoplatonic and Gnostic leanings. Like Irenaeus he ends up using the arguments and language of those he attempts to refute, and like all the schoolmen of the time he is more than a little embarassed and ashamed at the unsophisticated and unphilosophical nature of the faith of his simpler brethren. I think this embarassment is best expressed by Origen's contemporary Minucius Felix, whose Christian apologist, Octavius, goes to considerable pains to make clear to his educated pagan opponents that **they have really misunderstood Christianity by judging it from the behavior and beliefs of the ordinary members and officers of the Church. All Christians are not like that, he explains. Cultivated Christians really think just like cultivated heathens,** so that "anyone would think either that present-day Christians are philosophers or that the philosophers of yore were Christians."[30]

Some have argued that Origen's teachings, which were later repudiated by Augustine, were not really accepted by the church at large. This is not the case. In fact, Ambrose, the famed bishop of Milan, the saint and advisor to the emperor, provided the seven secretaries for Origen. This proves that the doctrines had official sanction.

> Starting from that time Origen's commentaries on the divine Scriptures had their beginning, at the instigation of Ambrose, who not only plied him with innumerable verbal exhortations and encouragements, but also provided him unstintingly with what was necessary. For as he dictated there were ready at hand more than seven shorthand-writers, who relieved each other at fixed times, and as many copyists, as well as girls skilled in penmanship; for all of whom Ambrose supplied without stint the necessary means.[31]

But the allegorical methods which Origen used were not his invention, nor were they the invention of Clement. They were merely copied from Philo Judaeus. And, whether we credit this theology to Origen, Clement or Philo, we are still dealing with speculation.

> Allegorizing of the Scriptures was not, of course, a novelty. The practice had been extensively employed by, for example, Philo. The point is, however, there was plenty of room for a philosophical or speculative interpretation of the Bible. In terms of a later distinction between theology and philosophy we can say that **Origen was developing Christian speculative theology with the aid of ideas derived from or suggested by philosophy.**[32]

Stephen was executed because some of the disciples of Philo from Alexandria objected to Christian doctrines. Now, a few centuries later in the same city where these disciples had come from, the ideas of Philo were being taught under the guise of being Christian doctrines. Is this merely a coincidence? I do not think so. The school of Pantaenus had assimilated the school of Philo. And the pagan doctrines of the latter were now being called Christian orthodox doctrines. Phillip Schaff points out that we should not have expected anything else in the Roman empire:

> The Roman state, with its laws, institutions, and usages, as still deeply rooted in heathenism, and could not be transformed by a magical stroke. The christianizing of the state amounted therefore in great measure to a paganizing and secularizing of the church. The world overcame the church, as much as the church overcame the world, and the temporal gain of Christianity was in many respects canceled by spiritual loss. The mass of the Roman empire was baptized only with water, not with the Spirit and fire of the gospel, and it smuggled heathen manners and practices into the sanctuary under a new name.[33]

The school of Alexandria had a dangerous rival in Antioch. The two schools differed fundamentally in their approach to theology.

Their Hearts Are Far From Me 137

Franz Funk, the Roman Catholic scholar, explains how they differed:

> The chief centers of scientific life were in the Orient at Alexandria and Antioch. Both names designated at the same time the most important theological schools and tendencies of the time. The difference between them shows itself merely in the field of exegesis. While the Alexandrians with preference devoted themselves to the **allegorical** interpretation, which earlier had found in Origen its most decided and learned representative, the Antiochians concerned themselves above all with the **grammatical-historical explanation** of the holy scriptures.[34]

As graduates from these two schools received appointments throughout the Christian theological structure, the viewpoints of the two schools were also spread. Disagreements among the bishops of that day were common, with each side following the doctrines espoused by their instructors. The situation was explosive, requiring only a minimal spark to set it off.

The spark was provided in Alexandria. This city had a number of bishops. The most influential bishop governed the others, being the regional head of the church (or metropolitan). Legend stated that the Alexandrine church was founded by Mark (Peter's scribe). It was one of several sites which argued (because of the connection with Peter) that they should govern the entire church. Accordingly, the Alexandrine Metropolitan was given the title of pope. This title was even accorded to them by the bishop of Rome.

A struggle ensued over the papal office of Alexandria. The favorite candidate was Arius, but he declined the office, preferring to be a mere presbyter. This caused a man named Alexander to be elected to the position. Alexander recognized that Arius was a dangerous rival. A serious dispute ensued which threatened to engulf all of Christianity.

Arius had studied at Antioch and Alexander had studied at Alexandria. They therefore disagreed over matters of doctrine. Alexander heard Arius state that Jesus was a creature. The pope of Alexandria denounced this premise and demanded that Arius stop preaching it. The disciples of Arius responded that Alexander had taught the same doctrines during a recent sermon. This, of course, shows that the differences between them at that time were so slight that it is unlikely that the differences between the two were theological. It seems more likely that the contest was primarily political.

...the subject was one which none but men trained in dialectic subtleties could possibly comprehend...yet the result was to set house against house and family against family, to fill cities with confusion and the whole empire with disorder, to arouse the most furious passions and to make men at enmity with each other on questions which not one in a thousand could understand.[35]

The pope of Alexandria had considerable influence in that area. He convened a council of approximately one hundred Egyptian bishops to discuss the ideas of Arius. It seems probable that most of these bishops had attended the school of Alexandria. At any rate, they deposed Arius for heresy.

The pope of Alexandria, Alexander (312?–328), heard these views presented in a debate between Arius and another teacher and gave his decision that Arius was in the wrong and must cease setting forth such opinions. Arius, however, was not without supporters among clergy and laity alike. He made it clear that he intended to continue disseminating his views. The scale of the controversy grew. In the end, about 320, Alexander had Arius and his associated deposed by a council of some one hundred Egyptian bishops; but by that time Arius had fled to Palestine, certain that outside of Egypt he would find sympathy for his views, as indeed he did.[36]

Why was Arius so sure that he could find others who felt as he did? Because he was teaching doctrines that had been formulated in the school of Antioch. One of the most famous teachers of that school was the martyr Lucian. A martyr, according to the teachings of that day, had received the baptism of blood by virtue of having died for the Faith, and unquestionably dwelt in the presence of God. Therefore, it was inconceivable to Arius that his teacher would have taught him falsehoods. He appealed to other theologians who had also attended this school. They sided with Arius and pressured Alexander to reinstate their comrade.

Among others, he won over the influential Eusebius of Nicomedia (d. ca. 342), bishop of the imperial capital of the east [and the favorite theologian of the Emperor Constantine's sister] and, like Arius, a former pupil of the martyr Lucian of Antioch. For a time, Arius stayed with Eusebius at Nicomedia, and it was there, in all probability, that he wrote his Thalia, a work (now known only in fragments) in which he presented his views

CHAPTER 8 REFERENCES

1. Joseph Smith History 1:19
2. Jeremiah 2:11–13
3. A Concise Bible Companion, 99
4. *Josephus—Complete Works,* 250
5. Ibid., 246
6. Roberts, *The "Mormon" Doctrine of Deity,* 1-82
7. Professor Schurer, of University of Giessen, Art. "Philo" in *Encyclo. Brit.* as cited in Ibid., 183–184
8. Talmage, *Jesus the Christ,* 69–70
9. Acts 6:9–12
10. Acts 7:55–58
11. Acts 17:18
12. *Collier's Encyclopedia,* 18:700, Article "Philo Judaeus"
13. Colossians 2:8
14. Robinson, *The Nag Hammadi Library in English,* 5
15. Galatians 1:6–8
16. 2 Timothy 4:3–4
17. Eusebius, *Ecclesiastical History,* Book III, Chapter 32 as cited in Talmage, *The Great Apostasy,* 39
18. Lortz, *History of the Church,* 141
19. Werner, *The Formation of Christian Dogma,* 303
20. *The Early Christian Fathers,* 83
21. Brumbaugh, *The Philosophers of Greece,* 44
22. Ibid., 45
23. Barker, *Apostasy From the Divine Church,* 229
24. Weber, *History of Philisophy,* 167
25. Ibid., 167, 171
26. Barker, *Apostasy From the Divine Church,* 222
27. Mourret, *Histoire Generale L'Eglise,* 1:275–276, cited in Ibid., 223
28. Nibley, *The World and the Prophets,* 72–73
29. Milner, *The History of the Church of Christ,* 94
30. Nibley, *The World and the Prophets,* 75
31. Quasten, *Patrology,* 2:43
32. Copleston, *A History of Medieval Philosophy,* 22
33. Schaff, *History of the Christian Church,* 3:93
34. Funk, *Lehrbuch der Kirkenqeschichte,* 195–196 as cited in Barker, *Apostasy From the Divine Church,* 224
35. Foakes-Jackson, *History of the Christian Church to A.D. 461,* 297
36. Walker, Norris, Lotz and Handy, *A History of Christianity,* 132
37. Ibid., 132

9
The Nicene Council

As we have noted, most of Christianity believes in the precepts which are affirmed in the Nicene Creed. In the view of these individuals, the creed was merely an affirmation of what Christians had always believed. We will demonstrate that this is not the case. We will also show that it was adopted by force, and that the majority of those who voted for it did not really believe in what they were voting for. Lastly, we will demonstrate that the motives and character of the participants are open to question. In other words, we are calling into question the credibility of that council and the creed which it adopted.

> The strength and validity of every testimony must bear proportion with the **authority of the testifier**; and the **authority of the testifier** is founded upon his **ability** and **integrity**: his **ability** in the knowledge of that which he delivereth and asserteth; his **integrity** in delivering and asserting according to his knowledge.[1]

Let us therefore examine the credibility of those who were the leading participants in the Council of Nicea. Let each of us determine whether these individuals had the authority, ability, and integrity necessary to codify a belief which would be binding upon Christianity for the rest of history. I must affirm that they did not.

Let us first consider the Roman Emperor Constantine, who assembled the council and presided at its sessions. He is generally perceived as the first Christian emperor, and the Greek Orthodox Church has declared him to be a saint. It is true that he legalized the Christian faith and showered it with expensive gifts. Basil Cooper, however, questions whether Constantine was really a fully converted Christian.

> ...in general, it may be said with truth, that **he was a tolerably good heathen, but a very sorry Christian.** Niebuhr's judgment

respecting him, in a passage in which the great historian is speaking of his execution of his brother-in-law, Licinius, and his murder of his son, Crispus, is not widely different. "Many judge of him by too severe a standard, **because they look upon him as a Christian; but I cannot regard him in that light.** The religion which he had in his head must have been a strange compound indeed. The man who had on his coins the inscription, Sol Invictus, who worshipped pagan divinities, consulted the haruspices, indulged in a number of heathen superstitions, and, on the other hand, built churches, shut up pagan temples, and interfered with the council of Nice, must have been a repulsive phenomenon, and **was certainly not a Christian.**"[2]

The judgment of the aforementioned author is confirmed by the fact that Constantine was not baptized until he was on his death bed. But while he was not a baptized Christian and had not been ordained to the ministry, Constantine did not hesitate to act as if he were the head of the Christian Church. By what authority did he do this? He did so by virtue of the fact that he was the Pontifex Maximus, or head of pagan worship, in the Roman empire.

The second individual who played a major part in the Council of Nicea was Athanasius. He was the student of Alexander and was a deacon in Alexandria. Since Alexander, as a pope, was expected to take a leading role in directing the council, Athanasius presented the case against Arius.

Athanasius was sainted because of his role in the adoption of the Nicene Creed. As a result, the historians of a later date have tended to describe this man in the most glowing of terms. However, many of those who knew the man did not see him in the same light. William Jones cites the description which was given by Constantine's son, Constantius.

> Constantius banished Athanasius from his bishoprick at Alexandria, and wrote a letter to the citizens in which he terms him "an impostor, a corrupter of men's souls, a disturber of the city, a pernicious fellow, one convicted of the worst crimes, not to be expiated by his suffering death ten times."[3]

Whether we agree with the enemies of Athanasius or not, we must agree that Athanasius was not an impartial observer on this matter. He was defending the opinions of his superior and teacher against an avowed enemy. The loser of this contest would be banished. Athanasius had no intention of allowing this fate to happen to Alexander—or to himself for that matter. As a result, compromises in the professed beliefs were made during the council

The Nicene Council

in order to gain allies. After all, the most important objective was not to defend a specific doctrine, but to crush Arius and his supporters! The truth of this statement can be illustrated by a description of the tactics which were used at this and other councils of that era.

> Nowhere is Christianity less attractive, and, if we look to the ordinary tone and character of the proceedings, less authoritative, than in the councils of the church. It is in general a fierce collision of rival factions, neither of which will yield, each of which is solemnly pledged against conviction. Intrigue, injustice, violence, decisions on authority alone, and that the authority of a turbulent majority decision by wild acclamation rather than after sober inquiry, detract from the reverence, and impugn the judgments of at least the later councils. The close is almost invariably a terrible anathema, in which it is impossible not to discern the tones of human hatred, or arrogant triumph, of rejoicing at the damnation imprecated against the humiliated adversary. **Even the venerable Council of Nicea commenced with mutual accusals and recriminations...but the more fatal error of that council was the solicitation, at least the acquiescence in the infliction of a civil penaty, against the recusant prelates.** The degeneracy is rapid from the Council of Nicea to that of Ephesus, where each party came determined by every means of haste, manoeuvre, court influence, bribery, **to crush his adversary...**[4]

Emperor Constantine had two spiritual advisors at his side during the deliberations. The first of these was Hosius of Cordoba (Spain), who sided with Alexander and Athanasius, and the second was Eusebius of Caesarea (Palestine), who was a moderate, but leaned toward the ideas of Arius.

> Among the bishops conspicuous for their rank were the patriarchs of Alexandria and Antioch, [Author's Note: These were, as we have already established, the cities where the chief Christian schools were located] Alexander and Eustathius, the former of whom bore the title of Pope (papa or Abba, i.e., Pater patrum [father of fathers]). These two patriarchs appear to have been the ordinary presidents of the Council in turn with **Hosius of Cordoba and Eusebius of Caesarea** (Metropolitan of Palestine), who were the special advisors of the emperor and sat at his right and left when he presided in person.[5]

Another individual who is often mentioned by religious historians is Sylvester, the bishop of Rome. They attempt to explain why he, who held the office that would later bear the title of pope over the entire Roman Catholic Church, would be absent from the most important council in the history of Christianity. Many have theorized that he did not attend because of his advanced age. However, the central issue still remains unresolved. Why was the appeal made to Constantine and not to Sylvester?

The Roman Catholic Church affirms that Sylvester was the man who stood at the head of the church at that time. Yet he was not asked to settle the dispute. Furthermore, the council was not even held in Rome. It is true that Sylvester did have several representatives attend the meetings, but no mention is made of their having taken an active role in the proceedings. In fact, all of the bishops present debated the matter and signed the Creed without even checking to see if Sylvester would concur.

> Most Catholic writers, looking back upon this event (the Council of Nicea), have felt positive that no such assembly could have taken place without the instigation or co-operation of the huge enterprises, even as he had been of the Council of Arles (called to settle the Donatst dispute). Eusebius gives him the sole credit, as do the letters issued by the Council itself, and he Himself, both then and afterwards, spoke of it as the council which he had summoned.[6]

The next participant who we needed to consider is Arius. Many of the textbooks of our day speak of him as he were a willing heretic who invented a new doctrine. This is a portrait which the winning side painted of him after he was dead [Author's note: Gibbon theorized that Arius was poisoned] and his writings were consigned to ashes. This propoganda was invented in order to prejudice the public concerning his ideas. By doing this, religious historians portray the Council of Nicea as merely ratifying documents instituted by Christ which had been since the meridian of time. This is not the case. In fact, Prestige points out that the teachings of Arius are copied from those of Origen.

> Origen, the common father of Arianism and of Cappodoican orthodoxy, is the obvious example.[7]

The ideas of Origen were also taught by Alexander. This shows that the beliefs of the two men were not really as far apart as history, in retrospect, claims. Nor was Arius really setting himself up in opposition to the authority of Alexander. Before his condemnation by the Egyptian synod, Arius wrote this letter, which acknowledges the authority of Alexander and claimed both parties were really teaching the same ideas:

The Nicene Council

> To our blessed pope and bishop Alexander the presbyters [comparable to the office of elder today] and deacons send greeting in the Lord.
> Our faith which we received from our forefathers and **have also learned from you is this.** We know there is one God, the only unbegotten, only eternal, only without beginning, only true, who only has immortality, only wise, only good, the only potentate, judge of all, governor, dispenser, unalterable and unchangeable, righteous and good, God of the Law and the Prophets and the New Covenant. Before everlasting ages he begot his unique Son, through whom he made the ages and all things...But as Monad and cause of all, God is thus before all. Therefore he is also prior to the Son, **as we learned from what you preached in the midst of the church.**
> So therefore, as he has being and glories from God, and life and all things were given him, accordingly God is his source. For he precedes him as "his God" and as being before him. But if the (phrases) "of him" and "out of the womb" and "I came forth from the Father and am come" are understood by some as (meaning) a part of the consubstantial himself and a projection, then according to them the Father is compound and divisible and alterable and a body, and according to them presumably, the bodiless God [is thought of as] suffering what belongs to a body.
> We pray that you may fare well in the Lord, blessed pope. Arius, Aeitheles, Achilleus, Carpones, Sarmatas, Menas, Helladius, Gaius. Bishops, Secondus of Pentepolls, Theanas of Libya, Pistus [whom the Arians installed at Alexandria].[8]

A review of Arius's letter shows how deeply both men were entrenched in the throes of apostasy. Each was proceeding under assumption that the Father and the Son were part of a universal substance and did not have a body. What they were arguing about was the time at which the Son had been begotten.

Having dealt with the leading participants of the Council, let us return to our account of history. As a result of Arius's appeal, a council of bishops at Bithynia denounced Alexander and declared the teachings of Arius to be orthodox. This decision meant that both parties now had been backed by a council.

Constantine was greatly disturbed by the dispute which was dividing all of Christianity. Therefore, the Roman emperor sent his religious councilor Hosius of Cordoba to deliver the monarch's view on the subject. A review of those instructions shows that at this point Constantine did not care who won. He merely did not want the dispute to destroy the peace. He told Alexander that he (Alexander) should not have asked the question and that Arius should not have answered it.

The unhappy spirit of discord which pervaded the provinces of the East interrupted the triumph of Constantine; but the emperor continued for some time to view with cool and careless indifference the difficulty of appeasing the quarrels of theologians, he addressed to the contending parties, to Alexander and to Arius, a moderating epistle; which may be ascribed with far greater reason to the untutored sense of a soldier and statesman then to the dictates of any of his episcopal counselors. He attributes **the origin of the whole controversy to a trifling and subtle question concerning an incomprehensible point of the law, which was foolishly asked by the bishop, and imprudently resolved by the presbyter.**

He laments that the Christian people, who had the same God, the same religion, and the same worship, should be divided by such inconsiderable distinctions; and he seriously recommends to the clergy of Alexandria the example of the Greek philosophers, who could maintain their arguments without losing their temper, and assert their freedom without violating their friendship.[9]

Hosius used this opportunity to condemn Arius. Arius objected to this treatment and demanded that he be given a chance to plead his case before Constantine in person. He was allowed to do so.

Nevertheless, the exasperated emperor did not refuse the personal conference which it would seem Arius had humbly craved; and, accordingly, such a meeting actually took place. At this interview, Constantine examined Arius in the presence of several prelates; but, of course, could make nothing of one so well practiced in the arts of logical evasion. Peace was not restored, and Constantine at length summoned the prelates of Christendom to meet at Nice, in Bithynia, to pronounce their judgment upon this question, as well as upon some others, such as the proper time for celebrating Easter, upon which a diversity of opinion prevailed.[10]

On what authority was Constantine doing all these things? He most certainly did not have any ecclesiastical authority. However, as the Roman emperor, Constantine could enforce his decisions. In addition, Constantine had bestowed huge sums of money upon the clergy. Could some of these bishops have been voting for what they thought the emperor wanted instead of voting their conscience? As we shall see, this became a factor in the form of the Creed that was adopted. At any rate, we are shown by the conduct of Constantine that he was in charge of the Council.

...the emperor arose in his turn in the midst of a universal silence. His glance ran over those assembled, meeting eyes fixed on him everywhere; then, in a very gentle tone of voice, he pronounced those words in Latin; an interpreter translated them as he did so:

...When, with the aid and the consent of the Almighty, I had triumphed over my enemies, I thought that all that remained for me to do was to praise God, and to rejoice with those (the Christians) whom he had delivered by my hand (by his defeat of Licinius). But as soon as I heard of the division that had appeared among you, I judged that it was an urgent matter, and **desirous of bringing a remedy for this new evil.** The division, not the ideas of either Arius or Alexander **I convoked you all without delay,** and it is a great joy to me to be present at your meeting. But I shall not think that I have arrived at the complete satisfaction of my desires, until I shall have seen all your hearts united in common sentiments, and united in that concord which must reign among you, and since it is your duty, consecrated to God, as you are, to preach it to others. Do not delay then, oh my friends, oh ministers of God, oh servants of a Master and oh of a common Savior, **do not delay to cause all roots of discord to disappear, and to resolve by peace the knot of all your difficulties.** It is thus that you will please the sovereign God, and me, your brother in the service of God, you will oblige me beyond all expression.

This discourse concluded, Adds Eusebius, he yielded to the presidents of the assembly.[11]

Constantine's address shows what the emperor's goal was when he organized the Council of Nicea. He wanted to have one side or the other win the argument. He did not care which side won. He assumed that all the disputes would stop when a decision was reached and that he would then be able to concentrate on other matters.

Arius was not granted a seat on the council. He was, however, allowed to present his case. Both he and Athanasius quoted scriptures in order to prove their point. James L. Barker cites some of their quotations:

"The Lord possessed me in the beginning of his way, before his works of old." Proverbs 8:22. "But of that day and that hour knoweth no man, no, not the angels which are in heaven, neither the Son, but the Father." Mark 13:32. "...for my Father is greater than I." John 14:28. "And this is life eternal, that they may know thee, and Jesus Christ, whom thou hast sent." John 17:3. "The Son can do nothing of himself." John 15:19. "Why callest thou me Good? There is none good, but one, that is God." Mark 10:18. "Wherefore God also hath highly exalted him, and given him a name which is above every name." Philippians 2:9. They also quoted passages representing Jesus as suffering, growing in wisdom, etc.: Luke 2:5; John 11:33, 38; Matthew 26:39.

Athanasius, for whom the Father and the Son were of "one substance" and who was the spokesman for Alexander, made use throughout the controversy, both before and after the Council of Nicea, of the following texts: "I and the Father are one." John 10:30. "...the Father is in me and I in him." John 10:38. "...he that hath seen me hath seen the Father." John 14:9.[12]

While the discussions were going on, Constantine was observing the strength of both sides. He soon noticed that there were more Athanasians present than Arians. The majority of the attendees were moderates (called Semi-Arians) who saw merits in the arguments of both sides. Constantine decided that the moderates could be induced to side with the winning group and began to intervene on the side of Athanasius. Fernand Mourret states:

> ...It was evident that [Arius's] cause was lost...The two Eusebiuses had to intervene with Constantine to prevent the emperor from taking measures against the person of the heretic. The tactics of the friends of Arius consisted henceforth in trying to get the Council to vote a formula that would leave the door open to speculations concerning the nature and origin of the Verb (Word—Jesus). To this end, the two Eusebiuses employed all their efforts. In consequence, the whole effort of Athanasius and his friends tended to reduce the third (moderate) party to the necessity of taking a position definitely for or against Arius, for or against the traditional (?) doctrine. All the struggles that follow are explained by those double tactics.[13]

Eusebius of Nicomedia suggested that a creed be composed out of quotations from the Bible. This was a reasonable request. Athanasius and his allies voted this idea down. Why? The Arians could use the same scriptural language and interpret it to justify their own ideas.

> At the Council itself the reason for the passage to the new ontological mode of conception was altogether practical. Athanasius is again explicit on this point. The old efforts to state the doctrine of the Son and Logos used scriptural formulas; this had been the traditional practice, visible in all the earlier (local) creeds. **The trouble was that the Arian party was quite willing to recite the scriptural affirmations at the same time that it read into them an Arian understanding,** the conception of the Son as a creature. The Fathers had, therefore, to go beyond the letter of the scriptural formulas to their sense. They stated the sense in new formulas, "out of the substance of the Father," "consubstantial with the Father".[14]

These formulas would not bear the Arian understanding. The latter was excluded from the formulas by the now mode of

The Nicene Council 149

understanding the Scriptures that the formulas embodied. What kind of new language was Athanasius introducing? He was utilizing language which had been gleaned from his philosophical studies. It contained the concepts that Plato and the other philosophers had taught. This is the reason that the concepts of the Trinity are not found in the Bible. Trinitarian theology was composed from other sources on purpose.

Athanasius introduced these phrases as a weapon against the Arians. However, their use provoked a storm of protest from the moderate majority. These men realized that the new language was unscriptural, and protested vigorously.

> A striking illustration is the difficulty which champions of novel theological terms like "of the same substance" or again ingenerate or "self-existent", and "without beginning," experienced in getting these descriptions of the Son's relationship to the Father, or of God's eternal being, generally admitted. They had to meet the damning objection, advanced in conservative as well as heretical quarters, that they were not found in the Bible. In the end, they would only quell opposition by painting out (Athanasius in the one case, Gregory of Nazianzus in the other) that, even if the terms themselves were non-Scriptural, the meaning they conveyed was exactly that of Holy Writ.[15]

But were the doctrines that Athanasius was introducing scriptural? The conservative factions at Nicea did not think so. They viewed this practice as being contrary to both the spirit and letter of the Bible.

> The prime objection of the Right was to the word, but the issue went much deeper, below the level of language, to an issue of most weighty substance. **The real issue concerned development in the understanding of the Christian revelation and faith. It concerned progress within the tradition.**[16]

Are we correct in our portrayal of the event? Let us review the testimony of Hilary. He sided with Athanasius and is an excellent witness of what actually happened at Nicea. Hugh Nibley quotes his account:

> Since the whole argument is about **words**, and since the whole controversy has to do with the subject of innovation (i.e., the introduction of philosophical terms not found in the scripture), and since the occasion of the discussion is the presence of certain ambiguities, and **since the dispute is about authority**, and since we are quarreling about technical questions, and **since our problem**

> is to reach a consensus, and since each side is beginning to be anathema to the other, **it would seem that hardly anybody belongs to Christ** [or is on Christ's side] **anymore**. We are blown about by winds of doctrine and as we teach we only become more upset, and **the more we are taught, the more we go astray**" (Hilary II, 5). What a commentary on Nicea! "We avoid believing that of Christ which He told us to believe, so that we might establish a treacherous unity in the false name of peace, and we rebel with new definitions of God against what we falsely call innovations, and in the name of the Scriptures we deitfully cite things that are not in the Scriptures: changeful, prodigal, impious, changing established things, abolishing accepted doctrine, presuming irreligious things" (Hilary II, 6).[17]

At this point, Eusebius of Caesarea attempted to find a solution by proposing that they adopt the baptismal formula which his church used. Many such formulas existed. However, none of these local formulas had ever been accepted by all of the individual churches. The Nicene Creed would be the first.

This creed was then presented to Constantine for his approval. The emperor accepted the creed on the condition that the bishops add the word *homoousios* (one substance) to the document.

> ...the emperor, speaking first, testified that it was irreproachable, and that it should be accepted and subscribed by all, **adding only the term** *omoousios* (one substance). The prince explained what he understood by this term, **which one should not take materially, but as is fitting with words that one applies to God**, it being well understood that the Son cannot subsist divided from or cut off from the Father...[18]

The Arians and the Semi-Arians did not want this word inserted. It had already been denounced as heretical and was associated with several heresies.

> The Sabellians had apparently already availed themselves of the expression, and Dionysius had rejected it as unscriptural in the same manner as did the Arians later. Again, somewhat later still, an Antiochene synod had also rejected *homoousios* in condemning the dynamic Monarchian, Paul of Samosata. The formula finally succeeded in establishing itself, yet only after, it proved, the suppression of a stony opposition within the camp of the Church itself.[19]

But Constantine wanted the word used. The moderates asked the emperor what definition he would attach to the word. This was important, because there were at least two different definitions.

The Nicene Council

Constantine replied that "one should not take materially, but as is fitting with words that one applies to God." What did this mean? The Arians and Semi-Arians decided that Constantine was giving them license to interpret it in any way they chose. The important thing was not to argue with the Athanasians and thus destroy the peace. The fact that Constantine threatened to banish all those who would not sign the creed helped to convince nearly everyone to sign.

> The Nicene creed was ratified by Constantine; and his firm declaration, that those who resisted the divine judgment of the synod must prepare themselves for an immediate exile, annihilated the murmurs of a feeble opposition; which, from seventeen was almost immediately reduced to two protesting bishops. The impious Arius was banished into one of the remote provinces of Illyricum; his person and disciples were branded by law, with the odious name of Porphyrians; his writings were condemned to the flames, and a capital punishment was denounced against those in whose possession they should be found.[20]

What did the original Nicene Creed say? The original text read:

> We believe in one God, the Father Almighty, Maker of all things, both visible and invisible: and in one Lord Jesus Christ, the Son (Word) of God, begotten of the Father, only-begotten, that is of the essence (substance) of the Father. God from God, Light from Light, (Life from Life), very God from very God, begotten not made, of one essence (substance) with the Father, (omoousion to Patri) through whom all things came to be, both things in heaven and things on earth; Who for the sake of us men and for our salvation came down, and was made flesh, and became man, suffered, and rose on the third day, ascended into the heavens (to the Father), is coming to judge living and dead; and in one Holy Spirit.[21]

A review of the language of this creed shows a big difference from that of later creeds. This one does not try to convince us that the Father, Son, and Holy Ghost are all the same being. Instead, it affirms that each one is God and states that they are all part of the same substance. We will explain in later chapters why Christianity abandoned this formula. We will also explain why the Nicene Creed represented a huge break with what Christianity had believed previously.

Constantine wanted Christianity to be a unifying force in his empire. This could not happen if there was constant fighting over doctrines and church positions. So a church structure was set up at

Nicea to establish a hierarchy of authority. The metropolitans (bishops over important cities like Rome, Constantinople, Alexandria, etc.) were given authority over the other bishops in their area. The emperor, of course, claimed authority over all church officers and treated them as civil servants.

> The council dealt with other matters beside the central issue of Arianism. For one, it passed a series **which for the first time defined a formal structure above the local level.** This structure, which took shape in the East much sooner than in the West, was based on the provincial divisions of the empire. The council limited the authority of local churches and their bishops by calling for regular provincial synods of bishops, by assigning to the bishop of the provincial metropolis a veto over the election and ordination of bishops in his area, and by insisting that no one could be made a bishop without the participation of at least three other bishops of the Province.[22]

The fact that it was necessary to codify new rules for the hierarchy of the church shows that a new church was being formed. If it was not, why did they not continue to operate under the old structure? In fact, all of the central doctrines of the church were being restructured.

The Council of Nicea redefined the nature of God the Father, his relationship to the Son, and the organization of the church. Other councils dealt with the nature of Christ, whether images should be allowed in the church, whether the Holy Ghost was God, predestination, grace, and the atonement of Christ. In fact, it is impossible to find a doctrine of orthodox Christianity which was not codified during the time of Nicea or after. Prior to that time, Christianity had been in existence for over three hundred years. Are we to believe that no beliefs had been established during all that time? If beliefs did exist, why was it necessary to define them again? It would only be necessary if Constantine organized a new church and established a set of doctrines for the church to teach.

Was Constantine really the head of the new church? He certainly acted as if he was. The other officers of the church confirm the fact that he was, for they accept his payments of money, obey his orders, and appeal to him to settle disputes on doctrinal matters.

> The business of the Council having been finished, Constantine celebrated the twentieth anniversary of his ascension to the empire, and invited the bishops to a splendid repast, at the end of which each of them received rich presents. Several days later the **emperor commanded that a final session be held,** at which he

The Nicene Council

assisted in order to exhort the bishops to work for the maintenance of peace; he commended himself to their prayers and **authorized the fathers to return to their dioceses.**[23]

Most religious manuals of our day portray the decision of the Nicene Council as a time of rejoicing. Basil Cooper sees it as a time when the church succumbed to the civil government and became a tool of the state.

> A more triumphant result than this was, **in appearance**, it is scarcely possible to conceive. Yet the subsequent history abundantly proved how hollow was the peace which this vaunted council—perhaps, actually the best of its kind—had brought about; and how little had really been done for the faith of the church by that assembly, which, after bartering away her freedom, deemed it fitting to revel at the feet of her ravisher, over the glory of its two-fold confession: of Christ as the fellow of the Almighty, and of his Bride as the toy of the Caesar.[24]

Constantine had backed Athanasius and his doctrines because he thought that they would bring peace. But they brought strife and contention in the years that followed.

As a result, the emperor switched his allegiance to the Arians and banished Athanasius. The next chapter will tell of the controversies which occurred in the following years. We will see that an examination of the historical events does not confirm that the right decision was made at Nicea.

> "Out of nothing nothing can come" is an axiom as true in history as in nature. A hundred weak arguments cannot make one strong argument. A dozen broken cisterns hold no more water than one. If every link of the chain is weak, the whole chain is weak, however long you make it.[25]

CHAPTER 9 REFERENCES

1. Pearson, *An Exposition of the Creed*, 5
2. Cooper, *The Free Church of Ancient Christendom*, 348
3. Jones, *History of the Christian Church*, 1:306–307
4. Milman, *History of Latin Christianity*, 1:227
5. Barker, *Apostasy From the Divine Church*, 251–252
6. Shotwell and Loomis, *The See of Peter*, 470
7. Prestige, *God in Patristic Thought*, xiv
8. Hardy, *Christology of the Latin Fathers*, 332–334
9. Gibbon, *The Decline and Fall of the Roman Empire*, 692
10. Cooper, *The Free Church of Ancient Christianity*, 372
11. Barker, *Apostasy From the Divine Church*, 249–251
12. Ibid., 257
13. Mourret, *Histoire Generale de L'Eglise*, 2:44 as cited in Ibid., 258
14. Murray, *The Problem of God Today and Yesterday*, 46
15. Kelly, *Early Christian Doctrines*, 46
16. Murray, *The Problem of God Today and Yesterday*, 47
17. Nibley, *The World and the Prophets*, 50
18. Hefele, *Histoire des Conciles d'Apres les Documents Origaux*, 1:449–450 as cited in Barker, *Apostasy From the Divine Church*, 269
19. Werner, *The Formation of Christian Dogma*, 159
20. Gibbon, *The Decline and Fall of the Roman Empire*, 693
21. Bartlett and Carlyle, *Christianity in History*, 265 as cited in Barker, *Apostasy From the Divine Church*, 263
22. Walker, Norris, Lotz and Handy, *A History of Christianity*, 135
23. *Catholic Encyclopedia*, 2:44–45
24. Cooper, *The Free Church of Ancient Christendom*, 373
25. Paine, *A Critical History of the Evolution of Trinitarianism*, 332

10
Defining *Homoousios*

A monk named Vincent of Lerins was sainted for writing a manuscript called the *Commonitorium* in 434 A.D. The premise which he invoked is now known as the Vincentian Rule. The Catholic Church now cites it as the authority for every doctrine which they affirm. Vincent argued that the true doctrines of Catholicism may be distinguished from the heresies by the fact that the church has always accepted them.

> Here, it may be, someone will ask, Since the canon of Scripture is complete, and is in itself abundantly sufficient, what need is there to join to it the interpretation of the Church? The answer is that because of the very depth of Scripture all men do not place one identical interpretation upon it. The statements of the same writer are explained by different men in different ways, so much that it seems almost possible to extract from it as many opinions as there are men. Novatian expounds it one way, Sabellius in another, Donatus in another, Arius, Eunomius and Macedonius in another, Photinus, Apollinaris and Priscillian in another, Jovinian, Pelagius and Caelestius in another, and latterly Nestorius in another. Therefore, because of the intricacies of error, which is so multiform, there is great need for the laying down of a rule for the exposition of Prophets and Apostles in accordance with the standard of the interpretation of the Church Catholic.
>
> Now in the Catholic Church we take the greatest care to hold **that which has been believed everywhere, always and by all.**
> That is truly and properly "Catholic," as is shown by the very force and meaning of the word, which comprehends everything almost universally. We shall hold to this rule if we follow universality (i.e. oecumenicity), antiquity, and consent. **We shall follow universality if we acknowledge that one faith to be true which the whole church throughout the world confesses;** antiquity, if we in no wise depart from those interpretations which it is clear that our ancestors and fathers proclaimed; consent, if in antiquity itself we keep the following the definitions and opin-

ions of all, or certainly nearly all, bishops and doctors alike.
 What then will the Catholic Christian do, if a small part of the Church has cut itself off from the communion of the universal faith? The answer is sure. He will prefer the healthiness of the whole body to the morbid and corrupt limb.
 But what if some novel contagion try to infect the whole Church, and not merely a tiny part of it? Then he will take care to cleave to antiquity, which cannot now be led astray by any deceit of novelty.
 What if in antiquity itself two or three man, or it may be a city, or even a whole province be detected in error? Then he will take the greatest care to prefer the decrees of the ancient General Councils, if there are such, to the irresponsible ignorance of a few men.
 But what if some error arises regarding which nothing of this sort is to be found? Then he must do his best to compare the opinions of the Fathers and inquire their meaning, provided always that, though they belonged to diverse times and places, they yet continued in the faith and communion of the one Catholic Church; and let them be teachers approved and outstanding. **And whatever he shall find; to have been held, approved and taught, not by one or two only but by all equally and with one consent, openly, frequently, and persistently, let him take this as to be held by him without the slightest hesitation.** (Vincent of Lerins, Commonitarium, [434] ed. Moxon, Cambridge Patristic Texts)[1]

Let us apply the Vincentian Rule to the doctrine of the Trinity as it is currently taught. Let us compare it to the Nicene Creed. Let us also determine what was taught by those before and after Nicea. For if the doctrine of the Trinity cannot stand this test, it must be acknowledged as a heresy, by definition. And all those who do not accept the orthodox doctrines of the Trinity have very good reasons for doing so.

The orthodox doctrines of today affirm that there is one God who is composed of three Persons. But the nature of these Persons is shadowy and undefined. The Father, the Son, and the Holy Ghost are all part of a divine substance. And yet they are not part of it, but each occupies the totality of the essence.

But the Council of Nicea did not define the three Persons in this way. It clearly separated the identity of each. Constantine had forced the bishops to insert the statement that the Son was *homoousios* with the Father. Athanasius envisioned the three Persons as being complete personages, who happened to be part of the same substance. Many of those who attended the council interpreted *homoousios* in a generic sense. Neither party thought that the three were numerically one. They were fighting over the nature of the substance.

> At first glance, Nicea appeared to have settled the question, but further arguments broke out almost at once. For one thing, though the Arians had lost a battle, they continued to fight the war. Later in Constantine's reign and even more under his son Constantius they secured considerable imperial support. **Even worse, it soon emerged that those who had signed the Nicene Creed could not agree on what it meant.** The crucial debate centered an the statement that the Son was "of the same substance (homoousios) with the Father." Perhaps an analogy can clarify the issue. Suppose I told you that the paperweight an my desk is made from the marble from which the Parthenon is constructed—the same substance. You might think I meant "the same substance" in the sense of the same type of marble, or you might think I had crept up to the Parthenon late one night and chipped off a piece of **that very substance. Most of the bishops at Nicea interpreted homoouisios in the first sense.** In effect, they thought that human beings, trees and rocks are made of changing, destructible stuff, while the Father is made of eternal, unchanging stuff, and the Son is made of the same sort of stuff as the Father.[2]

Athanasius combated the Arians by insisting that the word *homoousios* meant "that very substance." This idea touched off a rebellion which was to last in the church for many years. It is quite easy to understand why many refused to accept the definition which Athanasius used. It came from Greek philosophy and had never been used in the sense in which he was using it.

> The original signification of homoousios, apart from all theological technicality, is simply "made of the same stuff." Stuff, here bears a generic sense necessarily, since no objects of physical experience are composed of identical portions of matter.[3]

Levi Leonard Paine agrees with this assessment, and points out that *homoousios* was traditionally used in a generic sense.

> But still further, such a use of the word would have been altogether new in its history. Everywhere in Greek literature *homoousios* means generic likeness or sameness. Aristotle calls the stars homoousion. Plotinus uses the same term for souls, when arguing that they are divine and immortal. There is no evidence that any Greek Father ever gave the word any different meaning. Gregory of Nyssa calls not only "human souls," but also "corruptible bodies," *homoousios*...Chrysostom describes Eve as *homoousios* with Adam.[4]

A number of historians have investigated the meaning which the word *homoousios* had before Nicea. Edward Gibbon cites several authors who agree with the idea that it was used in a generic sense.

> According to Aristotle the stars were homoousion to each other. "That *homoousios* means of one substance *in kind*, hath been shown by Petavius, Curcellaeus, Cudworth, LeClerc, etc., and to prove it would be actum agere." This is the just remark of Dr. Jortin (vol. ii. p. 212), who examines the Arian controversy with learning, candor and ingenuity.[5]

Therefore, a great number of theologians began to use another word to describe the nature of the Father and the Son. This word was *homoiousion* and meant "like in substance." The dissenters were arguing that the Father and the Son did not occupy the same substance, but had the same nature. In other words, they were both made of the stuff that gods are made out of.

On the other hand, Athanasius was arguing that the Father and the Son were made from exactly the same substance. William Sherlock defends the Nicene Creed by explaining (as Athanasius did) that the three Persons are three real beings who happen to be located in the same substance.

> We must allow the divine Persons to be real substantial Beings, if we allow each Person to be God, unless we will call anything a God, which has no real Being, as that has not, which has not a real Nature and Essence, whereas all Men grant there are no Accidents (non-essential components), or Qualities or Modes in God, but a pure and simple essence, or pure Act; and therefore the Three Divine Persons are substantially distinct, though in One undivided substance.[6]

The idea that there was a substance which housed more than one individual was not Christian but pagan. Levi Leonard Paine points out that this was precisely what the pantheists (nature worshippers) believed.

> The pantheist holds that there is but one substance in the universe, and that personality is an accident or quality or mode of existence of substances, so that there may be and in fact are many persons included in the one universal substance of things.[7]

Having established a frame of reference, let us now see what happened after Nicea adjourned. Constantine sent a copy of the Nicene Creed to those bishops who had not attended the council.

One of these copies was sent to the bishop of Rome. Sylvester accepted the Creed without complaint, probably because the organizational changes gave him more power than he had before. At any rate, it was already signed and there was little that he could do about it.

Constantine banished several Arian supporters and waited for the furor to die down. To his surprise, it did not. Three years later, Constantine began to change his position in the dispute. He pardoned Eusebius of Nicomedia and Theognis of Nicea, whom he had banished. Arius was also pardoned and allowed to return. Hosius of Cordoba was dismissed as Constantine's advisor and Eusebius, at the urging of Constantine's sister, replaced him.

Why was Constantine changing his mind? Had the Arian side of the dispute become more credible to him? I do not think so. He had merely decided that the Arians could deliver the peace he wanted.

> Constantine's desire for peace and reconciliation, embroiled in the legislation of the Council of Nicea, did not flag after the close of the council. His manner of pursuing it, however, only brought about an increase of conflict. In 328, the very year in which the former deacon Athanasius succeeded Alexander as bishop of Alexandria, the emperor recalled Eusebius of Nicomedia (Whom he had exiled shortly after Nicee for communicating with Arius) as bishop of the imperial capital. A brilliant and resolute politician as well as an Arian, Eusebius soon became Constantine's principal ecclesiastical advisor. With the emperor's ear and confidence, he forthwith mounted a campaign to rid the church of the enemies of the subordinationist theology of the eastern tradition.[8]

Eusebius was able to depose Eusthanius of Antioch who was openly opposed to the teachings of Origen. He then decided to remove Athanasius from office.

Athanasius had made many enemies since he had become bishop of Alexandria. He had employed corporal punishment against those who did not agree with his theology. This included imprisoning a man named Arsenius. In fact, the general populace believed that Athanasius had actually killed Arsenius.

> Eusebius next, and more difficult, victim was Athanasius, the new Pope of Alexandria (328–373). A determined and single-minded champion of the Nicene formula, which he saw as representing the views of his predecessor, Alexander, Athanasius opened himself to attack by the high-handed methods he employed in dealing with the Melitians (heretics) and consolidating his authority over the Egyptian church. In 335, Athanasius was hauled

before a synod at Tyre composed entirely of his most bitter theological enemies. He was accused, among other things, of contriving the murder of a Melitian bishop named Arsenius. The charge was false (Athanasius had done no more than sequester Arsenius), but there was no hope for justice for Alexander's successor at such a council. Athanasius therefore fled Tyre secretly to appeal to the emperor in person at Constantinople (taking Arsenius with him to prove that the murder charge was false). In the end, however, the appeal accomplished nothing. Eusebius of Nicomedia and his associates persuaded Constantine that Athanasius had threatened to cut off the capital city's grain supply from Egypt. This amounted to a charge of treason, and Constantine, accepting it as proved without investigation, exiled Athanasius to Trier in Germany.[9]

Did Athanasius really use corporal punishment against the Melitians? The Roman Catholic historian Auguste Boulenger investigated the evidence and concluded that Athanasius was guilty. However, Boulenger says that such force was necessary because the Melitians would not yield without it.

> (Athanasius was accused) of having made use of the secular arm to have them (the Melitians) condemned to prison and to corporal punishment. That which they omitted to say is that, if rigorous measures had been taken, in applying the decisions of the Council of Nicea, it was the heresiarchs, obstinate and ungovernable as they were, who had rendered them necessary.[10]

A new council was convened after Athanasius was exiled. It was held in Jerusalem for the express purpose of re-admitting Arius to the church.

> ...having therefore left Tyre, they set forth with all dispatch to Jerusalem, where, after completing the ceremony of the consecration of the palace, they re-admitted Arius and his adherents to communion, in obedience, as they said, **to the wishes of the emperor,** who had signified in his communication to them, that **he (Constantine) was fully satisfied respecting the faith of Arius**...(Socrates, *Ecclesiastical History*, Ch. XXXIII)[11]

This decision was communicated to the bishops of all the churches in the Roman empire. Note that the Roman pope was not asked for his opinion on the subject. Whether he agreed or not was not deemed to be important. Constantine directed Alexander to admit Arius back into the church at Alexandria. This was so offensive to Alexander that he prayed for death to come. This incident shows how much they hated each other.

(Alexander) shut himself up in his church...and prostrating himself on the ground beneath the holy communion table, he poured forth his fervent intercessions mingled with tears...for several days and nights...for his petition was, that if the opinion of Arius was correct, he might not be permitted to see the day appointed for its discussion; but if he himself held the true faith, **Arius, as author of these evils, might suffer the punishment of his impieties**...It was then Saturday, and Arius was expected to assemble with the church the following day; **but divine intervention overtook his daring criminalities** (heresies).[12]

Did God kill Arius? Gibbon suggests that it is more likely that Athanasians committed murder.

On the same day which had been fixed for the triumph of Arius, he expired; and the strange and horrid circumstances of his death might excite a suspicion that the orthodox saints had contributed more efficaciously than by their prayers to deliver the church from the most formidable of her enemies...
We derive the original story from Athanasius (tom. i. p. 670), who expresses some reluctance to stigmatize the memory of the dead. He might exaggerate; but the perpetual commerce of Alexandria and Constantinople would have rendered it dangerous to invent. Those who press the literal narrative of the death of Arius (his bowels suddenly burst out in a privy) must make their option between **poison** and **miracle**.[13]

Shortly after this event Constantine died. Before the emperor died, Eusebius of Nicomedia baptized him. At last the emperor was a Christian (for a few moments anyway).

After the death of Constantine, all of his immediate family, with the exception of three sons and his nephews Gallus and Julian, were massacred. Constantius became the emperor of the east, while Constans and Constantine II were emperors in the west. The west was Athanasian and the east was Arian.

The three sons met and decided that some sort of accommodation had to be made to preserve the peace. So Athanasius and the other exiled Athanasian bishops were recalled from exile. This created more problems. The exiled bishops had been replaced by Arian bishops. The two bishops were thus contending for the same office and usually excommunicated each other. Armed conflicts between the followers of the two ecclesiastical authorities often resulted in a terrible loss of life.

Constantine II sent imperial letters to Alexandria to announce that Athanasius was being returned to his see (diocese). However, this position was already occupied by the Arian Pistus. Both men had considerable support among the clergy of the city. A fierce dispute raged concerning which one of them would occupy the position.

A council of Athanasian bishops was held at Alexandria to support the return of Athanasius. This council attacked the Council of Tyre because they had deposed Athanasius. A letter was addressed to "all the bishops of the world." One of these bishops was Bishop Julius of Rome. It was also sent to the three emperors.

The Arians sent out letters to "all their brethren of the episcopacy" as well. They argued that Pistus was the legal bishop.

Eusebius doubted that Pistus was strong enough to defeat Athanasius. He appealed to Constantius for some soldiers so that he could install Gregory of Cappodocia as the new bishop. Athanasius would not leave without a struggle and, in the mob scene that followed, many people were killed or wounded

The casual observer might wonder if this is the way that Christianity works. It is not. An apostasy had caused the true Church of Jesus Christ to leave the earth centuries before. This was a political struggle, with both sides failing to observe the principles which Christ established.

William Jones gives the following criticism:

> The Scriptures were no longer the standard of the Christian faith. What was orthodox, and what the decisions of fathers and councils; and religion propagated not by the apostolic methods of persuasion, accompanied with the meekness and gentleness of Christ, but by imperial edicts and decrees; nor were gainsayers to be brought to conviction by the simple weapons of reason and scripture, but persecuted and destroyed. It cannot surprise us, if after this we find a continual fluctuation of the public faith, just as the prevailing party obtained the imperial authority to support them; or that we should meet with little else in ecclesiastical history then violence and cruelties, committed by men who had wholly departed from the simplicity of the Christian doctrine and profession; men enslaved to avarice and ambition; and carried away with views of temporal grandeur, high preferments, and large revenues...
>
> The truth is, that **the clergy of the Catholic Church were now the principal disturbers of the empire**; and the pride of the bishops, and the fury of the people on each side had grown to such a height, that the election or restoration of a bishop seldom took place in the larger cities, without being attended with scenes of slaughter. **Athanasius was several times banished and restored at the expense of blood.**[14]

Defining *Homoousios*

Athanasius fled to Rome. He was joined there by Paul of Constantinople and Marcellus of Ancyra. Rome was becoming a haven for the followers of Athanasius. Therefore, Eusebius decided to ask Julius to condemn Athanasius. This would make the entire empire Arian. Julius welcomed the opportunity to make a ruling on the issue. This was the first time that a single bishop had ever called a council. Prior to this council, the eastern bishops refused to recognize the authority of the bishop of Rome over them.

> ...The Roman bishop investigated the case of each man and when he discovered that they all agreed upon the creed of the Council of Nicea [which had increased the power of the Roman pope], he received them as of one mind into communion...And he wrote to the bishops of the East, reproving them for their wrong judgment of these men and for the disturbance they had created in the Church by not upholding the decrees of Nicea. And he bade a few of them all to come to him on a certain day to show that they had arrived at a right decision. Otherwise, he said threateningly, he would not endure it in the future if they did not cease from innovations. Such was his letter. And Athanasius and Paul...**sent the letters of Julius** around among the eastern bishops. **But the latter were angered at them and met at Antioch and composed a reply to Julius...and they brought charges against Julius** for communing with the party of Athanasius and were indignant with him for disdaining their synod and annulling their verdict. **And they denounced his action as unjust and contrary to ecclesiastical law** [Julius was interfering in the affairs of other Metropolitans who held equal authority with him]. Then after upbraiding him in such style and declaring that he had done them grave injury, they offered Julius peace and communion if he would recognize the deposition of those whom they had expelled and the ordination of those whom they had elected instead, and **they threatened him with the contrary** [excommunication and deposition], if he overrode their decisions...[15]

Julius conducted the council even though the eastern bishops refused to attend. Since the Athanasian bishops were the only ones in attendance, it is not surprising that Athanasius was found innocent of all charges and declared to be the legal bishop. Julius then wrote a letter to the eastern bishops, thus informing them of his decision. Yet the Roman pope did not command them in his own name, but said that the bishops of Rome agreed with him.

> [Julius] points out how uncanonical all their proceedings had been. The deposition of Athanasius...was contrary to the established custom that no sentence could be pronounced against the

bishop of Alexandria (since he was a pope) without the consent of the bishop of Rome [Author's Note: Precedents existed for such depositions. For example, the bishop of Rome had been deposed without the consent of the other Metropolitans]; and the appointment of Gregory (by the pope of Constantinople) was utterly illegal, as an entire stranger ought never to be put over any church...Julius shows that nothing was done till after the most careful investigation, and that **he was expressing not his own personal convictions, but those of all the bishops of Italy.**[16]

The eastern bishops did not reply to Julius's letter. As a result, Gregory continued as the bishop of Alexandria and Athanasius remained in exile at Rome.

Constans defeated Constantine II in battle. This made the victor the most powerful emperor. As a result, Constantius urged the Arian bishops to make concessions to Constans with regard to a new creed which was being drafted (at the Synod of Antioch) to replace the creed of Nicea. They followed Constantius' wishes:

> ...Julius was proving unexpectedly formidable, now that the domain of his "Athanasian" ally, Emperor Constans, so far exceeded that of the Eastern emperor Constantius. Under these circumstances, the Synod of Antioch assumed a mild and defensive tone, issued letters protesting that **its members were not really Arian at heart and drafted four different, conciliatory forms of creed**, in which the most disputatious points were dexterously avoided and the most controversial terms quietly omitted...Before dispersing, the synod, at Constantius' request, appointed a deputation of eastern bishops...to wait upon Constans in the West, explain their attitude toward Athanasius, assure him of their pacific intentions and fidelity to the true faith and present to him a creed which explicitly repudiated several of the old Arian phrases, though still leaving somewhat indefinite the origin and character of the divine Son.[17]

Many different creeds were formulated in an attempt to find an acceptable substitute for the Nicene Creed. Each contained different phrases from the ones which came, before it.

> For fifty years after Nicea, the Church debated the affirmation, "Of one essence with the Father." Various alternatives were tried: "Exact image of the Godhead" (Second Creed of Antioch, 341); "Like the Father who begot Him according to the Scriptures" (Dated Creed, Fourth of Sirmium); "Of like essence with the Father" (Ancyra, 358); "Unlike the Father" (the teaching of Aetius and Eunomius and, by implication, of the Second Creed of Sirmium, 357).[18]

Defining *Homoousios*

Let us pause in our narrative to return for a moment to the central premises of the Vincentian Rule. Vincent said that Catholic truths have been believed "everywhere, always, and by all." In what sense has the premise of the *homoousion* been accepted everywhere, always and by all? It most certainly was not received by the Arians during the era of which we are speaking. But were the Arians really Catholics? Of course they were! They held positions of considerable importance in the church. Moreover, they called themselves Catholics. Both groups were present at the Council of Nicea as official delegates. Therefore, it does not make any sense to not call them Catholics. But this means that the doctrine of the *homoousios* was not universally received in that day. In fact, a large segment of the church refused to receive it at all.

Many of the Arians and Semi-Arians were the same bishops who had signed the Nicene Creed. Now they were trying to draft another creed. Why? Because they had not really believed it in the manner that Athanasius interpreted it. They had been forced to sign a document that they did not agree with, and they repudiated the *homoousios* concept as soon after that time as they could. Nathaniel Lardner writes:

> Tillemont has these words: "It was then, **fear of banishment**, and of having so illustrious an assembly the witness of their ignominy, that induced the Arians to make haste to renounce the doctrines that had been condemned, to anathematize them, and subscribe the consubstantial faith, after all the other bishops; being led by Eusebius of Nicomedia, to **confess with the mouth the faith of the church, without having it in the heart**, as the event showed."
> ...Those Arians confessed with the mouth, and signed with the hand, **what did they not believe**. For that they are to be blamed. But how came they to do so? It was owing to a fear of ignominy and banishment. But why were they put in fear?...Was there a necessity, that they should be required to sign, whether they believe them or not? Nay, is not this quite contrary to the design and example of the Lord Jesus...[19]

The fact that it was necessary to summon so many synods and councils after Nicea also casts doubts upon whether that creed was correct. Nibley writes of the feelings of Athanasius:

> ...why do the so-called clergy dash back and forth trying to find out how they should believe about our Lord Jesus Christ? If they had been believers all along they couldn't possibly be searching now for something they don't have! Everyone is laughing at the Christian leaders, Athanasius says, and is saying, "**These Chris-**

tians don't know what to think of Christ! Which of course weakens their authority." "What is the use of all these synods?" he asks. "In vain do they dash hither and yon under the pretext that synods are necessary to settle important matters of doctrine, for the Holy Scriptures are sufficient for all that." (Note where Athanasius finds the court of last appeal—not in any episcopal see, but simply in the scripture.) "We contradict those who were before us, depart from the traditions of our fathers, and think we must hold a synod. Then we are seized by misgivings, lest we simply come together and agree our diligence will be wasted; so we decide that the synod ought to be divided into two groups, so we can vote;...and so **we render ineffective what was done at Nicea under pretext of working for greater simplicity."**[20]

Therefore, the term *homoousios* was not received "everywhere, always and by all." This is important, for it is the concept of the *homoousion* which is at the heart of the doctrine of the Trinity. If the *homoousion* be false, then the Father, Son, and Holy Ghost must be three separate persons.

The Vincentian Rule suggests the criteria of universality, antiquity, and consent as ways to judge whether a doctrine is a Catholic truth. Let us now review the language of this famous rule in order to prove our premise further.

> **What then will the Catholic Christians do, if a small part of the Church has cut itself off from the communion of the universal faith? The answer is sure. He will prefer the healthiness of the whole body to the morbid and corrupt limb.**[21]

Traditional religious historians have chosen to regard the Arians as a "morbid and corrupt limb." But the unthinkable was about to happen. The doctrine of the Arians was about to be ratified by the entire church. This made the so-called heresy the entire body.

Constans had promoted the Athanasian cause and had succeeded in returning Athanasius to Alexandria. But a revolt occurred and Magentius was crowned emperor, so Constans committed suicide. A war was now inevitable between Magentius and Constantius. The Arian bishops did everything that they could to ensure the success of their champion. When Constantius did win, the event was used to prove that the Arian cause had been aided by the powers of heaven.

> The partiality which Constantius always expressed towards the Eusebian faction was insensibly fortified by the dexterous management of their leaders; and his victory over the tyrant Magentius increased his inclination, as well as ability, to employ the arms of

power in the cause of Arianism. While the two armies were engaged in the plains of Mursa, and the fate of the two rivals depended on the chance of war, the son of Constantine passed the anxious moments in a church of the martyrs, under the walls of the city. His spiritual comforter, Valens, the Arian bishop of the diocese, employed the most artful precautions to obtain such early intelligence as might secure either his favor or his escape. A secret chain of swift and trusty messengers informed him of the vicissitudes of the battle; and while the courtiers stood trembling round their affrighted master, Valens assured them that the Gallic legions gave way; and **insinuated**, with some presence of mind, **that the glorious event had been revealed to him by an angel**. The grateful emperor ascribed his success to the merits and intercession of the bishop of Mursa, whose faith had deserved the public and miraculous approbation of heaven. The Arians, who considered as their own the victory of Constantius, preferred his glory to that of his father. Cyril, bishop of Jerusalem, **immediately composed the description of a celestial cross** [much like the one which the other party claimed led to the conversion of Constantine], encircled with a splendid rainbow, which, during the festival of Pentecost, about the third hour of the day, had appeared over the Mount of Olives, to the edification of the devout pilgrims and the people of the holy city. The size of the meteor was gradually magnified; and the Arian historian has ventured to affirm that **it was conspicuous to the armies in the plains of Pannonia** and that **the tyrant**, who is purposely represented as an idolater, **fled before the auspicious sign of orthodox Christianity**.[22]

Constantius was thus convinced that the Arians taught the true doctrines of Christianity. He therefore acted to ensure that the language of *homoousios* was overthrown.

His first step in this direction was to rid himself of Athanasius. At synods held in Arles (353) and Milan (355), he forced the western bishops to abandon Athanasius and to resume full communion with the eastern churches. Those who resisted—Liberius of Rome (352–366), the aging Hosius of Cordova, and Hilary of Poitiers (ed. 367)—were promptly exiled. Athanasius was driven from Alexandria in 356 and took refuge for the next six years among the monks of the Egyptian hinterland. This much accomplished, the emperor proceeded, under the guidance of Arian advisers, to deal with the doctrinal problem. A synod held at the imperial residence, Sirmium, in 357 published a declaration which insisted that "there ought to be no mention" of terms like *substantia*, or *ousia*, or *homoousios*, which were unscriptural, or of phrases suggesting that the Son is "subordinated to the Father." This formula, which repudiated Nicea and in affect made room for Arianism, has gone down in history as "the blasphemy of

Sirmium," a label given it by Bishop Phoebadius of Agennum in Gaul. Despite opposition, however, Constantius did not relent. Through a series of councils and synods in 359, he compelled the unhappy assent of eastern and western bishops alike to a formula which was finally representing imperial orthodoxy by a synod held in Constantinople in 360.[23]

One of the councils which Constantius convened was the Second Council of Sirmium. This formula departed from the Nicene Creed even further. Athanasius had maintained that the *homoousios* meant that the Son was equal (of the exact same substance) to the Father. The new formula stated that the Father was greater. Some of the language which Hosius of Cordoba and other western bishops who had previously signed the Nicene Creed were forced to sign includes: "(the Father)...is greater; he surpasses the Son in honor, dignity, and glory, whence his name is Father."[24]

In 358, Constantius brought Liberius to the council of Sirmium. Fernand Mourret gives the following account of the proceedings:

> ...one saw arrive in this third assembly of Sirmium, almost exclusively composed of prelates who surrounded the emperor, a stranger, whose presence suddenly gave to the council a special importance. It was Pope (Bishop) Liberius...Constantius had just terminated his exile, and had asked him to take part in the council of Sirmium...One began by asking him—it is still Sozomen who is speaking—*to* **condemn the doctrine of** *homoousios* (one substance) that is to say the consubstantiality of the Verb. The old pontiff refused...(They) explained to him that the word *homoousios* was very dangerous, that it had served Paul of Samotsata and Photinus to propagate errors, that two councils had rejected it. **The** pope (Bishop Liberius) **yielded to these reasons and signed the formula.** Nevertheless, he judged it necessary to declare that...whosoever does not grant that **the Son is, as to substance and in all things, similar to the Father**, must be excluded from the Church. Even in his reservation he abandoned the strict Athanasian creed for the moderate Arian formula.[25]

Why did Liberius sign the formula? When he was exiled Constanius replaced Liberius with the Arian Felix. Liberius finally relented and struck a deal in order to escape banishment and regain his office. As part of this deal, he was to condemn Athanasius and the *homoousios*. Whether Liberius actually did keep this deal has been questioned.

Many Catholics have refused to believe that he did and state that he instead signed some other papers which did not condemn the *homoousios*. There are two reasons why I do not believe this explanation. First, signing other papers would not have released Liberius from exile or gotten his office back. Second, Athanasius states that Liberius did side with the Arians.

But Liberius gave way, after he had been two years in exile, and subscribed for fear of threatened death. Yet this shows only their violence and hatred of heresy and support of Athanasius as long as he had free choice. **For that which men do under torture, against their original intention, ought not be considered the will of these terrified persons but rather that of their tormentors.**[26]

It is interesting that Athanasius objects to the use of civil power against his cause but saw nothing wrong with the persecution of the Arians. But did Liberius really change sides because he was being tortured, as Athanasius says? A letter to several of the Arian bishops in Milan and Civita Vecchia indicates that he is glad to do so if it will allow him to be bishop again.

> Liberius in exile to Ursacius, Valens, and Germinius. I know you **are sons of peace and love the harmony of the Catholic Church, therefore, under no compulsion whatever**—as I call God to witness—but for the sake of the blessing of peace and concord, which is preferable to martyrdom, I approach you with this letter, my lords and dearest brethren, I hereby inform you that **I had condemned Athanasius**, who was bishop of the Alexandrine church, **before I wrote to the court of the Holy Emperor** that I was sending a letter to the eastern bishops. And **he (Athanasius) has been cut off from the communion of the Roman church** as all the Priesthood of the Roman church is witness...Wherefore, I approach you with this letter and adjure you by Almighty God and Christ Jesus His Son, our God and Lord, **to go graciously to our most clement emperor, Constantius** and ask him for the blessing of peace and concord, in which his reverence always finds delight, **he may order me to return to the church divinely committed to me**, so that in his time the Roman church may not endure tribulation. By this letter **you are to understand** fairly and honestly, dearest brothers, **that I am at peace with all you bishops of the Catholic Church.**[27]

Constantius returned Liberius and attempted to split the Roman church in two so that both Liberius and Felix could have a church to rule over. However, the people refused to allow this to happen.

> ...(Constantius) consented that the two bishops, Liberius and Felix, should govern in peace their respective congregations. But the ideas of toleration were so repugnant to the practice, and even

to the sentiments of those times, that, when the answer of Constantius was publicly read in the Circus of Rome, so reasonable a project of accommodation was rejected with contempt and ridicule...the Circus resounded with the shout of thousands, who repeatedly exclaimed "One God, One Christ, One Bishop." The zeal of the Roman people in the cause of Liberius was not confined to words alone, and the dangerous and bloody sedition which they excited soon after the departure of Constantius determined that prince to accept the submission of the exiled prelate, and to restore to him the undivided dominion of the capital. After some ineffectual resistance, his rival was expelled from the city by the permission of the emperor and the power of the opposite faction; the adherents of Felix were inhumanely murdered in the streets, in the public places, in the baths, and even in the churches; and the face of Rome, upon the return of a Christian bishop, renewed the horrid image of the massacres of Marinus and the proscriptions of Sylla.[28]

A new council was convened at Rimini. The formula which was debated at this time was that the Son was *homoiousios* (like in substance) to that of the Father. This meeting was a true general council of the church, since there were more clerics present than there were at Nicea.

...the memorable synod of Rimini, which surpassed in numbers the council of Nice, since it was composed of above four hundred bishops (Nicea had 318) of Italy, Africa, Spain, Gaul, Britain and Illyricum.[29]

Constantius required that all those who were in attendance sign the formula. The creed was then dispatched to all the churches throughout the empire and the bishops who were in exile were even required to sign. Roman Catholic historian Louis Duchesne writes:

Unity had now been brought about. Neither in the West nor in the East was there a single bishop in office who had not declared himself against Athanasius and the Nicene Creed.[30]

Jerome, in speaking of these events, remarks that, "the world groaned and wondered to find itself Arian!"[31]

Many find it difficult to believe that the decisions which were reached at Nicea are incorrect. They state that God would never allow the entire church to be led astray. Therefore, they agree with Socrates that the framers of the Nicene Creed were inspired by the Holy Ghost to reach the right conclusion. This same logic is applied to all of the other Catholic doctrines which were codified by a general council decision.

Such reasoning has serious flaws. First of all, why would such guidance be limited to a general council? Why would local councils not receive the same guidance? But if the judgments of Nicea are correct, then the Rimini Creed is false. But how can that be, for all the bishops who signed the second document (including the bishop of Rome) were members of the church in good standing? Every bishop in the church signed this creed. Did not this mean that the entire church was in heresy? Or was the church in heresy at Nicea? In reality, the true Church of Jesus Christ had not been on the earth for many centuries, so all of the warring factions of Christianity were in apostasy.

Bishop George Bull is acclaimed as one of the foremost champions of the Trinity. He uses another line of reasoning to try to establish that the Nicene Creed is correct. He argued that it would have been impossible for all of those bishops not to have known what the relationship between the Father and the Son was.

> ...it is incredible that so many holy and approved men, assembled from all parts of the Christian world (who, how defective soever in any other sort of knowledge), **could by no means be ignorant of the first and fundamental doctrine of the holy trinity,** a doctrine wherein the very catechumens were not uninstructed...**It was morally imposible that the Nicene fathers should have erred,** in the determination of the article before them.[32]

But, if one were to accept this argument, why would not the framers of the Rimini Creed be equally protected from error? As we have seen, the signers of the Nicene Creed also signed the Creed of Rimini. Had they suddenly become uninformed? Or were they now saying what they really thought?

A review of the historical accounts of Nicea shows that the framers of the Nicene Creed did not act as if they had received the Holy Ghost. Moreover, they did not act as if they knew what "the first and fundamental doctrine" was. Hilary of Poitiers tells of the uncertainty and change which characterized this era:

> "It is a thing," says Hilary, "equally deplorable and dangerous, that there are as many creeds as opinions among men, as many doctrines as inclinations, and as many sources of blasphemy as there are faults among us; because **we make creeds arbitrarily,** and explain them away as arbitrarily. **The homoousion is rejected, and received, and explained away by successive synods.** The partial or total resemblance of the Father and the Son is a subject of dispute for these unhappy times. **Every year, nay, every moon, we make new creeds to describe invisible mysteries.** We

repent of what we have done, we defend those who repent, we anathematize those whom we have defended. We condemn either the doctrine of others in ourselves, or our own in that of others; and, reciprocally tearing one another to pieces, we have been the cause of each other's ruin."[33]

We recognize that the Nicene Creed is accepted as a true doctrine by most of the Christian churches. The evidence, however, does not support these doctrines. Many people therefore try to discredit the documentation in order to keep the creed. Edgar Sheffield Brightman writes:

> Samuel Clarke in his work, *A Demonstration of the Being and Attribution of God* (1705), held that theology cannot prove an infinite and perfect cause of the world; and he was followed by the illustrious Immanuel Kant. But both these men, instead of accepting the idea of a finite God which is proved by the evidence, **discredited the proof because it did not demonstrate God to be the kind of being that they had supposed he was.** On any other question, we should be willing to admit that if the evidence does not conform with our ideas, **we should modify our ideas to conform to the evidence.** Why should this same rule not hold to the idea of God?[34]

Brightman also writes:

> In spite of the many religious persons from Pascal down who base religion on reasons of the heart instead of those of the head, the aim of religion has not been to make God conform to my desires, but, rather, to make my desires conform to God; not to let my heart have its way, but to discipline my heart; not to believe what is pleasant because I like it, **but to believe what is true because it is the only honest thing to do.**[35]

The evidence seems to indicate that Athanasius changed the doctrines of the day because of his own personal feelings. He originally used the word *homoousios* because the Arians would not accept it. He thought that by doing this, he would destroy them. But he was a stubborn man. The more others chided him for the use of the word, the more he insisted that it was the only true belief. And, as he sought to explain his doctrines, his own theology changed and evolved.

> Loofs goes farther. He thinks that the more St. Athanasius advanced in age, the more firmly he became attached to the Nicaean meaning of the homoousios: what is difficult to discern distinctly in his last writings, is not the unity of God, but the trinity of the divine Persons.[36]

Defining *Homoousios*

We have established that the two conflicting doctrines disagreed over the *homoousion*. Vincent had stated that when this happened, it was necessary to determine what the church believed in antiquity. If we do this, we see that the rank-and-file Christians were anthropomorphists who thought that God was a man. This definitely does not harmonize with the Nicene formula.

> The simpler class and the multitude depended upon the ipse dixit and cling to the literal sense with their "bare and unreasoning faith." They speak of God as the Creator, but **think of him as a coarse and unjust man**.[37]

> ...some of them indeed were themselves not content with the generally received doctrine. **They desired a God with eyes, ears and limbs**, a resurrection of the identical body, and a visible glorious kingdom of Christ at the end of the world.[38]

It is also a fact that many of the early Christians believed that the Father, Son, and Holy Ghost were separate beings. Nathaniel Lardner writes that, "On account of the doctrine of the Trinity, he (Athanasius) says, the heathen people of his time thought that the Christians taught a plurality of Gods."[39]

The pagans had good reasons to think that Christians worshipped several Gods. The ancient rank and file members believed that the three persons are individual beings. Those who preached this doctrine were known as Tritheists. Dionysius of Rome preached sermons against those who were Tritheists.

> Dionysius, bishop of Rome, who flourished about the year 259...thus proceeds to discourse against the contrary heresy of those "who divide and cut asunder, and overthrow the most sacred doctrine of the church of God, parting the monarchy in decree—certain powers and hypostases, separated from each other, and consequently into three Deities. For I hear that there are some catechists and teachers of the word of God among you, who also maintain this opinion"...
> What is Tritheism he also shows us plainly, viz. That it is to hold, that the three persons in the Trinity are of a different nature, or separated and divided from each other; or that there is more than one fountain or principle of the divinity.[40]

In fact, the proponents of the Sabellian heresy were the ones who thought that the Father, Son, and Holy Ghost were all the same being. In response to this idea, the early Christian Fathers had argued that the Son was numerically different from the Father. Acting on this premise, the Fathers charged the Sabellians with teaching falsehoods.

Therefore, the Nicene interpretation of the *homoousion* cannot pass the standard of Vincent's Rule with regard to antiquity. Nor can it pass the test of consent, since it required armed force to induce the bishops to accept it.

The observer may wonder why, since the Arians had now won the battle of Rimini, the *homoousion* finally was accepted as an official doctrine. It was accepted because the Athanasians then sued for peace and declared that both the Arian and Athanasian interpretations were right.

> Through the efforts of Athanasius and Hilary of Poitiers (d. 1-67), the Eusebians (the so-called *homoiousion* party) were eventually reconciled with the orthodox *homoousions*. Hilary contended in his On The Councils **that both sides were right** and had an obligation to recognize the essentially orthodox concerns of the other side... With Athanasius in the conciliar chair, the assembly legitimated the "three hypostases (persons)" formula of the Eusebian formula provided it merely expresses the separate subsistence of the three Persons in the Trinity. From this emerged a new orthodox formula: "one *ousia* (being, substance), three *hypostases* (persons)."[41]

Why, then, is the Nicene Creed considered to be the ultimate formula of truth? It was because later councils enlarged upon the Nicene Creed and made belief in its Canons mandatory. The theologians of that day chose to treat the Creed as if it were scripture, so eventually people became convinced that it must be contained within the Scriptures, even though it is not.

> Gratian, C. 2, D. XV (Friedberg, col. 35) cites the text where St. Gregory **directs that the first four ecumenical councils are to be venerated like the four gospels.**[42]

Eutyches speaks of the determination of the church officials to revere the Nicene Creed. Doing so became so important that anyone who criticized this formula was declared to be a heretic.

> Dioscorus states the matter more strongly: "We have heard," he says, "what this Council" of Ephesus "decreed, **that if any any one affirm or opine anything, or raise any question beyond the creed aforesaid**" of Nicaea "**he is to be condemned.**"[43]

Cardinal John Henry Newman has investigated the Creed of Nicea very carefully and attempted to apply the Vincentian Rule to the evidence. He found that history would not support the case.

Now let us look at the leading facts of the case, in appealing to which I must not be supposed to be ascribing any heresy to the holy men whose words have not always been sufficiently full or exact to preclude the imputation. First, the Creeds of that early day make no mention in their letter of the Catholic doctrine at all. They make mention indeed of a Three; but **that there is a mystery in the doctrine, that the three are one, that they are coequal, that the three are one, that they are all incomprehensible, is not stated, and never could be gathered from them.** Of course we believe that they imply it, or rather intend it. God forbid we should do otherwise. But **nothing in the mere letter of those documents leads to that belief.** To give a deeper meaning to their letter, we must interpret them by the times which came after.[44]

The doctrines which came after the era which we have just studied changed the doctrine of the Trinity even more. We shall discover in the next chapter how a new kind of trinity evolved.

CHAPTER 10 REFERENCES

1. Bettenson, *Documents of the Christian Church*, 117–119
2. Placher, *A History in Christian Theology*, 75
3. Prestige, *God in Patristic Thought*, 89
4. Paine, *A Critical History of the Evolution of Trinitarianism*, 50
5. Gibbon, *The Decline and Fall of the Roman Empire*, 87
6. Sherlock, *The Vindication of the Most Blessed and Holy Trinity*, 47
7. Paine, *A Critical History of the Evolution of Trinitarianism*, 117
8. Walker, Norris, Lotz and Handy, *A History of Christianity*, 136–137
9. Ibid., 136–137
10. Barker, *Apostasy From the Divine Church*, 279
11. Ibid., 280
12. Ibid., 280–281
13. Gibbon, *The Decline and Fall of the Roman Empire*, 694
14. Jones, *History of the Christian Church*, 1:306–307
15. Sozomen, *Histoiria Ecclesiastica*, III, 7–8 as cited in Shotwell and Loomis, *The See of Peter*, 505–506
16. Foakes-Jackson, *Hisotry of the Christian Church From the Earliest Times to A.D. 461*, 335
17. Shotwell and Loomis, *The See of Peter*, 494–495
18. Leith, *Creeds of the Churches*, 29
19. Lardner, *The Works of Nathaniel Lardner*, 4:66–67
20. Nibley, *The Worlds and the Prophets*, 48
21. Bettenson, *The Documents of the Christian Church*, 118
22. Gibbon, *The Decline and Fall of the Roman Empire*, 635
23. Walker, Norris, Lotz and Handy, *A History of Christianity*, 139
24. Poulet *A History of the Catholic Church*, 1:155
25. Mourret, *Histoire Generale de l'Eglise*, 1:146–147 as cited in Barker, *Apostasy From the Divine Church*,. 301
26. Shotwell and Loomis, *The See of Peter*, 586
27. Ibid., 584–585
28. Gibbon, *The Decline and Fall of the Roman Empire*, 716
29. Ibid., 691
30. Duchesne, *Histoire Ancienne de l'Eglise*, 2:262 as cited in Barker, *Apostasy From the Divine Church*, 306
31. Foakes-Jackson, *History of the Christian Church to A.D. 461*, 340

32. Bull, *The Works of George Bull*, 2:240–241
33. Gibbon, *The Decline and Fall of the Roman Empire*, 688
34. Brightman, *The Problem of God*, 128
35. Ibid., 91
36. Tixeront, *History of Dogmas*, 2:72
37. Seeberg, *Textbook of the History of Doctrines*, 1:148
38. Harnack, *History of Dogma*, 4:340
39. Lardner, *The Works of Nathaniel Lardner*, 4:152
40. Bull, *The Works of George Bull*, 2:2–3
41. McBrien, *Catholicism*, 2:294
42. Congar, *Tradition and Traditions*, 1:221
43. Newman, *An Essay on the Christian Doctrine*, 303
44. Ibid., 15–16

11

The Athanasian Creed Develops

The history of Trinitarian development only makes sense if we remember that an apostasy had occurred centuries before. The true organization of the Church of Jesus Christ had been taken from the earth. There were no more apostles and prophets to receive revelations from God. Therefore, men were adding new doctrines as they saw fit. Richard Hooker writes:

> Ye plainly hold that from the very apostle's times till this present age (1593) wherein yourselves imagine ye have found out a right pattern of sound discipline, **there never was any time safe to be followed.** Which thing ye thus endeavor to prove. Out of Egesippus ye say that Eusebius writeth, how although as long as the apostles lived the church did remain a pure virgin, yet after the death of the apostles, and after they were once gone whom God vouchsafed to make hearers of the divine wisdom with their own ears, the placing of wicked error began to come into the Church. Clement also, in a certain place, to confirm that **there was corruption of doctrine immediately after the apostles' times,** allegeth the proverb that "there are few sons like their fathers." Socrates saith of the Church of Rome and Alexandria, the most famous churches in the apostle's times, that about the year 430, **the Roman and Alexandrine bishops, leaving the sacred function, were degenerate to a secular rule or dominion.** Herein ye conclude that it is not safe to fetch our government form from any other than the apostles' times.[1]

Hooker especially notes with disapproval the degeneracy of the Alexandrine theologians. Yet it was because of the Alexandrians that the Nicene Council was convened, and they provided many of the ideas for that creed.

Hugo Grotius noted that those who wrote the Scriptures knew whereof they spoke. They had either heard the teachings of Jesus directly from him, or received revelations from him which conveyed such truths to them.

> Thus it being plaine that the bookes of the new covenant were written by those authors, whose names they beare, or by such as beare witness of themselves; if wee adde further that they **knew** well the **matters** whereof they wrote to be **true**, and had no purpose to lye or dissemble, it will follow that the **things** which they committed to writing were both **certaine** and **true**, because every untruth proceeds either from ignorance, or from a wicked desire to deceive.[2]

On the other hand, the theologians of the era we will now cover did not have this same assurance. Their doctrines are proclaimed as new and innovative. Moreover, those who formulate these ideas often have questionable credentials as far as having the authority to insert new doctrines into the church.

After the death of Constantius in 361, the political wars between the Athanasians and the Arians varied depending upon who the emperor was. Finally Gratian became the emperor of the west, and Theodosius (formerly a soldier of Gratian) was proclaimed the ruler in the East. This was extremely important because both of them favored the Athanasian party.

Athanasius died in 373 and leadership of the Athanasian party passed to Basil the Great. The new leader had a Semi-Arian background, but wanted to arrange an alliance between the Athanasian and Semi-Arians. In fact, many of the Athanasians of that day would have been accused of being Arians during an earlier era. Other outstanding theologians of this movement were Gregory of Nazianzus and Gregory of Nyssa (Basil's brother). They believed that the Son possessed a substance which was like the substance of the Father (*homoiousian*).

> The Athanasian Trinitarianism is seen in its completest form in the Cappadocian theologians, Basil and the two Gregories. The idea has recently been broached that these men formed a Neo-Nicene school, falling away from the homoousianism of Athanasius to the older homoiousianism of Origen.[3]

> St. Jerome discards the Cappodocian formula, three hypostases, which he thinks, smacks of Arianism. In his mind, the word hypostasis is the same as essence.[4]

The Cappodocian system was built around the idea that there was a Father, a Son, and a Holy Ghost. The Father was superior to the other two.

> The Cappodocians, while defending identity of substance, yet put their main emphasis on the three distinct hyposteses. This ele-

The Athanasian Creed Develops

ment of the composite dogma, moreover, they not merely affirmed, but endeavored to explore in theological understanding. What was distinctive, other, plural, hypastasis or Person in the Deity, the Cappodocians beginning with Basil (e.g., Adv. Eunom. 1.19) explained, was not what made Father and Son God, but what made Father precisely Father and Son precisely Son—the properties or marks of identification peculiar to each, "ungenerateness" and "generateness." These properties, as Gregory of Nyssa brought out more clearly, were entirely a matter of origin or procession, of the unique way in which the undiminished Godhead was communicated from the Father to both Son and Spirit.[5]

The Christian church was changing. Constantine had outlawed the pagan churches of that day. Even though they continued to exist for some time thereafter, many people could see the hand writing an the wall. It would be very advantageous politically for them to become Christians or, at the very least, to become catechumens. This would ensure that they remained in favor with the emperor.

An excellent example of this type of person is Ambrose. His mother was Catholic, and he was brought up in the presence of nuns. He was not, however, converted to the ideas of Christianity.

In 378, Auxentius, the Arian bishop of Milan, died. The congregation was a mixture of Athenasians and Arians. A prospect of strife or even bloodshed was present. As the civil ruler of the province, Ambrose attended in order to make sure that no violence occurred. As the debate was taking place, a child cried out "Ambrose bishop." Those present understood this to be a manifestation of the divine will, so they consecrated Ambrose bishop. However, he had not been baptized, so they performed the baptism thereafter. All this time the new bishop was protesting. He was now thirty-four. Would not you think that if he really wanted to be baptized that he would have done so on his own?

But although Ambrose was baptized, he was not a converted Christian. He did not believe that the Scriptures meant exactly what they said. Instead, he chose to interpret the Bible allegorically. Worse, he began to teach others to do the very same thing. It was he who communicated this method of interpreting the Scriptures to Augustine.

Ambrose became the favorite theologian of the emperor Gratian. Because of this connection, and because he had been a civil official himself, Ambrose became one of the most powerful bishops in the church. Acting under the influence of Ambrose, Gratian began to depose Arian bishops and replace them with Athanasian clerics.

Then, when the balance of power had shifted, Gratian convened the Council of Constantinople in 381.

One of the primary topics of discussion during this council was the question of whether the Holy Ghost was God. As William Shedd explains, the Nicene Creed had not fully defined who the paraclete was. Now a heretical group known as the Socinians was claiming that the Holy Ghost was not God at all.

> The Nicene Creed is remarkably reticent respecting the third Person in the Trinity. It contains but a single clause concerning Him, in these words: "And we believe in the Holy Spirit." But so little was the theological mind occupied with the discrimination and definition of this hypothesis, that after this brief statement respecting this Holy Spirit, it immediately recurs again to the second Person, and affirms, that 'those who say that there was once a time when the Son of God was not, or that before he was begotten, he was not in being, or that he became existent out of nonentity, or that he is of another substance or essence (than that of deity), or that he is created, or mutable, or changeable: all such, the catholic and apostolic Church anathematizes.[6]

The Council of Constantinople left no doubt concerning the fact that the Holy Ghost held the rank of deity. But it affirmed it in Biblical language, not philosophical jargon.

> It [the Creed of Constantinople] goes beyond Nicea in that it affirms the full deity of the holy Spirit, but in Biblical language rather than with the Nicene "homoousios." The clause "who with the Father and the Son is together worshipped and together glorified," leaves no doubt as to the authentic deity of the Holy Spirit.[7]

Not only was the Holy Ghost codified during this time, but the Nicene Council was glorified and its canons were declared to be binding as a rule of faith. The new creed which was generated became known as the Nicaeo-Constantinopolitan Creed, which is recited in the Sunday Mass. Pope Damasus of Rome did not participate in this council and there is no evidence that he actually approved its canons. The signature of Gratian was considered sufficient to give it the authority of law.

But these measures did not please everyone. Augustine knew that they fell short of what he hoped to accomplish. Athanasius had envisioned a Trinity which had three separate Persons in one divine substance. Augustine thought that this meant that there were three gods present. He therefore began constructing a new doctrinal system which would eliminate these difficulties. The fact that it took fifteen years to accomplish his task shows that the new system was an innovation and not merely a restructuring of existing beliefs.

> He knew that the Trinity was a stumbling block to the intellect, **for fifteen years he worked on his most systematic production—** De Trinitae—struggling to find analogies in human experience for three persons in one God.[8]

The approach of Augustine was completely unlike anything which had been formulated before in the Trinity. Richard McBrien explains what made his approach so unique.

> Unlike the Greek Fathers, Augustine does not begin with the three Persons as they function in history for our salvation and then work backwards, so to speak, to the unity of the Godhead. He begins rather **with the one divine nature itself and tries to understand how the three persons share in that nature without dividing it.**[9]

How was the theology of Augustine different from the doctrines expressed in the Nicene Creed? Levi Leonard Paine explains the difference between the two systems:

> Athanasius placed the Gordian knot of the problem not in the fact of the three persons, but in their metaphysical or ideal union. He held that the Father is the alone eternal, self-existent God, and that He eternally generated the Son and sent forth the Holy Spirit, so that while there are three divine beings in the Godhead, there are not three eternal self-existent Gods, since the Father is the source of being to the others who are thus dependent and subordinate, though receiving from the Father all divine attributes. Augustine seems to start from the same point of view, but as he proceeds we find that the problem discussed is just the reverse. It is not how the three are one, but **how the one is three.** The explanation of this change of front, of which Augustine himself seems not to be aware, is to be found in the fact that he began by treating the Trinity as a problem of faith; **but it soon developed into a problem of reason.** His whole argument starts an the basis of Scripture and revelation, but gradually passes into the remotest regions of philosophy.[10]

Augustine theorized that allowing each member of the Trinity to be a being produced three gods. So he tried to redefine the Father, Son, and Holy Ghost as a trinity in which the meaning of the word "person" has become so shadowy that it loses its meaning. In fact, Augustine himself cannot define what the Father, Son, and Holy Ghost are.

He enters into a curious discussion of the question whether, since God is one essence, he is not also properly called one person, and an the other hand whether, if there are three persons, it is not proper to call them three essences or three Gods. He allows the logical truth of these conclusions, but refuses to accept them in the explanation of the Trinity, and frankly acknowledges that the problem is insoluble. "It is feared" to "say three essences," nor "can it be said that there are not three somewhats." It is plain that all through this discussion Augustine is playing with words. In fact he confesses it. "Such words are employed," he says, "that there may be something to say;" and again, "from the necessity of speaking, when copious reasoning is required against the devices or errors of the heretics."

What then did Augustine mean by "three persons" or "somewhats" if not three personal beings? Was he a Sabellian without knowing it, and even while striving to distinguish his doctrine from that of Sabellius? This cannot be affirmed without some explanation. Augustine did not start from the Sabellian premise of an evolution in God from unity to trinity; nor did he develop a Sabellian doctrine of Christ. But while he did not adopt the Sabellian premise, his own monistic New Platonic premise led him to the Sabellian conclusion, viz., that the "three somewhats" or "persons" so-called of the Trinity are only triple modes or relations of the one essence or being of God. The critical test of Sabellianism versus the Nicene doctrine is **whether the Trinity is essentially one being or three beings**. Sabellianism says one Being; Athanasianism says three Beings. Hence Sabellianism is monistic, while Athanasianism is trinitarian. Here Augustine plainly sides with Sabellius. A remarkable passage in his "Tractae an the Fourth gospel" brings out his position clearly: **"The Trinity is one God; three, but not three gods"**. Three what, then? I reply: "The Father, and the Son, and the Holy Spirit." But can the three be numbered, as three man can be? Here Augustine wavers. 'If you ask: "three what?" number ceases. When you have numbered, you cannot tell what you have numbered. Only in their relations to each other do they suggest number, not in their essential existence...When the Trinity is spoken of, "number fails." This must mean that Augustine did not regard the "three" as real and distinct existences or individuals which, of course, can be numbered, but only as modes or relations "in triple form, of one existence or individual."[11]

But Christianity had been teaching for centuries that the Godhead could be distinguished by number. Hippolytus, who had been elected as bishop of Rome and is revered as a saint, taught that they were three.

> If, again, he alleges his own word when he said, "I and the Father are one," let him (Noetus) attend to the fact, and understand that

The Athanasian Creed Develops

> he did not say, "I and the Father am one, but are one." For the word (esmen) is not said of one person, but it refers to two persons and one power. He has himself made this clear, when he spake to the Father concerning the disciples, "The glory which Thou gavest me I have given them; that they may be made perfect in one; that the world may know that Thou hast sent me." What have the Noetians to say to these things? Are all one body in respect of substance, **or is it that we become one in the power and disposition of unity of mind?**...A man, therefore, even though he will it not, is compelled to acknowledge God the Father Almighty, and Christ Jesus the Son of God, who, being God, became man, to whom also the Father made all things subject, himself excepted, and the Holy Spirit; **and that these therefore, are three.**[12]

Hippolytus was not the only Father who thought that the members of the Godhead could be numerically differentiated. Most of the Apologists had firmly declared that the Father, the Son, and the Holy Spirit were each numerically one.

> Following the custom of the Apologists and in conformity also with his own view that the Holy Ghost proceeded from the Father through the Son and is not equal with God, though it is worthy of honors and dignity, Origen takes only the Father and the Son as the subject of his discussion of discussion and unity in the Trinity. Still what he says of the Son would be true also of the Holy Spirit. Like Justin Martyr, he maintains that God and the Logos are real beings and **argues against those who believe that the distinction between them is not in number but only according to certain thoughts. This criticism of those who deny that God and the Logos were numerically distinct means, of course, that he himself believes that they are are numerically distinct and many,** so each one of them is numerically one.[13]

But Augustine was so influential that his precepts were accepted in preference to those who came before. It was encapsulated in the Quicumque, or Athanasian Creed.

> The so-called Athanasian Creed (Quicumque) of the late fifth century clearly bare the stamp of Augustinian thought. Falsely attributed to St. Athanasius, the creedal formula has stood ever since as the Western Church's classical statement of Trinitarian faith.[14]

This formula contains a great many contradictions. A statement is affirmed as a truth, and then its exact opposite is also stated as a truth. It reads:

THE ATHANASIAN CREED

Whoever will be saved: before all things it is necessary that he hold the Catholic Faith. Unless he keep this faith whole and undefiled, without doubt he will perish everlastingly.

And the Catholic Faith is this: we worship one God in Trinity, and Trinity in unity, neither confounding the Persons, nor dividing the Substance. For there is one Person of the Father, another of the Son, another of the Holy Ghost. But the Godhead of the Father, of the Son, and of the Holy Ghost is all one: the Glory co-equal, the Majesty co-eternal. Such as the Father is, such is the Son, and such is the Holy Ghost. The Father uncreated, the San uncreated, and the Holy Ghost uncreated. The Father incomprehensible, the Son incomprehensible, and the Holy Ghost incomprehensible. The Father eternal, the Son eternal, and the Holy Ghost eternal. **And yet they are not three eternals, but one eternal. As also there are not three incomprehensibles, nor three uncreated, but one created and one incomprehensible.** So likewise the Father is almighty, the Son is almighty, and the Holy Ghost is almighty; **and yet they are not three almighties, but one almighty.** So the Father is God, the Son is God, and the Holy Ghost is God; **and yet they are not three gods, but one God.** So likewise the Father is Lord, the Son Lord, and the Holy Ghost Lord; **and yet not three Lords, but one Lord.** For like as we are compelled by the Christian truth to acknowledge every Person by Himself to be God and Lord, so are we **forbidden by the Catholic religion to say, there are three gods or three lords.**

The Father is made of none, neither created nor begotten. The Son is of the Father alone, not made, nor created, but begotten. The Holy Ghost is of the Father and the Son, neither made, nor created, nor begotten, but proceeding. So there is one Father, not three Fathers, one Son, not three Sons, one Holy Ghost, not three Holy Ghosts.

And in this Trinity none is before or after the other; none is the greater or less than another; but the whole three Persons are co-eternal together, and co-equal; so that in all things the Unity in Trinity, and the Trinity in Unity is to be worshipped. **He therefore that will be saved must think of the Trinity.**[15]

There are several objections which we must raise against the Athanasian Creed. The first, of course, is that it establishes a great many contradictions. William Cunningham explains why the presence of a contradiction disproves a premise. He then attempts to apply this to the Nicene Creed.

> The first part of the allegation—namely, that the doctrine directly and in itself involves a contradiction—is very easily disposed of, as it is manifestly destitute of any solid foundation. In order to constitute a contradiction, it is necessary that there be both an affirmation and a negation, not only concerning the same thing,

but concerning the same thing in the same respect. To say that one god is three gods, or that three persons are one person, is, of course, an express contradiction, or, as it is commonly called, a contradiction in terms. To affirm, directly or by plain implication, that God is one in the same respect in which he is three, would also amount to a plain contradiction, and, of course, **could not rationally be believed.** But to assert that God is in one respect one, and in another and different respect three—that He is one in nature, essence or substance—and that He is three with respect to personality, or personal distinction (and this is all that the received doctrine of the Trinity requires or implies), can never be shown to contain or involve a contradiction.[16]

The Athanasian Creed does plainly contain many contradictions. For example, it acknowledges that the Father, Son, and the Holy Ghost each enjoy the status of God. It follows that statement by declaring that they are only one god. What is happening here? The author of the Creed is utilizing the theory of Augustine that deity cannot be numbered. Yet, if we grant three beings the status of godhood, they are three. A contradiction is created if by granting the divine status to each member individually, and refusing to grant it to a group. And this, according to Cunningham, "could not rationally be believed."

But while the Athanasian Creed does grant deity on an individual basis (in principle), it concentrates on the message that the Father, Son, and Holy Ghost are one. It returns again and again to that principle. Paine states that this shows that this shows that the formula is really Sabellianism in disguise.

This creed, which is clearly a product of the Augustinian school, declares that "We worship one God in trinity, and trinity, neither confounding the persons, nor dividing the substance." The language assumes that the substance or Being is one, while the persons are three. **But does the creed hold to three real persons? Plainly not.** It plays with the term "person," as Augustine did. Its doctrine, under all its verbal antinomies, is that of the essential Divine unity. God, it declares, is unus Deus, that is, **one personal being.** This creed has recently been charged with tritheism. In fact its position is at the opposite pole. "There are not three Gods, but one God." True, its Sabellianism is veiled under tie assumption that God may be one Being and yet be three persons, **but its real position is that God is one Being,** whatever explanation be given of the three persons. Thus its Trinitarianism is only a disguise. Its hands indeed are those of Esau, but its voice is the voice of Jacob. **The doctrine of numercal unity of essence is monistic,** not tritheistic...[17]

Is Paine right in his assessment? Yes, he is. Let us, for example, consider the case of William Sherlock. He wrote a book called *The Vindication of the Most Blessed and Holy Trinity and the Incarnation of the Son of God.* In this publication, he attempted to demonstrate that the Father, Son, and Holy Ghost were each real beings.

> It is plain that the Persons are perfectly distinct, far they are Three distinct and infinite Minds, and therefore Three distinct Persons; **for a person is an intelligent being**, and to say, they are Three Divine Persons, and not three distinct Minds, is both heresie and nonsense; The Scripture, I'm sure, **represents Father, Son and Holy Ghost, as three intelligent beings, not as three powers or faculties of the same being,** which is down-right Sabellianism; for faculties are not Persons, no more than memory, will and understanding [all used by Augustine in his explanations of how the Trinity worked] are Three Persons in one Man: **when we prove the Holy Ghost to be a person"** against the Socinians, who make him only a Divine Power, **we prove that all properties of a person belong to him,** such as Understanding, Will, Affections and Actions; which shows that our Notion of a Person is, such a Being as has Understanding, and Will, and Power of Action, and it would be very strange, that we should own Three Persons, each of which Persons is truly and properly God, and not own Three infinite Minds; as if anything could be a God, but an infinite Mind.[18]
>
> **We must allow the divine persons to be real substantial beings,** if we allow each Person to be God, unless we will call any thing a God, which has no real Being, as that has not, which has not a real Nature and Essence, whereas all Man grant there are no accidents (non-essential parts), or Qualities or Modes in God, but a pure and simple Essence, or pure Act; and therefore the Three Divine Persons are substantially distinct, though One in undivided Substance.[19]

The statement of Sherlock is really a recapitulation of the Nicene Creed, in which the three members of the Godhead are portrayed as existing in a divine essence or substance. But each of them is portrayed as a real being. Many theologians took exception to what he wrote, because they felt that three real beings would really be three gods.

> In the English Church the error of tritheism was revived by Dean Sherlock in his "Vindication of the Holy and Ever Blessed Trinity." He maintained that, with the exception of a mutual consciousness of each other, which no created spirits can have, the three divine persons are "three distinct infinite minds" or

"three intelligent beings." He was opposed by South, Wallis, and others.[20]

By attacking the statements of Sherlock, these other theologians were refusing to agree that the Father, Son, and Holy Ghost are real beings. Instead, they were ready to acknowledge only one being—God.

> But there exists in God only one power, one will, one self-presence, one activity, one beatitude, and so forth. Insofar as the individual Persons can even be described as "self-conscious" (which at best is an analogical attribution), it is a self-consciousness which derives from the one divine essence and is common to the divine Persons. Our modern psychological and philosophical notions of subjectivity (viewing the Godhead as three distinct beings), therefore, must be kept strictly away from the concept of person as applied to the Trinity.[21]

The Augustinian theory of the Trinity is a very difficult idea to grasp. Not even its author understood it. This is the reason that it was called incomprehensible. Michael Schmaus gives several examples of this type of logic.

> The Fathers passionately rejected Eunomius's thesis that God can be comprehended from the aspect of uncreated being. Chrysostom calls this godlessness. "What you understand is not God," said Augustine. This ignorance is not the ignorance of the person who knows little, but of him who knows much, it is a docta ignorantia. According to Augustine, **God is better known through igorance than through knowledge.**[22]

Should the character and attributes of God be incomprehensible? Nathaniel Lardner explains why they should not.

> All I affirm is, that it is obscure, and difficult to be conceived and understood, if it be not absolutely incomprehensible.
> Secondly, I would observe, that obscure doctrines ought not to be made necessary to salvation. They who consider the general tenure, and great design of the preaching of Christ and his apostles, to all sorts of men, in order to bring them to repentance and holiness, and thereby to everlasting happiness, by the good will and appointment of God, **will be easily led to think that there should not be any doctrines, necessary to be believed, which are of such a nature, that the most metaphysical and philosophical minds can scarcely know what they are, or reconcile them to reason.** Therefore, the commonly received doctrine of the Trinity, if it be obscure, should not be made a necessary article of a Christian's faith. And yet this is the introduction to the Athanasian

creed: "Whosoever will be saved, before all things it is necessary, that he hold the Catholic faith. Which faith, except every one do keep whole and undefiled, without doubt he shall perish everlastingly. And the Catholic faith is this, that we worship one God in Trinity, and Trinity in Unity:" And the more fully to enforce the necessity of this doctrine, it is repeated again at the end: "This is the catholic faith. **Which except a man believe faithfully, he cannot be saved.**"[23]

Is it really fair to have a man perish because of a doctrine which is so complicated that he cannot possibly comprehend it? I do not think so. In fact, such a premise seems to be absolutely foreign to the god of the Bible. He wants people to know him and to covenant with him. Such a relationship is not merely far a few elite people, but for all.

> Behold, the days come, saith the Lord, that I will make a new covenant with the house of Israel, and with the house of Judah:
> Not according to the covenant that I made with their fathers in the day that I took them by the hand to bring them out of the land of Egypt; which my covenant they brake, although I was an husband unto them, saith the Lord:
> But this shall be the covenant that I will make with the house of Israel; After those days, saith the Lord, I will put my law in their inward parts, and write it in their hearts; and will be their God, and they shall be my people.
> And they shall teach no more every man his neighbor, and every man his brother, saying, Know the Lord: **for they shall all know me, from the least of them unto the greatest of them,** saith the Lord: for I will forgive their iniquity, and I will remember their sin no more.[24]

Many people can understand how God the Father could be incomprehensible. But they forget that Jesus Christ is part of the Godhead. This would mean that the Savior is incomprehensible. Such a doctrine was totally unknown before the Nicene Creed.

> ...Bishop Bull allows that "**nearly all the ancient Catholics who preceded Arius have the appearance of being ignorant to the invisible and incomprehensible (immensam) nature of the Son of God;**" an article expressly taught in the Athanasian Creed under the sanction of its anathema.[25]

The Athanasian Creed also teaches that each of the three Persons is equal to each of the others. This is the same as saying $x = y = z$. But Jesus expressly taught that his Father was greater than he (John 14:28). This is one contradiction.

But the Athanasian Creed also teaches that the three Persons are equal to one God. This is the same as saying *1+1+1=1*. Mathematically, this does not work. The Creed also states that any one of the three is equal to the entire essence. This is even a bigger contradiction. Friedrich Schleiermacher, the father of modern religious thought, explains why this system does not work:

> The ecclesiastical doctrine of the Trinity demands that we think of each of the three Persons as equal to the Divine Essence, and vice versa, and each of the three Persons as equal to the others. **Yet we cannot do either one or the other**, but can only represent the Persons in a gradation, and thus either represent the unity of the Essence as less real than the three Persons, or vice versa.[26]

The same creed also states that the essence cannot be divided. What does this mean? Later writers would decide that this means that each member of the Trinity has taken part in every action which any member performs. This would, of course, mean that the Father also took part in the crucifixion of the Savior.

This same doctrine had been denounced before this time. The Patripassians taught that the Father suffered along with the Son.

> ...when Praxeas said, Filius patritur, pater vero compatitur, he asserted indirectly, if not directly, **that the Father suffered**: and hence **the heretics**, to whom Praxeas belonged, acquired the name of Patripassians. Origen describes the Patripassians as persons, "who with more superstition than religion, **that they may not appear to make two gods**, nor on the other hand to deny the divinity of the Savior, **assert that there is one and the same existence of the Father and Son**:" i.e., that one hypostasis exists, which receives two names according to the difference of causes: i.e., **one person answering to two "names."**[27]

> Hippolytus wrote a treatise against him, which is still extant; and as they were contemporaries, we can hardly question the authority of Hippolytus, when he represents Noetus as saying, "**that Christ is himself the Father, and that the Father himself was born and suffered and died.**" He also informs us, that Noetus reasoned as follows: "Since I acknowledge Christ to be God, he must be himself the Father, since he is God; **therefore the Father suffered, for he was himself the Father.**"[28]

As we have before stated, the Athanasian Creed was built upon the premises of Augustine. Those who followed him developed his line of reasoning. As they did so, maintaining the unity of substance became the important principle. In fact, writers like Anselm were really unsure of what the Father, Son, and Holy Ghost really were.

> All the rest sing the same Augustinian song. Anselm may speak for them. "Although necessity compels that there be two, still it cannot in any way be expressed what two they are" (quid duo sint); and again, "one essence, yet a trinity, on account of three **I know not what**" (tres nescio quid). It is noticeable that in these passages Anselm refuses to use the term "person," though it is still employed by Augustinians generally, with the express understanding, however, that it is in a negative or relative sense. The great question with the Schoolmen was whether the Trinity is one being (uns res) or three beings (tres res). Roscelin held that three real persons involved three real beings (tres res). This was allowed by Anselm, who accepted, with Augustine, the principle that nature and person are coincident; and hence **he denied that there are three real persons in the Trinity.** "As God is one in substance, He cannot be several persons (ita nec plures personoe)." Hence his frank confession, ¦tres nescio quid.[29]

As we have often said, Augustine contributed more to the Trinitarian doctrine than any other man in history.

> He developed the Nicene dogma of the Trinity, completed it by the doctrine of the double procession of the Holy Ghost, and gave it the form in which it has ever since prevailed in the West, and in which it received classical expression from his scholar the Athanasian Creed.[30]

> ...He is, indeed, the most important figure in Church history since St. Paul, and his influence on Western Christendom still endures.[31]

> ...he contributed to the incipient divergence between the Christianity of the western and eastern portions of the Mediterranean world. His thought was dominant in Latin Christianity for at least eight centuries, has since remained prominent in the Roman Catholic Church, and was to make major contributions to Protestantism.[32]

But the ideas of Augustine did not come from the Bible or from revelation. They came from the teachings of Plato and other philosophers.

> Augustine was a Platonist, as were most of the Christian thinkers of antiquity; his Platonism, however, was colored by the new religion and was filled with its spirit. In his eyes Plato is the foremost of all pre-Christian philosophers. In the same place he declares Aristotle a: vir excellentis ingenii et eloqui Platoni quidem impar, sed multos facila superans. Among the Neoplatonists he distinguishes Plotinus, Jamblichus, Porphyrius and Apuleius. **It is the Platonists who came closest to the true**

The Athanasian Creed Develops

> philosophy, which is that of Christianity...Seeking after God, they rightly rose above the world of sense, above the soul and the changeful realm of spirits...his Christian Platonism manifests itself particularly in his demonstration of the existence of God...From these truths Augustine concludes that God exists; it is true that he frequently seems to identify them with the divine essence itself...The Platonic ideas, therefore, according to Augustine, are identical with the creative ideas of God.[33]

Many people of the era in question recognized that new doctrines were being formulated. They denounced the ideas of Augustine. Vincent of Lerins wrote an article to expose Augustine as a heretic. This was the Vincentian formula.

> Far from accepting the Augustinian doctrine as that of the Church, he (Vincent of Lerins) represented its author as one of those "heretics fond of novelties," who merit condemnation, for it is indeed to Augustine that he alluded when he spoke of those who dared to teach "the existence of a grace of God such that, without effort, without even asking for it," the predestined may effect their salvation. And it is against Augustine, that he laid down as an indisputable sign of orthodoxy, the celebrated axiom: Quod semper, ubique et ab omnibus creditum est. (That which always, everywhere and by everybody has been believed). Any doctrine is orthodox that has been believed at all times, in all places and by all.[34]

Augustine had many enemies. There was a full-scale dispute between him and Pelagius which resulted in councils being held and many bishops being excommunicated. Furthermore, the teachings of Origen were denounced and those who were suspected of believing in his teachings were driven from the church. Canons were written to extol the teachings of Augustine which declared that no one had ever disagreed with his precepts. And the part of Vincent's writings which denounced Augustine was deleted.

> We have always held Augustine a man of holy memory because of his life and also of his services in our communion, **nor has even report ever sullied him with unfavorable suspicion.** We recall him as having once been a man of such great knowledge that even by my predecessors in the past he was always accounted among the best teachers.[35]

Yet the qualifications of Augustine to define the true faith for anyone must be questioned. After all, he was only the bishop of Hippo, a remote area in Africa. Why should his teachings be viewed as binding upon the entire Christian Church? Why should his premises be viewed as more authoritative than those of Origen, that had been accepted by the church since before the Council of Nicea? Even Augustine himself did not think that he was infallible, but freely admitted that people should reject his writings if they found error.

> I would not wish anyone to so esteem my [writings] that he would follow me except in those matters in which he has clearly seen I do not err...[36]

Therefore, we are fully justified in questioning both the doctrines of Augustine himself, and of the Athanasian Creed, which contains many of those same doctrines. What, then, can we use as a standard? As William Cunningham points out, we must use the Scriptures themselves and the revelations of God. Only in these is there safety. All else are the ideas and theories of men.

> There are one or two obvious reflections, suggested by the general nature and character of the subject, to which it may be proper to advert, though it is not necessary to enlarge upon them. The subject, from its very nature, not only relates immediately to the infinite and incomprehensible Godhead, but concerns what may be regarded as the penetralia or innermost recesses of the divine nature, the most recondite and inaccessible department of all that we have ever learned or heard concerning God. It is a subject about which reason or natural theology—in other words, the works of nature and providence, with the exercise of our faculties upon them—**give us no information**, and about which we know, and **can know nothing, except in so far as God himself may have been pleased to give us a direct and imediate revelation concerning it**. These considerations are surely well fitted to repress any tendency to indulge in presumptuous speculations with respect to what may be true, or possible, or probable, in regard to this profoundly mysterious subject; and to constrain us to preserve an attitude of profound humility, while we give ourselves **to the only process by which we can learn anything with certainty regarding it,—namely, the careful study of God's word**—anxious only to know what God has said about it, what conceptions he intended to convey to us regarding it—and ready to receive with implicit submission whatever it shall appear that he has declared or indicated upon the subject.
> The way in which this question ought to be studied is by collecting together all the statements in Scripture that seem to be in any way connected with it—that seem, or have been alleged, to assert or to indicate some distinction in the Godhead or divine nature—**to investigate carefully and accurately the precise meaning of all these statements by the diligent and faithful application of all the appropriate rules and materials**—to collect their joint

or aggregate results—and **to embody these results in propositions which may set forth accurately the substance of all that scripture really makes known to us regarding it.** It is only when we have gone through such a process as this, that we can be said to have done full justice to the question—that we have really formed our views of it from the word of God, the only source of knowledge respecting it—and that we can be regarded as fully qualified to defend the opinions we may profess to entertain upon it.[37]

As we have seen, Augustine does not meet these criteria. Instead, he used the teachings of Plato. Yet even these teachings would later be revised by Thomas Aquinas, who used the doctrines of Aristotle.

CHAPTER 11 REFERENCES

1. Hooker, *The Laws of Ecclesiastical Polity*, 28–29
2. Grotius, *True Religion Explained and Defended*, 161
3. Paine, *A Critical History of the Evolution of Trinitarianism*, 55
4. Tixeront, *History of Dogmas*, 2:271
5. *New Catholic Encyclopedia*, 14:301, Article "Holy Trinity"
6. Shedd, *History of Christian Doctrine*, 1:355
7. Leith, *Creeds of the Churches*, 32
8. Durant, *The Age of Faith*, 68
9. McBrien, *Catholicism*, 2:298
10. Paine, *A Critical History of the Evolution of Trinitarianism*, 71
11. Ibid., 74–75
12. Hippolytus, *Against the Heresy of Noetus*, verses 7–11
13. Wolfson, *The Philosophy of the Church Fathers*, 317
14. McBrien, *Catholicism*, 2:300
15. Brantl, *Catholicism*, 70–71
16. Cunningham, *Historical Theology*, 2:208
17. Paine, *A Critical History of the Evolution of Trinitarianism*, 93
18. Sherlock, *The Vindication of the Most Blessed and Holy Trinity*, 66–67
19. Ibid., 47
20. Schaff, *History of the Christian Church*, 3:675
21. McBrien, *Catholicism*, 2:356
22. Schmaus, *Dogma*, 2:24
23. Lardner, *The Works of Nathaniel Lardner*, 9:581
24. Jeremiah 31:31–34
25. Newman, *An Essay on the Christian Doctrine*, 18
26. Schleiermacher, *The Christian Faith*, 742
27. Burton, *An Inquiry Into the Heresies of the Apostolic Age*, 588
28. Ibid., 589
29. Paine, *A Critical History of the Evolution of Trinitarianism*, 94–95
30. Schaff, *History of the Christian Church*, 3:1017
31. Foakes-Jackson, *History of the Christian Church From the Earliest Times to A.D. 461*, 490
32. Latourette, *A History of Christianity*, 174
33. Bardenhewer, *Patrology*, 496–497
34. Boulenger, *Histoire Generale de l'Eglise*, 3:160 as cited in Barker, *Apostasy From the Divine Church*, 488–489

35. Denzinger, *The Sources of Catholic Dogma*, 52
36. Ibid., 52
37. Cunningham, *Historical Theology*, 2:193–194

12

Aquinas and Luther

Augustine changed the concept of the Trinity forever. By defining the Father, Son, and Holy Ghost as one being, he made Christianity monotheistic. But he also created great confusion. People were never really sure how to conceive of any of the members of the Godhead from that time on. As a matter of fact, Anselm and others like him began to teach that Jesus Christ was the whole Trinity.

> ...so confounded Christ with God the Father that instead of making him the expression and representation of Divine mercy and intercession, as the earlier intercession had always done, it made him rather the representative of Divine justice and punishment. Mediaeval art is an this point a true and telling witness. The face of Christ, which in early art was benignant and compassionate, becomes hard and severe, and in the frequent judgment scenes he is pictured on the throne wrathful and vengeful, and in the act of punishing the guilty. No wonder that the cult of the Virgin Mary became so popular. Its growth, with all the superstitions involved, was the protest of heavy-laden souls, longing for some way of access to the mercy of God, when the old and living way through Christ had been closed. Anselm's "Cur Deus Homa"— a work which was epoch-making in its influence upon the mediaeval views of the atonement—illustrates forcibly the effect of the Augustinian type of doctrine. The treatise is pervaded with a thinly-disguised Patripassianism and Monaphysitism (a heresy that acknowledged only a divine nature in Christ). The very title is suggestive. It is not "Why the Christ," but "Why the God-man?" **Anselm's redemmer is God himself, not another mediating being, such as the Logos of Greek theology.** The question raised at the outset is, "By what necessity and for what reason God, since He is omnipotent, took upon himself the humiliation and weakness of human nature far the sake of its restoration?" Here the mediating element is wholly absent. A mediator implies two parties. Anselm confounds one party and the mediator together. He represents God as "descending to the Virgin's womb" and

"enduring weariness, hunger, thirst, strokes, crucifixion, and death." God "the Creator," who "made Adam," "redeemed" us "by his own blood" "from sin and from his own wrath." Such language runs through the whole book. Sometimes it becomes grossly Patripassian or monistic. Speaking of the death of Christ, he says; "No one would knowingly kill God." The point of all this mode of speech is explained by Anselm himself. Christ, he says, is "the whole trinity." "In one person the whole godhead is meant." "Since he himself is God, the son of God, he offered himself for his own honor to himself, as he did to the Father and the holy Spirit." Thus the whole gospel idea of a daysman between God and men, a Messiah and mediator whom, "in the fullness of time," God sent, "because he so loved the world," is dissolved into the crude materialism of the early heretics. God is made to send himself, to be born, to suffer and die, **and this to save men from the effects of his own wrath.** Is it any wonder that modern discussions on the atonement could never reach a satisfactory result an the Anselmic basis? Anselm's God—man is both the Being to be propitiated and the Being that propitiates, **a kind of Dr. Jekyll and Mr. Hyde,** now the omnipotent and eternal God and anon the "man of sorrows."[1]

This was a new type of trinity. The earlier Trinity (that of Father, Son, and Holy Ghost) was known as the Economic Trinity. The one God who had three somethings somewhere inside it was termed the Immanent Trinity. It had been invented by Augustine and would now be perfected by Thomas Aquinas.

San Tomasso d'Aquina was born in Italy in 1224 or 1225. He was a brilliant scholar who studied and taught at the University of Paris. He is best known because he borrowed the Moslem interpretation of the teachings of Aristotle (a Greek pagan philosopher) and modified them to conform with the idea of the Immanent Trinity.

> When Thomas Aquinas arrived at the University of Paris, the influx of Arabian-Aristotelian science was arousing a sharp reaction among believers; and church authorities tried to block the naturalism and rationalism that were emanating from this philosophy and according to many ecclesiastics, seducing the younger generations. Thomas did not fear these new ideas, but like his master Albertus Magnus (and Roger Bacon, also lecturing at Paris), he studied the works of Aristotle and eventually lectured publicly on them...
> The works of Averroes, the outstanding representative of Arabic philosophy in Spain, who was known as the great commentator and interpreter of Aristotle, were just becoming known to the Parisian masters. **There seems to be no doubt about the Islamic faith of the Cordovan philosopher;** nevertheless, he asserted that the structure of religious knowledge was entirely

heterogeneous to rational knowledge: **two truths—one of faith, the other of reason—can, in the final analysis, be contradictory**...Thomas Aquinas rose in protest against his colleagues; nevertheless, the parties retained a mutual esteem.[2]

By championing the ideas of Aristotle, Aquinas was making a dramatic break with the theology of his day. Augustine had built his doctrines upon the precepts of Plato. Therefore, in many respects, he was abandoning all that had come before.

His [Aquinas'] philosophical indebtedness to Aristotle should not be minimized. One has only to read his theological works to realize the esteem in which he held the philosopher...In order to preserve the wisdom of Augustine, Thomas disputed with its professed protagonists and **urged them to abandon the whole Platonic approach, while in order to save the philosophy of Aristotle, he commented on it and recast it.**[3]

Aristotle had theorized that God was the First Cause. In other words, every other thing owes its existence to this First Cause.

The eternal actual Being is both the motive or generating cause, the form, and the final goal of things.
It is the first mover and itself immovable. The existence of this first mover is the necessary consequence of the principle of causality. Every movement implies, in addition to the thing moved, a moving principle, which, again, receives its motion from a higher motive force. Now, since there can be no infinite series of causes, we are obligated to stop at a first mover. To deny this and at the same time to assume the reality of motion, to assume with Leucippus, Democritus, and others, an infinite series of effects and causes without a first cause, is to violate one of the most fundamental laws of thought.[4]

This First Cause of Aristotle was not God the Father, however. He was the creator of everything. As such, he was not available to help the worshipper.

Although Aristotle frequently calls the prime mover "God" and sometimes refers to his first philosophy as a theology, later critics have often pointed out **that this is not the sort of God that religious believers worship**. It is more like a scientific principle of actuality than a religious God.[5]

Whitehead, SMW, opens his chapter on God with a discussion on Aristotle, and finds the latter's God "not very available for religious purposes." (See also Ross, *Aristotle*, pp. 179–186).[6]

Aquinas, therefore, was making a very serious error by building his theories about God upon the philosophies of Aristotle. The results of this type of theology is to distance deity from man to the point where people question whether deity exists at all. It is not surprising that Aquinas expands a great deal of time and effort, therefore, in an attempt to convince everyone that God does exist.

> Aquinas's understanding of the Being and action of God is consistent with his famous "five ways" to prove the existence of God: the argument from **motion** (there must be a prime mover), the argument from **causality** (every affect must have a cause), the argument from **necessity** (all beings are possible" but one must be necessary if there are to be any beings at all), the argument from gradation or **exemplarity** (our ideas of more or less, of better or worse, presuppose some standard of perfection), and the argument from **design** (the consistent and coherent operation of the whole universe demands some intelligent and purposeful designer). (See Summa Theologica, 1, q. 3, a. 3). These arguments were not original with Aquinas. He was largely indebted to Plato, Aristotle, Avicenna, Augustine and especially the Jewish philosopher Moses Maimonides. All of the arguments are reducible to one: the argument from causality. No one argument "proves" the existence of God. They are simply ways in which the believer can begin to "make sense" of his or her belief in God after the fact.[7]

Several flaws exist with the reasoning of Aquinas. First of all, the god which he is talking about could be any god, not just the Christian one. It is, in fact, a generic god.

Secondly, these arguments do not prove the existence of God. In fact, the idea of exemplarity was attacked by Sigmund Freud as wishful thinking. He argued that people came to invent a god because they reasoned that someone must be better than the beings with which they were associated. Aquinas admits that his premise is the same upon which agnosticism is built: namely, that mankind can never really understand who or what God is.

> In Aquinas's account of our natural knowledge of the divine nature there is, then, **a certain agnosticism**...But we cannot provide any adequate description of the content, so to speak, of this infinitely higher degree; we can only approximate towards it by employing the way of negation. What is affirmed is positive, but the positive content of the concept in our minds is determined by our experience of creaturely wisdom, and we can only attempt to purify it or correct its inadequacies by means of negations. Obviously enough, **this process will never lead to an adequate positive understanding of the objective meaning of** (that is, of what is objectively signified by) **the terms predicated of God. But**

Aquinas never claimed that it would. On the contrary, he did not hesitate to draw the logical conclusion. "The first cause surpasses human understanding and speech. He knows God best who acknowledges that whatever he thinks and says falls short of what God really is" (In librum De Causis, lactio 6). **Aquinas would have been quite unmoved by the accusation that he could not give the exact significance of the terms predicated of God; for he never pretended to be able to give it.**[8]

Thirdly, such arguments ignore the real witness which is present in the Scriptures. The written accounts do describe what a member of deity looks like. Many miracles are ascribed to his intervention in the affairs of men. He speaks to his prophets and his words give us real insights into his personality. In fact, no exercises of the type which Aquinas indulges in can be found in the sacred writ. The prophets bear solemn witness that he lives because he has revealed himself to them. Let us refer to several of these accounts:

> In the year that king Uzziah died I saw also the Lord sitting upon a throne, high and lifted up, and his train filled the temple.
> And I heard the voice of the Lord, saying, Whom shall I send and who will go for us? Then said I, Here am I; send me.[9]

> Then answered Amos, and said to Amaziah, I was no prophet, neither was I a prophet's son: but I was a herdman, and a gatherer of sycamore fruit;
> And the Lord took me as I followed the flock, and the Lord said unto me, Go, prophesy unto my people Israel.[10]

> That the Lord called Samuel: and he answered, Here, am I.
> And he ran unto Eli, and said, Here am I; for thou calledst me. And he said, I called not; lie down again. And he went and lay down.[11]

We might cite hundreds of more passages, but the point is established. The prophets testified that the voice of God was heard, as in the cases of Isaiah, Amos, and Samuel. He was seen as he was in the case of Isaiah. There was no need for the apostles and prophets to use philosophical proofs to establish the existence of God, for they were eyewitnesses. It is the function of all Christians (or it should be) to proclaim these truths and preserve them in their purity. This is the purpose of the church of the Savior.

> For, first, it is acknowledged by all Christians, that in order to our being saved by Christ, it is necessary that we know and believe His Gospel, and the fundamental truths revealed in it. And therefore, as God would have all men to be saved, so for that purpose, He

would have them come to the "knowledge of the truth." But it is as plain also, that, as things now stand, **we cannot come to the knowledge of the truth, but only by the Church, which is the witness and keeper of holy writ,** and so, as the Apostle saith, "the pillar and ground of the truth," by which the truth is upheld and maintained in the world, the Gospel preserved and propagated; and so true religion, and the way of salvation by Christ, is divulged and made known to mankind.[12]

Aquinas built upon the premise that there is one god. In order to make his system work, he had to make the three Persons less real. As Moltmann points out, this poses a great danger to Christianity.

> Strict monotheism has to be theocratically conceived and implemented, **as Islam proves.** But once it is introduced into the doctrine and worship of the Christian church, **faith in Christ is threatened:** Christ must either recede into the series of the prophets, giving way to the One God, or he must disappear into the One God as one of his manifestations. The strict notion of the One God really makes theological Christology impossible, for the one can neither be parted nor imparted. It is ineffable. The Christian church was therefore right **to see monotheism as the severest inner danger,** even though it tried on the other hand to take over the monarchical notion of the divine lordship.[13]

Having a Father, Son, and Holy Ghost who are real beings is extremely important. In fact, without the assurance that the person that you are praying to is real, the whole purpose of worship is defeated.

> ...a theology like that of the Athanasian Creed may discover as many mysteries as it pleases in the nature of God as long as it does not deny that God is real, as a person is real with whom we may enjoy a reciprocal personal intercourse.
> **It is upon the possibility of this reciprocal intercourse that the whole question turns.** A child will offer sweets from its pocket to an elder friend with the intent to give him the pleasure the like offer would give to the child himself. He may feel disappointed that his sweets are not appreciated, or baffled by the inexplicable preoccupations which divert the attention of his elders from his own concerns; but, whatever momentary distress these things may cause, **he is sure that he has to do with a real person,** who, however strange his tastes and pursuits may be to the child's apprehension, **can answer the child and understand him and perhaps care for him.** It would be a very different thing if he came to find that there was not really any person there at all, that he was no more in communication with any one other than himself than when talking to himself and consciously "making believe."[14]

Aquinas does not consider the Father, Jesus Christ, and the Holy Ghost to be real beings. When describing how the Immanent Trinity works, the following description is given. You will note that we seem to be dealing with processes or modes of operation instead of actual historical entities.

> 1. There are two **processions** and only two processions in God: generation and spiration (breathing).
> 2. There are four **relations**, (paternity, filiation, active spiration, passive spiration), but only three **subsistent relations**, i.e., three relations which are mutually opposed and, therefore, distinct from one another (without, however, being distinct from the very being of God): paternity, filiation, and passive spiration. Active spiration (which involves Father and Son) is not opposed to either paternity or filiation, and, thus, does not constitute a fourth subsistent relation.
> 3. In God all things are one except what is opposed by the opposition of relations. Those relations which are opposed and, therefore, distinct one from the other are called, as noted above, subsistent relations, or **hypostases**. **They give rise, in turn, to the trinity of persons within the godhead: Father, Son, and Holy Spirit.**
> 4. Because of the unity of the divine essence, of the processions and of the relative oppositions, **which constitute the persons**, there is a mutual indwelling (circumincession) of the Persons, one in the other two, the other two in the one, so that the Son is for all eternity in the Father, and the Father from all eternity in the Son, and so on.[15]

Sabellianism was condemned because it reduced the members of the Godhead to names, modes of operation, or some other concept which made the three less than real beings. This is precisely what Aquinas does. He even refused to use specific terms when he spoke of God the Father, referring to him as a principle.

> The word **principle** signifies only that from which something proceeds: for we call anything from which anything in any way proceeds a principle, and vice verse. Since the Father is the one from which another proceeds, it follows that the Father is a principle.
> ad. 1. The Greeks use indifferently the words "cause" and "principle" when referring to God; on the contrary, the Latin doctors avoid the word "cause" and use only that of "principle." This is the reason. "Principle" is more general than "cause," the latter being itself more general then element; in fact, the first term or even the first part of a thing is called the "principle" but not the "cause." But **the more general a term, the more it can be used of God**, for the more specialized names are, the more appropriate they are to the creature.[16]

What does Aquinas mean when he distinguishes the three Persons by relations? Normally the term is used to describe the connection between two things as a frame of reference. Please note that Aquinas refers to the Father as a "thing" in the proceeding quotation. God the Father, therefore, is being distinguished from Jesus Christ by the relation of paternity (fatherhood). The Son is distinguished from the Father by reason of filiation (sonship). These terms describe the connection between the two, but they do not define who they are. As we have already established, he does not know. He knows only that the two are connected in some way, and considers it to be his duty to explain what that connection is. Since he lacks specific information about the individual members of the Godhead, Thomas attempts to disguise this ignorance by playing with words. In fact, reading his writings will soon confuse most readers due to the contradictions in which Aquinas indulges.

Let us use as an example the statement that the Father is a principle. What is a principle? Aquinas defines it as "anything from which anything in any way proceeds." Yet he also declares that there are times when the Father and the Son are one principle and other times when they are not.

> Augustine says (On the Trinity XIV) that the Father and the Son are not two principles but one principle of the Holy Spirit.
> The Father and the Son are one **in everything when there is no distinction between them of opposite relation.** [Implying, of course, that they are two principles when there is relative opposition.] Thus since there is no relative opposition between them as the principle of the Holy Spirit, it follows that the Father and the Son are one principle of the Holy Spirit.[17]

But Aquinas does not follow this thought through to its logical conclusion. The more he attempts to explain the differences between the three Persons, the more he retreats to the subject of their origins. In fact, he declares that the only difference between the persons is their origin.

> To the question what does person signify when applied to God, he answers: person in any nature signifies what is distinct in that nature...and **distinction in God is only by relation of origin**...therefore a divine person signifies a relation as subsisting (St 1a, 29. 4). To Thomas this is the logical, inevitable, ultimate answer **to someone who is convinced that a person is essentially a distinct center of consciousness, this answer that Thomas gives must seem very unsatisfactory.**[18]

Why is the answer of Aquinas unsatisfactory? He had built upon a Moslem copy of the teachings of Aristotle. Islam has no place in its theology for Jesus Christ. Therefore, we would expect any adaptation of those teachings to be confused and unsatisfactory.

One may wonder why the theories of Thomas Aquinas were accepted as authoritative if they were not correct. They were codified because the office of the papacy had moved its headquarters from Rome to France. The French pope had established certain teachers in the University of Paris as his experts in doctrinal matters. Thomas Aquinas was one of these. This Parisian influence was still in existence during the time of Martin Luther. The doctors of the Sorbonne declared:

1. The Scriptures are obscure.
2. The Scriptures cannot be used by themselves.
3. The Scriptures must be interpreted by Masters, and **especially by the Masters of Paris.**
4. The Fathers are obscure.
5. The Fathers cannot be interpreted by themselves.
6. The Fathers must be interpreted by Masters, and **especially by the Masters of Paris.**
7. The Sentences are obscure.
8. The Sentences cannot be used by themselves.
9. the Sentences must only be interpreted by Masters, and **especially by the Masters of Paris.**
10. Therefore, **the University of Paris is the chief guide in matters of scriptural interpretation,** for its decrees against Luther and Melanchthon are clear and can be understood by everyone.[19]

Merely designating the staff of a particular university as your scriptural experts does not make their interpretations correct, however. In order for such a determination to be valid, it must be given by revelation. It cannot merely be an adaptation of pagan thought. Yet Thomas Aquinas built his doctrinal system upon pagan thought.

> Thomas Aquinas (d. 1274), "the clearest thinker and the boldest innovator in scholasticism," integrated Aristotelian philosophical principles with traditional speculative theology, and...created, by remolding and rethinking existing materials and old problems. **A wholly new and original Christian philosophy.**[20]

As we have mentioned, the theology of Thomas Aquinas was built around the idea that the Trinity was really one god. We will now consider the contributions of a man who decided to name this being.

Martin Luther was a monk of the Augustinian order. However, he was later ordained a priest and then was appointed a professor of philosophy in the University of Wittenberg. Then an event happened which changed the life of Luther forever.

> In late 1517, Luther felt compelled to speak up against a crying abuse. Pope Leo X (1513–1521) had earlier issued a dispensation permitting Albrecht of Brandenburg (1490–1545) to hold at the same time the archbishopric of Mainz, the archbishopric of Madeburg, and the administration of the bishopric of Halberstadt. This dispensation from church regulations against "pluralism" (multiple offices) cost Albrecht a great sum, which he borrowed from the Augsburg banking house of Fugger. To repay this loan, Albrecht was also permitted to share half the proceeds from his district from the sale of indulgences that the papacy had been issuing, since 1506, for building that new basilica of St. Peter which is still one of the ornaments of Rome. A commissioner for this collection was John Tetzel (1470–1519), a Dominican monk of eloquence, who, intent on the largest possible returns, painted the benefits of indulgences in the crassest terms.[21]

Because he denounced this practice and others, Martin was excommunicated from the Roman Catholic Church. He soon set up a new system of theology which was patterned after that of Augustine (since Luther was of the Augustinian order). Like his hero, Luther believed that the Trinity was one god. However, the reformer (like Anselm before him) decided that the name of this one god was Christ: "Know that there is no other God but this man Christ Jesus."[22]

This did not mean that Luther did not speak of the Father and the Holy Ghost. He did speak of them a great deal. However, he accepted the statements of Augustine that there was only one God. Luther thought that, since there was only one God, it was easier to use the name of Christ to designate the Trinity. After all, he argued, the whole Trinity was present in any one person.

> The term "Trinity" (Dreifaltigkeit, three-foldness) does not please him, because God is "the supreme Unity"...he had a vigorous consciousness of the absolute unity of God, and **this enabled him to see in each trinitarian person the entire godhead. God is therefore fully revealed through Christ...where one part is, there is certainly the entire godhead**... The theoretical problems which arise in this connection never presented themselves to his mind.[23]

Many Protestant churches have followed the ideas of Martin Luther and, while affirming the reality of the Trinity, largely acknowledge Jesus as the only God. Richard Niebuhr warns that those who follow this course of action are, in reality, denying the reality of the Father.

> ...it is hardly necessary to await the outcome of many inquiries before concluding that substantial error involving many further confusions is present when the proposition that Jesus Christ is God is converted into the proposition that God is Jesus Christ...however the doctrine of the Personae is stated it must still be affirmed that **the Father is not the Son and the Son is not the Father and the Spirit cannot be equated with either.** Yet in many churchly pronouncements the faith of Christians is stated **as if their one god were Jesus Christ**; as if Christ's ministry of reconciliation to the Creator were of no importance; as if the Spirit proceeded only from the Son; as if the Christian Scriptures contained only the New Testament; as if the Old Testament were relevant only insofar as it contained prophecies pointing to Jesus Christ; as if Jesus Christ were man's only hope. **When this is done the faith of Christians is converted into a Christian religion for which Jesus Christ in isolation is the one object of devotion and in which his testimony, his very character, his sonship, his realtion to the one with whom he is united, are denied.**[24]

Many Protestant ministers have severely criticized the Church of Jesus Christ of Latter-Day Saints because the latter's refusal to accept the doctrine of the Trinity. It is alleged that you must believe in that premise to be a Christian.

> ...they declare it necessary, after the pattern (forsooth) of the ancient Fathers and councils (whom they have imitated not half so well as an ape doth a man) to premise the symbol, or rule of faith, used by the holy church of Rome, (which is indeed the creed of Constantinople) and beginning with these words "I believe in one God," and this creed they judge necessary to be in so many express words professed by their whole assembly, as the principle **wherein all Christians do "necessarily agree,"** they plainly intimate (if we poor Protestants may presume to understand their meaning by their words,) that there is no absolute necessity that all Christians should agree in other things. But their following words are express, wherein they acknowledge this creed to be **"the only foundation,"** and consequently, that nothing is to be laid as a foundation beside; nay, that this creed is **"the only firm foundation, against which the gates of Hell shall never prevail"**.[25]

Even the most dogmatic supporter of the Trinitarian dogmas must admit that a man may cling to the letter of the Nicene Creed and yet fail to serve the Lord in other matters. James taught that mere belief was not enough.

> Thou believest that there is one God; thou doest well: the devils also believe and tremble.
> But wilt thou know, O vain man, that faith without works is dead?[26]

Moreover, as we have seen, not all Christians believe in the Trinity. There are those who do not believe that it is a Christian doctrine at all.

> ...some there are, namely, the Arians in reformed Churches of Poland, which imagine the canker to have eaten so far into the very bones and marrow of the Church of Rome, as if it had not so much as a sound belief, no, not concerning God himself, but that the very belief of the Trinity were a part of Antichristian corruption, and that the wonderful providence of God did bring to pass that the Bishop of the See of Rome should be famous for his triple crown—a sensible mark whereby the world might know him to be that mystical beast spoken of in the Revelation to be that great and notorious Antichrist in no one respect so much as in this, that he maintaineth the doctrine of the Trinity.[27]

In his book *The Belief of 700 Ministers*, Dr. George Herbert Betts cited the results of a questionnaire which polled five hundred active ministers and two hundred theological students. The ministers were from Chicago while the students were from five different theological schools in different parts of the country. What did these Protestants say concerning their own personal beliefs concerning the nature of divinity? The results are very revealing:

> On the question whether God is three distinct persons in one, 44 percent of students as against 80 percent of ministers-in-service accept this view; 21 percent as against 7 percent of ministers are uncertain; 35 percent of students as against 13 percent of ministers [or almost 20 percent of those surveyed] disbelieve the proposition.[28]

Quotations like these show that many who have studied the evidence find real reasons to question whether the Trinity can really be one being. And, as we shall see, there is a viable alternative—that the Father, Son, and Holy Ghost are really three beings.

CHAPTER 12 REFERENCES

1. Paine, *A Critical History of the Evolution of Trinitarianism*, 84–85
2. *Encyclopedia Britannica*, 28:637, Article "Thomas Aquinas"
3. *Collier's Encyclopedia*, 2:376, Article "Thomas Aquinas"
4. Weber, *History of Philosophy*, 116
5. Brumbaugh, *The Philosophers of Greece*, 194
6. Ibid., 251
7. McBrien, *Catholicism*, 2:305
8. Copleston, *Thomas Aquinas*, 136
9. Isaiah 6:1, 8
10. Amos 7:14–15
11. 1 Samuel 3:4–5
12. Beveridge, *The Theological Works of William Beveridge*, 1:63
13. Moltmann, *The Trinity and the Kingdom*, 131
14. Webb, *God and Personality*, 131
15. McBrien, *Catholicism*, 2:355
16. Aquinas, *Summa of Theology* I, 9. 33 a. 1, c as cited in Aquinas, An Aquinas Reader, 431
17. Ibid., q. 36, a. 4, c, Ibid., 437
18. Fortman, *The Triune God*, 208–209
19. Schweibert, *Luther and His Times*, 436
20. Fortman, *The Triune God*, 204
21. Walker, Norris, Lotz and Handy, *A History of the Christian Church*, 425
22. Dunstan, *Protestantism*, 127
23. Seeberg, *Textbook of the History of Doctrine*, 2:305–306
24. Niebuhr, *The Purpose of the Church and Its Ministry*, 44–45
25. Bull, *Works of George Bull*, 2:220
26. James 2:19–20
27. Hooker, *The Laws of Ecclesiastical Polity*, 252
28. Betts, *The Belief of Seven Hundred Ministers* as cited in Howells, *His Many Mansions*, 6

13

They Are Real Beings

During the last twelve chapters, we have examined the doctrines of the Trinity from the standpoints of historical development and doctrinal content. In both areas this idea was found to be deficient. But it is not enough to prove that an idea is wrong. It must be replaced with another idea which is right.

If the Trinity is not found in the Bible, it follows that some other doctrine must be contained therein. It appears self-evident that God would not dictate sixty-six books of revelation to his children without giving them some definition concerning his nature. We must, therefore, be prepared to define what this nature is. And, as Cardinal John Henry Newman points out, we must also be prepared to demonstrate that such doctrines were perceived in that manner by the members of Christ's ancient church.

> And now in like manner the Tridentine Creed is met by no rival developments; there is no antagonist system. Criticisms, objections, protests, there are in plenty, but little of positive teaching anywhere; seldom an attempt an the part of any opposing school to master its own doctrines, to investigate their sense and bearing, to determine their relation to the decrees of Trent and their distance from them. And when at any time this attempt is by chance in any measure made, then an incurable contrariety does but come to view between portions of the theology thus developed, and a war of principles; an impossibility moreover of reconciling that theology with the general drift of the formularies in which its elements occur, and a consequent appearance of unfairness and sophistry in adventurous persons who aim at forcing them into inconsistency; and, further, a prevalent understanding of the truth of this representation, authorities keeping silence, eschewing a hopeless enterprise and discouraging it in others, and the people plainly intimating that they think both doctrine and usage, antiquity and development, of very little matter at all; and, lastly, the evident despair of even the better sort of men, who, in consequence, when they set great schemes on

foot, as for the conversion of the heathen world, are afraid to agitate the question of the doctrines to which it is to be converted, lest through the opened door they should lose what they have, instead of gaining what they have not.[1]

Yet there is another doctrine concerning the Godhead which can meet the criteria of doctrine, usage, antiquity, and development. Lowell L. Bennion writes:

> Latter-day Saints believe that the Father, Son and Holy Ghost are unified in purpose and one in influence for good, but that they remain separate and distinct persons, each with his own personality, work, and mission in relation to man. God the Father is the supreme intelligence, the head, worshipped and honored by Jesus, by the Holy Ghost, and by men. Jesus Christ is the Son of God, chosen to lead the children of men, his brethren, to salvation and eternal life. The Holy Ghost bears witness of the Father and the Son and guides mankind to understand and live the teachings of the Son.[2]

These doctrines are clearly very different from those of the Trinity and have been sharply denounced by most Christian churches of our day. Yet, as we have demonstrated, these ideas are in harmony with the Scriptures. This raises a perplexing question. How was Joseph Smith able to learn this great truth when all of the theologians of his day were teaching that the Trinity was true?

Joseph testified that he had received revelations from God and that these truths had been communicated by that medium.

Joseph was very concerned about which church was right. He went to the woods and knelt in prayer. As he was praying, an unseen power tried to prevent him from praying. But then a light appeared:

> It no sooner appeared than I found myself delivered from the enemy which held me bound. When the light rested upon me I saw two Personages, whose brightness and glory defy all description, standing above me in the air. One of them spake unto me, calling me by name and said, pointing to the other, **This is My beloved son. Hear him!**[3]

Joseph then asked which church was right. The answer which the Savior gave surprised him.

> I was answered that I must join none of them, for they were all wrong; and the Personage who addressed me said **that all their creeds were an abomination in his sight**; that those professors were all corrupt; that: "they draw near to me with their lips, but their hearts are far from me, **they teach for doctrines the com-**

mandments of men, having a form of godliness, but they deny the power thereof."[4]

What did Jesus mean when he called the Christian creeds an abomination? An abomination is something which was connected with paganism or idol worship. As we have already established, the modern-day Trinity was built upon the doctrines of Plato and Aristotle. These philosophers were pagans. It therefore makes perfect sense that Jesus would call their doctrines abominations.

But just as Jesus denounced false doctrines, he also taught great truths. He taught that he was the son of God the Father. The Father and Jesus are not the same being nor have they ever claimed to be.

> In our Articles of Faith we declare our belief in God the Eternal Father, and in His Son, Jesus Christ, and in the Holy Ghost—in other words, the Trinity. We accept the scriptural doctrine that they are separate and distinct personages. This is one distinguishing and, to some, disturbing doctrine of the Church. We do not believe that He is incomprehensible, immaterial, and without body or parts. While we agree that finite man cannot fully comprehend God, there is ample support in the Bible for our faith that we may progressively increase our knowledge and understanding of Him. In fact, our eternal life is dependent upon our knowing Him. Note the words of Jesus:
> "And this is life eternal, that they might know thee the only true God, and Jesus Christ whom thou hast sent.—John 17:3"[5]

The strengths of these doctrines are awesome. First of all, they claim to have been received by revelation through the prophet Joseph Smith. Their premises were known and taught throughout the Church during the period from 1830–1844. The governing principles were not evolved over a period of hundreds of years.

Nor were its tenets codified through the rancor and debate of endless councils. Joseph Smith presented the revelations which he received to the members of the Church. He asked the Saints to pray to God the Father in order that they might receive a witness of the truth of these things. After having received a confirmation from the Holy Ghost, the Saints were then asked to signify their acceptance of the revelations by raising their right hands in support of the prophet.

This sign of support was not a vote. The doctrines were revelations from God, regardless of whether the listeners received them. What was being signified was the willingness of each individual member to submit to the will of the Lord and to receive them as scripture.

Nor was acceptance secured through governmental edicts, threat of exile, torture, public executions or conquest (in stark contrast to the doctrines of the Trinitarian Creeds). Converts were allowed to be baptized only if they received a spiritual witness that its teachings were true.

No speculations about God being dead are promulgated within the theology of The Church of Jesus Christ of Latter-Day Saints, for the very presence of revelation proves that he does exist. Heresy is also non-existent because the principles of the gospel are fully defined therein. In contrast, the heresies connected with the development of Trinitarian doctrines occurred because new doctrines had been introduced which raised unanswered questions concerning the nature of God.

The Persons of the Godhead are fully protected. The Father is not the Son, the Son is not the Father, and the Holy Ghost cannot be equated with either one. All three have the powers and characteristics which constitute God.

The roles of the three are protected. God the Father is the judge. Jesus Christ is our intercessor with the Father. No earthly man "robs" God by trying to perform this function. The Holy Ghost bears witness of the truth when sent forth by the Father.

A strict hierarchy is maintained. The Father is greater than the Son. It was the Son who died on the cross and was resurrected, not the Father or the Holy Ghost. In all of these doctrines, the promises are identical to the original teachings of Jesus Christ and to that of the Tritheists, who existed prior to the Council of Nicea.

There is no universal substance which fills the immensity of space. The Father and the Son have bodies. This doctrine was taught prior to the time of Augustine. The existence of this doctrine in ancient Christian theology has already been established during earlier chapters. Gordon B. Hinckley explains why this doctrine makes sense:

> Each of us is a dual being of spiritual entity and physical entity. All know of the reality of death when the body dies, and each of us also knows that the spirit lives an as an individual entity and that at some time, under the divine plan made possible by the sacrifice of the Son of God, there will be a reunification of spirit and body. Jesus' declaration that God is a spirit no more denies that he has a body then does the statement that I am a spirit while also having a body.
>
> I do not equate my body with God's in its refinement, in its capacity, in its beauty and radiance. His is eternal. Mine is mortal. But that only increases my reverence for him. I worship him "in

spirit and truth." I look to him as my strength. I pray to him for wisdom beyond my own. I seek to love him with all my heart, might, mind, and strength. His wisdom is greater than the wisdom of all men. His power is greater than the power of nature, for he is the Creator Omnipotent. His love is greater than the love of any other, for his love encompasses all of his children, and it is his work and his glory to bring to pass the immortality and eternal life of his sons and daughters of all generations. (See Moses 1:39.) "He so loved the world, that he gave his only begotten Son, that whosoever believeth in him should not perish, but have everlasting life." (John 3:16.)

This is the Almighty of whom I stand in awe and reverence. It is he to whom I look in fear and trembling. It is he whom I worship and unto whom I give honor and praise and glory. He is my Heavenly Father, who has invited me to come unto him in prayer, to speak with him, with the promised assurance that he will hear and respond![6]

In short, every problem encountered during the period when Trinitarian doctrines were installed is avoided by the affirmation of the teachings of the LDS Church upon this subject.

To a Latter-Day Saint, it is essential that they know the Savior so that he can emulate him. For unless we do this, we cannot re-enter the presence of our Father in Heaven. The strength of the LDS theology is that it makes such knowledge possible, rather than standing in the way.

Vagueness about the true nature of God—what we worship—has taken a terrible toll in the world. Such vagueness subtly feeds faithlessness and adds to the sense of purposelessness that needlessly permeates so many lives. Someday we shall see how much boredom and drift (as well as both dread and disdain of death) are rooted in the incorrect and inadequate perceptions of God. Those in ancient Israel were not alone in following false gods "to [their] hurt." (Jeremiah 7:6)

Besides, the teachings of Jesus Christ have never been rejected because His standards are imprecise or insufficiently high. His teachings have, in fact, been disregarded by some because they are viewed as being too precise and impractically high! Yet such lofty standards, when followed, produce the truest and highest happiness. There is no other individual to compare with Jesus Christ, nor any other message to rival that of Jesus—a message that is so holistic, so consistent, and so explanatory of what we earthlings are experiencing in mortality.

Passive acknowledgment of an aimless and diluted deity does little to improve the human condition. And militant followership of tribal deity who issues no equivalent of the second commandment is dangerous. But sincere followership of the living God—who urges us to be like Him in love, justice, kindness, mercy, and purity—can redeem both the individual and mankind. Understanding what we worship is, thus, no trivial theological point-it is purpose itself![7]

We bear testimony that Jesus does live! He has appeared to prophets in our day and given them commandments. Joseph Smith gave the following testimony:

> And now, after the many testimonies which have been given of him, this is the testimony, last of all, which we give of him: That he lives!
> For we saw him, even on the right hand of God; and we heard the voice bearing record that he is the Only Begotten of the Father.[8]

Let us examine this matter with logic. Joseph Smith was an individual with a very meager education. Yet he went against the tide of public opinion in this matter. In fact, the Trinity was being used as the litmus test to determine if a minister could be licensed. To the clergy, a statement that the three were not the same being was considered to be idiotic.

> The historical cycle has run out, and we are back once more at the point where Christian history began, the first stage in the evolution of Christian theology, viz., the question of the man of Nazareth. Who is he? And that question has evolved to its final answer, that Jesus is God, the only highest God. It is no longer the historical question of his birth, life, character, teaching, and moral power over the men of his own generation, but rather the subtlest question that human thought can raise, that of the metaphysical relation of the human Jesus to the absolute Deity, and the answer to this question is made the test of evangelical faith. The young minister may be at his ease as to his theological system besides, if he can only give as his own the "new trinitarian" version of Christ's true Godhead.[9]

But the young prophet did not teach the popular ideas which were current during his era. This brought him scorn from the Catholic and Protestant ministries, and many accused him of not being a Christian. Yet Joseph defended his teachings by saying:

> ...I had actually seen a light, and in the midst of that light I saw two Personages, and they did in reality speak to me; and though I was hated and persecuted for saying that I had seen a vision, yet it was true; and while they were persecuting me, reviling me, and speaking all manner of evil against me falsely for so saying, I was led to say in my heart: Why persecute me for telling the truth? I have actually seen a vision; and who am I that I can withstand

God, or why does the world think to make me deny what I have actually seen? For I had seen a vision; I knew it, and I knew that God knew it, and I could not deny it, neither dared I do it; at least I knew that by so doing I would offend God, and come under condemnation.[10]

We have seen that those who instituted the Trinity did not agree with the descriptions that were written in the Bible but chose to follow the teachings of philosophers like Plato and Aristotle. The Fathers were so confident of their own academic skills that they chose to set aside the message of the Scriptures.

O that cunning plan of the evil one! O the vainness, and the frailties, and the foolishness of men! When they are learned they think they are wise, **and they hearken not unto the counsel of God, for they set it aside, supposing they know of themselves,** wherefore, their wisdom is foolishness and it profiteth them not. And they shall perish.
But to be learned is good if they hearken unto the counsels of God.[11]

This prophecy has been literally fulfilled. Men have adapted the theory of anthropomorphism, which states that any passages in the Scriptures which state or imply that God has a body, parts or passions are there merely because the people of that era were too primitive to be able to comprehend that God was only a spirit. Therefore, whenever the Scriptures began to portray a view of God which they thought was anthropomorphic, the Fathers dismissed the passages as unlearned superstition. Clement of Alexandria summarizes this attitude by saying, "We must not even **think** of the Father of all as having a shape, or as moving, or as standing or sitting, or as being in some place, or as having a left and a right hand, **even though the scriptures say these things about him.**"[12]

Many people have accused the LDS Church of ignoring the meaning of the Bible because the Trinity is not affirmed. As we have already demonstrated, the very opposite is true. Trinitarian doctrines are not in the Bible. Those who formulated those theories ignored the content of the scriptures. It was Joseph Smith and the Saints who captured what the Bible really meant.

In reality, the doctrines of the Trinity were known during the early days of Christianity. Those who taught them were regarded as heretic, however. Simon Magus (otherwise known as Simon the Sorceror (Acts 8:9–20)) taught that God did not have a body. Sabellius said that the Father, Son, and Holy Ghost were all the same being. Either Praxeas or Noetus was the originator of the idea that all three members of the Godhead did everything which one of them did. All of these individuals were denounced as heretics, yet today their theories are enshrined in the Trinitarian Creeds.

Those present at the Council of Nicea (318 bishops) protested that the words and ideas being debated were not scriptural. When Constantine threatened exile, two chose banishment in preference to signing the document. Within a short time later, 1800 bishops signed creeds repudiating the premises of the Nicene Creed. Once again, these dissenters expressed the view that the Trinitarian doctrine (that God was one substance) was heretical. Yet the Nicene Creed is revered today as orthodox.

Moreover, such ideas as the ones which these men espoused do absolutely nothing to explain anything about the nature of God. However, they do raise a whole host of questions which even their brightest champions have never been able to answer.

But the revelations which Joseph Smith received answer questions instead of creating more. This information does not contradict Bible message, but instead confirms and clarifies it. For example, consider the clear and concise information which is available concerning each member of the Godhead and his purpose.

Father:
God the Father is our "Father which art in heaven" (Matthew 5:9) and we were his "offspring" (Acts 17:29) "before the world was." (Abraham 3:22) One peculiar contribution of the Father, then, was to beget us in the spirit before we "were naturally upon the face of the earth." (Moses 3:5)

Another function of the Father was that he was the father of Jesus after the manner of the Flesh. (Luke 1:30–37)

Further, the Father prepared the plan of salvation. (Moses 4:1–4)

Son:
Jesus is the Son of God (John 10:36). Because of this, He has made many contributions to us. Salvation is in Him (John 3:13–18). He is our redeemer (2 Ne. 2:25–26). He is our Intercessor (Romans 8:34–39) and Advocate with the Father (D&C 45:3–4).

He is the "light of the world" (John 8:12).

He is the perfect example of all mankind to follow (3 Ne. 27:27).

Holy Ghost:
"The Holy Ghost...beareth record of the Father and the Son" (D&C 20:27). One of the great functions of this third member of the Godhead is to testify in men's hearts of the other two. Our

Lord taught that when the Holy Ghost would come to minister unto men "he shall testify of me" (John 13:26).
He further bears witness of "the truth of all things" (Moro. 10:5) pertaining to salvation.
Another function of the Holy Ghost is to cleanse and sanctify the souls of the righteousness (3 Ne. 27:20).[13]

As you will note, the above citations come from the Bible, Book of Mormon, Doctrine & Covenants, and Pearl of Great Price. Yet the message of the four books of scripture is the same: they all bear witness that the Father, Son, and Holy Ghost are real beings. None of the members of the Godhead are incomprehensible—in fact, we can be as close to the Savior as we choose.

> He [Jesus] lifted up His hands and blessed them, and, even as He blessed them, was parted from them, and as He passed from before their yearning eyes a cloud received Him out of their sight.
> Between us and His visible presence—between us and that glorified Redeemer who now sitteth at the right hand of God—that cloud still rolls. **But the eye of faith can pierce it; the incense of true prayer can rise above it;** through it the dew of blessing can descend. And if He is gone away, yet He has given us in His Holy Spirit a nearer sense of his presence, a closer enfolding in the arms of His tenderness, then we could have enjoyed even if we had lived with Him of old in the home of Nazareth, or sailed with him in the little boat over the crystal waters of Gennesareth. We may be as near to Him at all times and more than all when we kneel down to pray—as the beloved disciple was when he laid his head upon His breast.[14]

We can, however, only be truly close to the Lord when we understand who and what he is. Let us use an example to illustrate this point.

Suppose that I was expecting a visit from an exchange student named Leslie. I go out and buy pretty dresses, lots of dolls, and other items which are sure to appeal to a young girl. The day finally comes when Leslie is to arrive and a taxi stops in front of our house. Out steps a young boy named Leslie. Will he like all of the presents which I got him? Obviously he will not. I could have saved myself a lot of money and effort by finding out what gender he was before I made my purchases. Similarly, we can save ourselves a lot of wasted motion if we understand more about the Lord. Elder Bruce R. McConkie wrote:

> **Faith unto life and salvation centers in Christ.** There is no salvation in that general principle of faith alone, that moving

cause of action, which causes the farmer to plant his seed with the unseen hope that it will bear grain. But there is faith unto salvation when Christ is the focal point in which the unseen hope centers. Accordingly the Prophet explained "that three things are necessary in order that any rational and intelligent being may exercise faith in God unto life and salvation." These he named as: 1. "The idea that he actually exists"; 2. "A **correct** idea of his character, perfections and attributes"; and 3. "An actual knowledge that the course of life which he is pursuing is according to his will."

It follows that **a knowledge of the true and living God is the beginning of faith unto life and salvation,** "for faith could not center in a being of whose existence we have no idea, because the idea of his existence in the first instance is essential to the exercise of faith in him" (Lectures on Faith, p. 33). So a faith in a false god can engender no faith in the human breast. If a person believes that an idol is God, or that Deity is a power or essence that fills the immensity of space, or if he has any other false concept, he stops himself from gaining faith, because faith is a hope in that which is not seen which is true. **Faith and truth cannot be separated; if there is to be faith, saving faith, faith unto life and salvation, faith that leads to the Celestial world, there must first be truth.**[15]

We can therefore understand why it is so important to God that we have a correct understanding of him and of what he is. History is full of incidents where people committed terrible atrocities because they had an incorrect idea of who God was and what he wanted from them. For example, the Moabites thought that Chemosh was God and, after heating the idol until it was red hot, placed children in its arms. Many Hindus thought that Kali was a goddess and went around strangling others in an attempt to make her happy. We Christians may poke fun at those who believe in these practices, but we must admit that they are sincere people who wanted to please someone whom they thought was God. Many of them wanted this so badly that they laid on beds of nails, walked on red-hot coals, and even killed themselves because they thought that this was what God wanted them to do!

Christian history shows the same pattern. Saint Symeon of the Stylites erected a platform on a pole and lived there, exposed to the elements, for sixty-three years. Rome was sacked because the Arian Goths were sure that God wanted them to punish the Athanasian Romans. Constantinople was sacked because the Crusaders thought God wanted them to punish the "heathen" Greek Orthodox Church. People bought indulgences, not only because they thought it would rid them of their sins, but because they thought that God had sanctioned this innovation. The institution of death bed repentance, infant baptism, the worship of saints, and many other practices which we look down upon today were all practiced because people had a false idea of who God was. It was natural that these misconceptions would translate into an extreme course of action which God neither sanctioned nor wanted.

The key to knowing what God wants from us is to know who and what he is. He is the Father of our spirits. We are made in his image. And, just as we look somewhat like him, he looks something like us.

Believing that God the Father is the father of our spirits throws the vengeful god theory out the window. Gone is the bully who dangles the sinner over the hell fires, trying to decide whether to save him or throw him in. Instead, we see a loving Father, who loved us enough to send his only begotten son to die for us. Once we understand this, we begin to comprehend that all of the commandments which we have been given are really for our benefit—to teach us how to be better people. As we keep these divine laws we become more like their author.

Mankind has seldom understood this. He has usually performed the ordinances of God and thought that the mere actions themselves pleased deity. This was the attitude which became present when the children of Israel offered sacrifices. But the Lord denounced these ordinances because the intent behind them (helping us to be better people and doing it in memory of the fact that Jesus would be sacrificed for our sins) was missing.

> **To what purpose is the multitude of your sacrifices unto me?** saith the Lord: I am full of the burnt offerings of rams, and the fat of fed beasts; and I delight not in the blood of bullocks, or of lambs, or of he goats.
>
> When ye come to appear before me, who hath required this at your hand, to tread my courts?
>
> Bring no more vain ablations; incense is an abomination unto me; the new moons and sabbaths, the calling of assemblies, I cannot away with: it is iniquity, even the solemn meeting.
>
> Your new moons and your appointed feasts my soul hateth: they are a trouble unto me; I am weary to bear them.
>
> And when ye spread forth your hands, I will hide mine eyes from you: yea, when ye make many prayers, I will not hear: your hands are full of blood.
>
> Wash you, make you clean; put away the evil of your doings from before mine eyes; cease to do evil;
>
> Learn to do well; seek judgment, relieve the oppressed, judge the fatherless, plead for the widow.
>
> Come now, and let us reason together, saith the Lord: though

your sins be as scarlet, they shall be as white as snow; though they be red like crimson, they shall be as wool.[16]

After the apostles were killed, the Fathers reinstated the idea of merely performing the ordinance. It was taught that a person had to have seven sacraments performed in order to be saved. But the heart of the worshipper was not required as a part of this bargain. The infant was baptized when he had no comprehension of what was happening. The mass was performed in Latin so that the worshippers could not understand what was being said. People were taught that they could be forgiven of their sins if they confessed their sins before a priest. And the most reprobate sinner could have the transgressions of a lifetime blotted out because some priest gave him the last rites. What was the message which was being taught? It was that God was interested in the ceremony and that performance of the ceremony made one acceptable before God. No wonder that the time when these practices reigned is called the dark ages. No wonder that Joseph Milner exclaims that, "We are penetrating into the regions of darkness, and a 'land of deserts and pits, a land of drought, and of the shadow of death,' and we are carried by every step into scenes still more gloomy than the former. Here and there, indeed a glimmering ray of the sun of righteousness is discernible, but it is vain to look for any steady luster of evangelical truth and holiness, amidst this dismal darkness."[17]

Believing that God the Father is really our father and that he loves us gives us a different perspective. We come to have faith in Jesus Christ because we are sure that he lives today and intercedes with the Father in our behalf. We repent of our sins because we know that they cannot be washed away until we do so. At our baptism we covenant with the Father that we will take upon us the name of Jesus Christ and always remember him and keep his commandments. In return, the Father promises us that we will always have the guidance of the Holy Ghost if we live worthily. But all human beings sin. This breaks the covenant. Therefore, we partake of the sacrament to renew the covenants which we have made. Even our temple ordinances were established by the Father to help us return to his presence.

Can we now understand why it is so important that we understand what the true nature of God is? When we understand that the Father has a body which is in forms like ours, we also understand that, if we keep all his laws, we shall be given all that he has.

> Beloved, what manner of love the Father hath bestowed upon us, that we should be called the sons of God: therefore the world knoweth us not, because it knew him not.
> Beloved, now are we the sons of God, and it doth not yet appear what we shall be: but we know that, when he shall appear, **we shall be like him**; For we shall see him as he is.
> **And every man that hath this hope in him purifieth himself,** even as he is pure.[18]

Those who purify themselves because they have this hope are known as children of the covenant. They look forward to dwelling with the Father and enjoying an intimate relationship with him.

> Therefore are they before the throne of God, and serve him day and night in his temple: and he that sitteth an the throne shall dwell among them.
> They shall hunger no more, neither thirst any more; neither shall the sun light an them, nor any heat.
> For the Lamb which is in the midst of the throne shall feed them, and shall lead them into living fountains of waters: **and God shall wipe away all tears from their eyes.**[19]

Yes, God the Father and his son, Jesus Christ, and the Holy Ghost are real beings. We look forward to the time when we shall be in their presence. For this purpose we have established our covenant with the Lord. We look forward to these events not in any allegorical sense, but as something which will happen. Jeremiah was told:

> Behold, the days come, saith the Lord, that I will make a new covenant with the house of Israel, and with the house of Judah:
> Not according to the covenant that I made with their fathers in the day that I took them by the hand to bring them out of the land of Egypt; which my covenant they brake, although I was an husband unto them, saith the Lord:
> But this shall be the covenant that I will make with the house of Israel; After those days, saith the Lord, I will put my law in their inward parts, and write it in their hearts; and will be their God, and they shall be my people.
> And they shall teach no more every man his neighbor, and every man his brother, saying, Know the Lord: For **they shall all know me,** from the least of them unto the greatest of them, saith the Lord: for I will forgive their iniquity, and I will remember their sin no more.[20]

We can know the Lord. I bear witness that the Father is not the Son, that the Son is not the Father, and that the Holy Ghost cannot be equated with either one. Such knowledge makes the above promise a beautiful one. I look forward to its fulfillment, when I shall see the face of my Master, and touch the wounds in his hands, face, and side, and with whom I may converse forever more.

CHAPTER 13 REFERENCES

1. Newman, *An Essay on the Development of Christian Doctrine*, 95
2. Bennion, *An Introduction to the Gospel*, 29
3. Joseph Smith—History 1:17
4. Joseph Smith—History 1:19
5. Brown, *The Abundant Life*, 312–313
6. Hinckley, *Faith: The Essence of True Religion*, 21–22
7. Maxwell, *Even As I Am*, 3
8. Doctrine & Covenants 76:22–23
9. Paine, *A Critical History of the Evolution of Trinitarianism*, 173
10. Joseph Smith—History 1:25
11. 2 Nephi 9:28–29
12. Stromata V, 4 as cited in Lonergan, *The Way to Nicea*, 116
13. McConkie, *God and Man*, 16–17
14. Farrar, *The Life of Christ*, 671
15. McConkie, *Mormon Doctrine*, 262
16. Isaiah 1:11–18
17. Milner, *The History of the Church of Christ*, 361
18. 1 John 3:1–3
19. Revelation 7:15–17
20. Jeremiah 31:31–34

Bibliography

1. Aland, Kurt. *A History of Christianity.* 2 Volumes. Translated by James C. Schaaf. Fortress Press: Philadelphia, 1980–82
2. *Ante Nicene Fathers.* Edited by Alexander Roberts and James Donaldson. William B. Eerdmans Publishing Co.: Grand Rapids, 1951.
3. *An Aquinas Reader: Selections From the Writings of Thomas Aquinas.* Edited by Mary T. Clark. Image Books, A Division of Doubleday and Co.: Garden City, New York, 1972.
4. Augustine. *Great Books of the Western World.* No. 18. Edited by Robert Maynard Hutchins. Encyclopedia Britannica, Inc.: Chicago, 1952.
5. Augustine, Saint. *The Trinity.* Translated by Stephen McKenna. The Fathers of the Church. Vol. 45. The Catholic University of America Press: Washington, DC., 1970.
6. Bardenhewer, Otto. *Patrology: The Lives and Works of the Fathers of the Church.* Translated by Thomas J. Shahan. B. Herder Book Co.: St. Louis, 1908.
7. Barker, James L. *Apostasy From the Divine Church.* Bookcraft, Inc.: Salt Lake City, 1984.
8. Bennion, Lowell L. *An Introduction to the Gospel.* The Utah Printing Co.: Salt Lake City, 1960.
9. Bethune-Baker, J. F. *An Introduction to the Early History of Christian Doctrine to the Time of the Council of Chalcedon.* Methuen and Co., Ltd.: London, l958.
10. Bettenson, Henry. *Documents of the Christian Church.* Oxford University Press: New York, 1954.
11. Beveridge, William. *The Theological Works of William Beveridge.* Vol. 1. John Henry Parker: Oxford, 1842.
12. Bloesch, Donald G. *The Battle For the Trinity: The Debate Over Inclusive God-Language.* Vine Books, Servant Publications: Ann Arbor, Michigan, 1985.
13. Brightman, Edgar Sheffield. *The Problem of God.* The Abingdon Press: New York, Cincinnati, Chicago, 1930.
14. *The New Encyclopedia Britannica.* 29 Volumes. Encyclopedia Britannica, Inc.: Chicago, l986.
15. Brown, Hugh. *The Abundant Life.* Bookcraft, Inc.: Salt Lake City, 1965.

16. Brown, William Adams. *Christian Theology in Outline.* Charles Scribner's Sons: New York, 1906.
17. Browne, Peter. *Things Divine and Supernatural.* Garland Publishing Co.: New York and London, 1976: *British Philosophers and Theologians of the 17th and 18th Centuries*, Vol. 9, Reprint of 1733
18. Brumbaugh, Robert S. *The Philosophers of Greece.* Thomas Y. Crowell Co.: New York, 1964.
19. Bull, George. *The Works of George Bull.* 2 Volumes. The University Press: Oxford, 1846.
20. Burton, Edward. *An Inquiry Into the Heresies of the Apostolic Age in Eight Sermons.* Samuel Collingwood: Oxford, 1960, Reprint of 1829 Edition.
21. *Catholic Encyclopedia, The.* 15 Volumes. Robert Appleton Co.: New York, 1907–1912.
22. *Catholicism: Great Religions of Modern Man.* Edited by George Brantl. George Braziller: New York, 1962.
23. Clarke, William Newton. *The Christian Doctrine of God.* Charles Scribner's Sons: New York, 1925.
24. *Collier's Encyclopedia, The.* 24 Volumes. MacMillan Ed. Corp.: New York, 1978.
25. *A Concise Bible Dictionary Based on the Cambridge Companion to the Bible.* Published by the Syndics of the Cambridge University Press: London.
26. Conger, Yves M. J. *Tradition and Traditions.* Vol. 1. Translated by Michael Naseby. MacMillan Co.: New York, 1967.
27. Cooper, Basil A. *The Free Church and Its Subjugation Under Constantine.* Albert Cockshaw: London, 1843.
28. Copleston, F. C. *A History of Medieval Philosophy.* Harper and Row: New York, I974.
29. Copleston, Frederick. *Thomas Aquinas.* Barnes and Noble: Harper and Row, Publishers: New York, 1976.
30. Cudworth, Ralph. *The True Intellectual System of the Universe.* 2 Volumes. Garland Publishing: New York and London, 1976, Reprint of 1678.
31. Cunningham, William. *Historical Theology.* Vol. 2. T and T Clark: Edinburgh, 1864.
32. Danilou, Jean and Henri Marrow. *The Christian Centuries: A New History of the Christian Church, The First Six Hundred Years.* Vol. 1. Translated by Vincent Cronin. Paulist Press: New York, 1964.
33. DeChateaubriand, Viscount Rene. *The Genius of Christianity.* Vol. 1. John Murphy and Co.: Baltimore, 1854.
34. Denzinger, Henry. *The Sources of Catholic Dogma.* Translated by

Bibliography

Roy J. Defarrari from the 13th Edition of *Enchiridion Symbolorum*. B. Herder Books Co.: St. Louis, 1957.

35. Dodds, E.R. *Pagan and Christian in An Age of Anxiety*. W.W. Norton and Co.: New York, 1985.

36. Durant, William James. *The Age of Faith*. Vol. 4 of The Story of Civilization. Simon and Schuster: New York, 1950.

37. *The Early Christian Fathers: A Selection From the Writings of the Fathers From St. Clement to St. Athanasius*. Translated by Henry Bettenson. Oxford University Press: New York, 1956.

38. Farrar, Frederick W. *The Life of Christ*. Fountain Publications, H. W. Shank Publishers: Portland, Oregon, 1980.

39. Foakes-Jackson, Frederick John. *History of the Christian Church From the Earliest Times to A. D. 461*. Deighton, Bell and Co.: Cambridge, 1942.

40. Fortman, Edward J. *The Triune God: A Historical Study of the Doctrine of the Trinity*. Westminister: Philadelphia, 1972.

41. Gibbon, Edward. *The Decline and Fall of the Roman Empire: The Modern Library*. 2 Volumes. Random House, Inc.: New York.

42. Grillmeier, Aloys. *Christ in Christian Tradition*. Translated by J. S. Bowden. A.R. Mowbray and Co.: London, 1965.

43. Gonzalez, Justo L. *A History of Christian Thought*. 3 Volumes. Abingdon Press: Nashville, 1970.

44. Grotius, Hugo. *True Religion Explained and Defended*. DaCapo Press and Theatrum Orbis Terrarum, Ltd.: Amsterdam and New York, 1971. Reprint of 1632.

45. Hardy, Edward Rochie. *Christology of the Later Fathers*. The Library of Christian Classics. Westminster Press: Philadelphia, 1985.

46. Harnack, Adolph. *History of Dogma*. 7 Volumes. Translated by Neil Buchanan. Peter Smith: Glouster, 1976.

47. Hastings, James. *Hastings Encyclopedia of Religion and Ethics*. 13 Volumes. T and T Clark: Edinburgh, 1908–1926.

48. Hinckley, Gordon B. *Faith: The Essence of True Religion*. Deseret Book Co.: Salt Lake City, 1989.

49. Hooker, Richard. *The Laws of Ecclesiastical Polity*. George Rutledge and Sons: London, 1888.

50. Hooper, Finley. *Roman Realities*. Wayne State University Press: Detroit, 1989.

51. Hopkins, Richard R. *Biblical Mormonism: Responding to Evangelical Criticism of LDS Theology*. Horizon Publishers and Distributors, Inc.: Bountiful, 1994.

52. Howells, Rulon S. *His Many Mansions*. Ensign Press, Funk and Wagnalls: New York, 1967.

53. Hunter, Milton R. *The Gospel Through the Ages*. Deseret Book Co.: Salt Lake City, 1958.
54. Illingworth, J. R. *The Doctrine of the Trinity*. MacMillan and Co.: London, 1907.
55. Jones, William. *History of the Christian Church*. Vol. 1. William Jones: London, 1983 Reprint of 1826 (by Church Research and Archives, Gallatin, Tenn.)
56. *Complete Works of Josephus*. Translated by William Whiston. Krigel Publications: Grand Rapids, 1981.
57. Jungmann, Josef A. *The Mass: A Historical, Theological and Pastoral Survey*. Translated by Julian Fernandes. the Liturgical Press: Collegeville, Minnesota, 1970.
58. Kaufman, Gordon D. *The Theological Imagination: Constructing the Concept of God*. The Westminister Press: Philadelphia, 1981.
59. Keller, Roger R. *Reformed Christians and Mormon Christians: Let's Talk*. Pryor: Pettingill, 1986.
60. Kelly, J. N. D. *Early Christian Doctrines*. Harper and Row: New York, 1978.
61. Kung, Hans. *On Being A Christian*. Translated by Edward Quinn. Doubleday and Co.: Garden City, New York, 1976.
62. Lardner, Nathaniel. *The Works of Nathaniel Lardner*. Volumes 3, 4, 5, 9. S. William Ball: London, 1838.
63. Latourette, Kenneth Scott. *A History of Christianity. Beginnings to 1500*. Vol. 1. Harper and Row: New York, 1975.
64. Latourette, Kenneth Scott. *Christianity Through the Ages*. Harper and Row: New York, 1965.
65. Leith, John H. *Creeds of the Churches*. John Knox Press: Atlanta, 1977.
66. Leland, John. *A View of the Principal Deistical Writers*. 3 Volumes. Garland Publishing: New York and London, 1978. Reprint of 1757.
67. Lonergan, Bernard. *The Way to Nicea: The Dialectical Development of Trinitarian Theology*. Translated by Conn O'Donovan. The Westminister Press: Philadelphia, 1976.
68. Mansel, Henry Longueville. *The Limits of Religious Thought Reexamined in Eight Lectures Delivered Before the University of Oxford*. Gould and Lincoln: Boston, 1859.
69. Martos, Joseph. *Doors to the Sacred: A Historical Introduction to Sacraments in the Catholic Church*. Doubleday and Co.: Garden City, New York, 1982.
70. Maxwell, Neal A. *Even As I Am*. Deseret Book Co.: Salt Lake City, 1982.
71. McBrien, Richard P. *Catholicism*. 2 Volumes. Winston Press: Oak

Bibliography

Grove, Minnesota, 1980.

72. McConkie, Bruce R. *Mormon Doctrine*. Bookcraft, Inc.: Salt Lake City, 1986.

73. McConkie, Bruce R. *The Promised Messiah: The First Coming of Christ*. Deseret Book Co.: Salt Lake City, l981.

74. McConkie, Joseph Fielding and Robert L. Millet. *The Holy Ghost*. Bookcraft: Salt Lake City, 1989.

75. McConkie, Oscar W., Jr. *God and Man*. The Corporation of the Presiding Bishop of the Church of Jesus Christ of Latter-Day Saints: Salt Lake City, 1963.

76. McGavin, E. Cecil. *Cumorah's Gold Bible*. The Deseret News Press; Salt Lake City, 1940.

77. McSorley, Joseph. *An Outline History of the Church By Centuries*. B. Herder: St. Louis, 1957.

78. Milman, Henry Hart. *History of Latin Christianity*. John Murray: London, 1867.

79. Milner, Joseph. *The History of the Church of Christ*. Abridged From the First Five Volumes of Milner's Church History by Jesse Townsend. Camp, Merrill and Camp: Utica, 1816.

80. Moltmann, Jurgen. *The Trinity and the Kingdom: The Doctrine of God*. Harper and Row: San Francisco, 1981.

81. von Mosheim, James Lawrence. *Institutes of Ecclesiastical History: Ancient and Modern*. Volumes 1–2. Translated by James Murdock. Harper and Brothers: New York, 1839.

82. *New Bible Commentary*. Edited by Francis Davidson. William B. Eerdmans Publishing Co.: Grand Rapids, 1953.

83. *New Catholic Encyclopedia*. Vol. 14. McGraw-Hill Books: San Francisco, 1989.

84. Newman, John Henry. *An Essay on the Development of Christian Doctrine*. Longmans, Green and Co.: New York, 1916.

85. Nibley, Hugh. *The World and the Prophets. The Collected Works of Hugh Nibley*. Vol. 3. Mormonism and Early Christianity. Deseret Book Co. and Foundation For Ancient Research and Mormon Studies: Provo, Utah: 1987.

86. Nibley, Hugh. *Old Testament and Related Studies*. Deseret Book Co.: Salt Lake City, 1986.

87. Niebuhr, H. Richard. *The Purpose of the Church and Its Ministry*. Harper and Brothers: New York, 1956.

88. O'Brien, John A. *The Faith of Millions: The Credentials of the Catholic Religion*. Our Sunday Visitor, Inc.: Huntington, Indiana, 1974.

89. Paine, Levi Leonard. *A Critical History of the Evolution of Trinitarianism and its Outcome in the New Christology*. Houghton,

Mifflin and Co.: Boston, 1900.

90. Pearson, John. *An Exposition of the Creed*. D. Appleton and Co.: New York, 1853.

91. Pelikan, Jaraslav. *The Christian Tradition: The Emergence of the Catholic Tradition (100–600)*. Vol. I. The University of Chicago Press: Chicago, 1971.

92. Placher, William C. *A History of Christian Theology*. The Westminister Press: Philadelphia, 1983.

93. Poulet, Charles. *A History of the Catholic Church*. Vol. 2. Translated by Sidney A. Raemers. B. Herder Book; St. Louis, 1948.

94. Prestige, G. L. *God in Patristic Thought*. S.P.C.K.: London, 1952.

95. Priestley, Joseph. *A History of the Corruptions of Christianity*. The British and Foreign Unitarian Association: London, 1871.

96. Priestley, Joseph. *Disquisitations Relating to Matter and Spirit*. Arno Press: New York, 1975. Reprint of 1777.

97. Quastan, Johannes. *Patrology*. 3 Volumes. Christian Classics: 1983.

98. *Protestantism: Great Religions of Modern Man*. Edited by J. Leslie Dunstan. George Braziller: New York, 1982.

99. Rather, Karl. *The Trinity*. Translated by Joseph Donceel. Herder and Herder: New York, 1970.

100. Richards, LeGrand. *A Marvelous Work and a Wonder*. Deseret Book Co.: Salt Lake City, 1973.

101. Roberts. *Mormon Doctrine of Deity: The Roberts Van Der Donckt Discussion*. Published by B. H. Roberts, Salt Lake City, 1903 and Horizon Publishers: Bountiful, Utah:

102. Robinson, James H. *The Nag Hammadi Library in English*. Harper and Row: San Francisco, 1977.

103. Royce, Josiah, Joseph LeContes, G. H. Howison and Sidney Edward Mazes. *The Conception of God*. The MacMillan and Co.: New York, 1902.

104. Schaff, Phillip. History of the Christian Church. Vol. 3. William S. Eerdmans Publishing Go.: Grand Rapids, 1910.

105. Schaff, Phillip and Henry Wace. *A Select Library of Nicene and Post Nicene Fathers of the Christian Church*. Second Series. William S. Eerdmans Publishing Co.: Grand Rapids, 1975.

106. Schleiermacher, Friedrich. *The Christian Faith*. Fortress Press: Philadelphia, 1976.

107. Schmaus, Michael. *Dogma*. 3 Volumes. Sheed and Ward: New York, 1971.

108. Schwiebert, E. G. *Luther and His Times: The Reformation From a New Perspective*. Concordia Publishing House.: St. Louis, 1950.

109. Seeberg, Reinhold. *Textbook of the History of Doctrines*. Trans-

Bibliography

lated by Charles E. Hay. Vol. 1. Baker Book House: Grand Rapids, 1964.

110. Shedd, William T. *A History of Christian Doctrine*. Vol. 1. Klock and Klock Christian Publishers: Minneapolis, l978. Reprint of 1889. (Charles Scribner's Sons).

111. Sherlock, Richard. *The Practical Christian or the Devout Christian*. R. Royston: London, 1682.

112. Sherlock, William. *The Vindication of the Most Blessed and Holy Trinity and The Incarnation of the Son of God*. W. Rogers: London, 1694.

113. Shotwell, James T. and Louise Roper Loomis. *The See of Peter*. Columbia University Press: New York, 1927.

114. Skousen, W. Cleon. *The First 2000 Years*. Bookcraft: Salt Lake City, 1981.

115. Strong, Thomas B. *A Manual of Theology*. Adam and Charles Black: London and Edinburgh, l892.

116. Talmage, James E. *Jesus the Christ*. The Church of Jesus Christ of Latter-day Saints: Salt Lake City, 1962.

117. Talmage, James E. *The Great Apostasy*. Deseret News Press; Salt Lake City, 1910.

118. *The Teaching of Christ: A Catholic Catechism For Adults*. Edited by Ronald Lawler, Donald W. Wuerl and Thomas Comerford Lawler. Our Sunday Visitor, Inc.: Huntington, Indiana, 1976.

119. Tixeront, J. *History of Dogmas*. 3 Volumes. Translated by H. L. B. Christian Classics: Westminister, MD, 1984.

120. Tymms, T. Vincent. *The Evolution of Infant Baptism and Related Ideas*. The Kingsgate: London.

121. Walker, Williston, Richard A. Norris, David W. Lotz, Robert T. Handy. *A History of Christianity*. Charles Scribner's Sons: New York, 1985.

122. Ursenbach, O. F. *The Quest*. Bookcraft Publishers: Salt Lake City, 1945.

123. Waterland, Daniel. *Works of Daniel Waterland*. 11 Volumes. Reprint of 1828. AMS Press: New York.

124. Webb, Clement C. *God and Personality*. Books For Library Press: Freeport, New York, 1972. Reprint of 1919.

125. Weber, Alfred. *History of Philosophy*. Translated by Frank Thilly. Charles Scribner's Sons: New York, 1896.

126. Welch, Claude. *The Trinity in Contemporary Theology*. SCM Press, Ltd.: London, 1953.

127. Werner, Martin. *The Formation of Christian Dogma, A Historical Study of Its Problems*. Translated by S.G.F. Brandon. Beacon Press: Boston, 1965.

128. White, David Manning. *In Search of God: A World Treasury of*

Quotations About the Eternal Quest. MacMillan Publishing Co.: New York, 1983.

   126. Wolfson, Harry Austryn. *The Philosophy of the Church Fathers.* Vol. 1. Harvard U. Press: Cambridge, Mass, 1956.

Index

absolute being   75, 79
abstractions   21, 43–44, 47, 52, 132
Alexander   137–138, 142–143, 145–147, 159–161
Ambrose   8, 61–62, 115, 135–136, 181–182
angels   95–96
Anselm   4, 191–192, 199–200
anthropomorphism   9, 38, 52, 55–57, 219
anthropomorphists   59–61, 173
Apolloniris of Laodicea   100, 155
Apologists, did not teach Trinity   6–7, 34
apostasy   123, 127–129, 162, 171, 179, 224
Aquinas, Thomas   vii–viii, 82, 195, 199–207
Aristotle   9, 52, 75, 78, 82–83, 86, 88–89, 127, 131, 132, 157–158, 195, 200–202, 207, 219
Arius   22, 55, 92, 137–138, 144–149, 157–158, 190
Arnobius   23, 88
Athanasian Creed   26–28, 38–39, 85, 179–195, 204
Athanasius   4, 24, 44, 55–56, 115–116, 119, 142–150, 153, 156–169, 172–174, 180, 182–183, 185
Athenagoras   35
attributes   55, 80–81
Augustine   vii, 4, 8, 24–26, 28–30, 38–39, 43–44, 60–61, 76, 86, 95–96, 119, 135, 179–195, 199, 202, 206, 208
Averoes   200

Basil   4, 54, 180–181
Bible (Trinity not found in)   2–4, 52, 81, 149–150, 219
body of God   2, 9, 51–71, 216–217, 219
Buddhists   81, 130

Catholic Church, formed after 300 A.D.   7, 151–153
Christ, did not teach Trinity   3–4
Christ, natures of   2, 85–103
Christians, did not understand Trinity   17
Chrysostom   157
Clement of Alexandria   8, 52, 53, 55, 62, 118, 133–135, 219
Clement of Rome   6, 96
Comminitorium   24, 155–157
Constans   161, 164, 166
Constantine   8, 44, 138, 141–148, 150–153, 158–161, 167, 181
Constantine II   161–162, 164
Constantius   142, 161–170, 180
consubstantial   55, 101
corporal punishment   1
council of heaven   108–109
creations, many   107–109
creature, Jesus was   92–93, 137
crude   59–60
Cudworth, Ralph   54, 158
Cyprian   9

de Beausobre, Isaac   58–60, 62–63
designation of Jesus as one god   16, 208–209, 218
devil   110–112
Didache   6
Dionysius of Alexandria   92
dividing the substance   26–27, 55, 150, 191
doctrinal changes seen in history   6

Economic Trinity   24, 200
Epistle of Barnabas   6
evangelical challenge   1
Eusebius of Caesarea   22, 92, 143–144, 147–148, 150, 179
Eusebius of Nicodemia   138, 148, 159, 162–163, 165
Eustathius   143
Eutychianism   99

Father, is not the Son   vii, 15–30
Fathers, were converted pagans   78
Fathers, invented Trinitarian doctrines   4–6, 43–44, 55–56, 90
Felix   168–170
First Cause   42–43, 79–80, 82, 201, 203

Index

First Vision 2, 12, 82, 123, 214–215
foreordination 112–114
Freud, Sigmund 202

Gnostics 86–87, 100, 135
Godhead, doctrines of in first 300 years 6
Godhead, nature of 2, 220–221, 224
Godhead, numerically differentiated 19–21, 34–35
Godhead, one in purpose 33–48
God is Dead theory viii
God, must be known 75–83, 221–226
Gratian 174, 181–182
Gregory of Cappodocia 162–163
Gregory of Nazianzus 4, 8, 96, 115, 149, 180
Gregory of Nyssa 54, 93, 113, 157, 180–181
Gregory the Great 8

Hegesippus 129, 179
helenization 123–129
Heraclitus 52–53, 78, 130–131
heresies, caused by Trinitarian doctrines viii, 18–21, 85–103, 171, 188, 199–200, 216, 219–220
Hermes 8
Hilary of Poitiers 8, 115, 149–150, 167. 171–172, 174
Hindus 81
Hippolytus 184–185, 191
history, rewriting of 8
Homer 8, 86
homoiousios 170, 180
homoousios 7, 55, 150–151, 155–175
homoousios, rejected as heresy 7, 59, 150
Hosius of Cordoba 143, 145–146, 167–168

Ignatius 6, 22, 68, 78
Immanent Trinity 24, 200
immaterial spirits not possible 59–61, 90–91
inheritance, man's 107–119, 223–224
Irenaeus 6, 22, 78, 86

Jehovah 24
Jerome 135, 170, 180
Jesus, intercedes in our behalf viii, 199–200

John of Damascus   9, 54
Julius of Rome   162–164
Justin Martyr   22, 34–35, 43, 130–131, 185

Lactanius   9, 43–44, 78, 118
Liberius   167–170
Luther, Martin   viii, 207–210

Maccabees, revolt of   124
Martin, Dr. Walter   1
mathematical contradiction   20, 26–27, 186–188, 190–191
Melito   56, 63, 78
Menedus   124–125
Methodius   118
Moslem   200–201, 204, 207
mystery, God is not a   77–79, 213–226

negation   60, 76–77, 93–94
Neo-Platonism   75, 135
Nestroianism   99
Nicea, 300 years after death of Jesus   7–8
Nicene Council   141–153, 160, 170, 182, 188, 220
Nicene Creed, codified in 325   1, 6, 139
Nicene Creed, signed by 316 bishops   7, 220
Nicene Creed, terms of not scriptural   7, 9, 149–150, 167, 220
Noetus   184–185, 191, 219–220
Novatian   vii, 18, 23, 33, 155

one god in three personages   2, 15–30
omnipresence by extension disproved   69–71
Opatus   9
Origen   4, 21, 33–34, 39, 43, 53, 57, 78, 92, 114–115, 119, 133–136, 144, 159, 180, 185, 191, 193–194

pagan trinities   53–54, 158
Pantanaenus   133–134, 136
Pantheism   2, 26, 53–55, 158
Papias   6
Paris, University of   200–201, 207
parts, none in Trinity   41–44, 219–220
Patripassionism   20–21, 191, 199–200, 219
Paul   9, 86, 102, 116, 127–129

Index

Paul of Samotsa   150, 168
Pelagius   119, 155, 193
Persons, are they real?   25, 41–42, 44–48, 81, 158, 187–189, 192, 204–205, 210, 213–226
Peter   15, 96
Philo Judaeus   125–127, 136
philosophers, Paul warned against   10
Plato   8, 9, 43, 52–53, 75, 78, 83, 86–87, 124, 127, 131–132, 149, 184, 192–193, 195, 201–202, 219
Plotinus   131–132, 157
Polycarp   6, 133
pre-existence   108–114
Priestley, Joseph   20, 23, 43, 58–60, 62–63, 86
problems in Trinity   2, 23, 100–101, 220
procession   26–27, 39–41, 45–46, 94–95, 205–207
pseudo-Aeropagite   95
Ptolemy Philadelphus   124–125

rejection of Nicene Creed   7
restoration, desire for   11–12
results of Trinitarian doctrines   viii–ix
resurrection disproves substance theory   65–69, 101
revelation, true doctrines by   10–11, 179–180, 194–195, 203–204, 213–226
Rimini   170–171

Sabellianism   18–21, 25–26, 39–41, 45–48, 150, 155, 173–174, 184, 187, 205, 219
sacraments, have changed   5
saints, worship of   viii, 18, 199–200, 223
school of Alexandria   55, 125–127, 132–139, 179
school of Antioch   132–133, 136–139
seventy elders   124
Shepherd of Hermas   6
Sherlock, William   41, 45, 69, 158, 188–189
Simon Magus   59, 219
Sirmium   164, 167
Smith, Joseph   82, 90–91, 107–108, 114, 118–119, 139, 214–215, 218–220, 222
sons of God   107–119
spiritual body   57–60
spoiling the Egyptians   8–9

Stephen   126–127, 136
Stoics   126, 127
subordinationism   23, 216
substance, idea of divine   vii, 26–28, 36, 54–55, 60, 62, 69–71, 79, 86, 155–175, 216, 220
Sylvester   143–144, 159

Tatian   35
Tertullian   4, 21, 33, 59, 63, 78, 88, 107
Tetzel, John   208
Theophilus   4, 35, 43
traditions, of Fathers   4–6
transcendent being, pagan in origin   75
Trinitarian ideas, speculation   76, 93–94, 133, 136, 216
Trinitarian ideas, taken from pagans   8–10, 81
Trinitarian doctrines, took hundreds of years to develop   6, 81, 134, 215
Trinity, defined in Nicene and Athanasian Creeds   vii
Trinity, destroys Father, Son, and Holy Ghost   16–30, 80–81, 204–205, 208–209
Trinity, word first used by Tertullian   4
Tritheists   22–24, 36–38, 173
Two Natures theory   85–103

Ulysses   8
Unitarians   22, 102
unity of God   33–48

Victorinus   8
Vincentian Rule   155–175, 193
Vincent of Lerins   24, 155, 193
vulgar   60

Wesley, John   79

About the Author:

Ramon D. Smullin attended the University of Utah where he studied history. He served a full-time mission for the LDS Church in the Alaskan-Canadian Mission. He is married to the former Louise Benson, and has three children. Ray resides in Salt Lake City, Utah, where he owns and operates a mergers and acquisitions consulting business. He has been honored nationally for his public speaking and writing skills.

Ray is available to speak to your congregation or group about the fascinating subject of the Trinity. Should you wish to have him speak or desire an autographed copy of this book, please contact Camden Court Publishers at the address listed on the legal page.